Not
All Superheroes
Wear Capes

by

Danny Bent

ISBN-13:978-0996015202
ISBN-10:0996015205

Content Editor: Kate Treleaven

Danny Bent's website can be found at:
www.dannybent.com

This book is dedicated to all whose lives were affected by the Boston Marathon bombings on April 15, 2013

Foreword:

I ran the 2013 Boston Marathon, though I never reached the finish line. Like about 5000 others, I was stopped a mile away by police and race officials who told us several bombs had exploded just yards from the famous finish.

Huh? What? None of us could believe the words we were hearing. They simply didn't equate. We couldn't imagine anything so tragic happening to the Boston Marathon, the world's most welcoming and historic 26.2 miler.

As a former Boston winner (1968) and longtime Runner's World editor, I spent the next several days on TV and radio shows explaining the shock we all felt. I was so busy I don't think I realized the whole world was watching.

I certainly didn't know that three British citizens, Danny Bent, Kate Treleaven and Jamie Hay, were following the news on the internet. Nor could I have guessed that they would be seized by a crazy and outsized thought - that they could honor the dead and injured in Boston by organizing a fundraising relay right across the USA.

These things have been done before. But almost always by people who spent years in the planning. After all, the logistics of covering 3300 miles from the Pacific shores of Los Angeles to Boston Harbor are mindboggling, especially if you don't know anyone in the U.S.

But Danny, Kate and Jamie refused to sweat the small stuff. They only knew that they wanted to help heal Boston's shattered soul and raise funds for the victims. Also, and a very key point, they had Facebook – and weren't afraid to use it!

They were overwhelmed by the response and just seven weeks after the Boston Marathon, they were in California, ready to begin the One Run For Boston. Driving a support vehicle quickly dubbed 'The Stinkmobile,' Danny and Kate headed eastward.

A steady stream of relay runners ran nearby, 24 hours a day, seven days a week, through the deserts, mountains, cornfields, and rolling hills that make America so magnificent. The runners themselves were young, old, black, brown and white. Some had run the Boston Marathon at one time or another. Most hadn't.

They simply wanted to reach out. They wanted to show that they cared, that they hadn't forgotten Paul Revere and the Minutemen; that they shared Boston's pain and the need for healing, even if they lived thousands of miles away.

The marathon race itself is a tough individual challenge. You don't reach the finish line unless you get there under your own power, be it on foot, in a wheelchair, or on crutches. It's a test of will and character.

A relay is different. It's like a chain that's only as strong as its weakest link. The One Run For Boston had some difficult moments. It had some bizarre ones, and it certainly included its share of belly laughs. The One Run proved itself worthy of the tough men and women who have been running from Hopkinton to Boston for 117 years. It had high goals, precise planning, great endurance and the heart of a champion.

Amby Burfoot
1968 Boston Marathon winner
Editor At Large, Runner's World Magazine

Chapter 1

Right on Hereford, left on Boylston…

Patriots' Day. Marathon Monday - a day when a stream of color runs from Hopkinton Common all the way to the heart of Downtown Boston; destination Boylston Street. Here, outside the public library, a sacred blue-and-yellow painted line spans the street all year round, marking the finish of an epic feat of endurance for the 30,000 runners who take part each year in the oldest, most prestigious marathon on the planet.

The colorful stream that floods the streets is made up of individuals representing nearly a hundred nationalities. Merged together, in one unstoppable current are the young and the old, marathon veterans and first timers, charity runners in bright t-shirts and elites in team vests. Side by side, shoulder-to-shoulder, they run as one.

Within it, people's dreams become reality, barriers are broken down and legends are crowned. If they look hard enough, runners find the meaning of courage, dedication and triumph, and the most sacred of treasures, themselves.

A marathon is the pinnacle of many running careers. Boston is the pinnacle of Marathons. It is the Marathon of Marathons, the Super Bowl of running. People spend their whole lives training so that one day they might just get their place on the most hallowed of start lines.

On race day, often having been unable to sleep, runners rise early to complete their pre-race rituals and make their way to Hopkinton. Huddled together in groups, some of them stand in silence, consumed by the enormity of the day, hiding from buzzing photographers and reporters. Others talk incessantly, deep within the throng, unaware of what leaves their lips.

In 2013, the weather was perfect. The sun shone but the temperature was cool. A light wind meandered through the crowds causing the leaves and grass to dance. A man wielding a megaphone called the first wave of runners forward to the start line at 9.50am.

Pumped with adrenaline, the runners jostle over to the line. The air is thick with anticipation. This is the moment - *their* moment. This is why they have woken at 4:30am to train before the kids wake, before work. This is the reason why day after day they have pounded the streets, through the wind and the rain, increasing their lung capacity, their strength, their endurance, while their friends are out eating, drinking and having fun.

At 10am the starting pistol fires. The urge to expend all that pent-up excitement in the first mile has to be controlled and the frustration of being hemmed in behind so many runners must be contained. *Keep calm, save your energy. You'll need that later on.*

The Boston Marathon was first run in April 1897, inspired by the revival of the marathon for the 1896 Summer Olympics in Athens. In those days, the only prize awarded for winning the race was a wreath woven from olive branches. In 2013, the winner received $100,000. It's incentive indeed for the fastest of runners who float over the course at a pace we mortals can only dream of.

For the rest of the runners, money plays no part. It's about personal glory, about achieving what you thought impossible. For many marathoners to qualify for Boston (to 'BQ') is both a goal and an achievement in itself. A BQ is earned through determination, sweat and very often tears and is on the bucket list of not just every runner in the States, but runners around the world.

The Boston Marathon course is divided into three parts, 14 miles of fun, 8 miles of sweat and 4.2 miles of hell. A host of legendary landmarks line the route. There's the rail road at Framingham, where a freight train once blocked the course for two minutes, stopping all but the lead pack of runners. Next up is the lake at Natick where two-time winner of the Boston Marathon, Ellison "Tarzan" Brown is said to have stopped for a dip to cool off during a particularly warm race in the 1930s. Then at mile 13, just short of halfway, the 'Wellesley Scream Tunnel', for many the most highly anticipated landmark on the course. Here, students from the all girls' college line the street to cheer on the runners. Clutching posters proclaiming "I'm Single / I'm from California / I major in kissing" the girls vie for attention whilst screaming so loud that the runners can hear them a mile out.

Then, it's on to the Newton hills. The last of these, Heartbreak Hill, is the point many dread. It's not the biggest of climbs but it comes at a point in the marathon, at about the 20-mile mark, where energy stores run out. Runners call it 'hitting the wall', and that's what it feels like, but worse. It's one of those fascinating facts of evolution that each human can store only 20 miles worth of energy, irrespective of your size, weight, speed or time. It's at 20 miles when you get nailed. You feel like you're running through treacle, that you have weights on your legs and arms. The pain is evident on every runner's face. This is why at Heartbreak Hill the crowds are crazy. The force of their breath alone is enough to keep you moving.

As the runners move on, leaving the cheers behind them, their minds begin to take over. The voice that is telling them to stop and curl up in a ball on the soft grass verge is trying to derail them. And many *are* derailed. Bodies can line the street at this point, especially on hot days. You have to lock that voice up in the little black box inside your head and tell it, sometimes out loud, to shut the heck up. You feel like your blood is laced with glass and with each heartbeat your legs are being lacerated from the inside out. Hitting the wall can cause nausea, dizziness and even hallucinations.

The iconic Citgo sign looms large above the runners as they hit the outskirts of Downtown. The sight of it sends a shiver up the spine and, even though dehydration has them in its grip, many runners spare a tear. Those lone tears, that navigate their way down sweaty faces encrusted with crystallized salt, symbolize tidal waves of relief. They know they're going to make it!

The runners reach Kenmore, home to Fenway Park and the Boston Red Sox, as the traditional Patriot's Day game is ending. 30,000 baseball fans spill out of the stadium onto Commonwealth Avenue to cheer the runners as they enter the last mile. Then all that remains are those famous final turns.

Right on Hereford, left on Boylston...

Now the screaming of the lactic acid in your legs is drowned out by the crowd screaming with joy at your achievement. They fill every gap on the sidewalk on Boylston Street, ten-deep at points. You are almost there. It's almost time to throw your hands in the air to celebrate. One more push, one more surge, and one more cry from the crowd...

Then an angry metallic sound rings out and how quickly life changes.

Chapter 2

A blinding flash, followed by a thunderous boom knocks runners off their feet. Shrapnel and debris rain down onto their faces from a mushroom cloud of smoke as they look up to the sky.

The voices that once screamed the runners' names, urging them on to the finish, are screaming for their lives. And now everyone is running. Tears of joy and relief have turned to tears of fear and tragedy.

At 2:49 on April 15 2013, a bomb exploded outside the Marathon Sports store, just yards from the Boston Marathon finish line.

The barriers bearing the flags of every runner's nationality are thrown onto the street, across the marathon course. Behind the barriers, a hole is left. The thronging crowd, waiting for the sight of their loved ones, just moments previously, is gone.

One block away, outside the Forum restaurant, a man dressed in jeans and a Red Sox sweater goes to leap the barriers. The only thought on his mind is to help with the injured from the first blast. But as he jumps, a second bomb explodes outside the restaurant where he and four friends have been standing. They are picked up and thrown through the air in slow motion, as razor sharp pieces of shrapnel find soft flesh. Delirious, and with horrific injuries visible through his torn pants, he gets to his feet and heads for the finish line, oblivious to the runners around him.

*****

Dust fills the air clouding vision. Ears are ringing from the blasts, and nostrils begin to burn with the stench of sulphur, burnt plastic, dust and hatred. Those who are able to move, run, for fear of another explosion. With debris filling the air, there is no way to see what's around them. In their panic they trip, falling over what they will later know to be bodies. Just visible through the smoke, moving quickly in the opposite direction against the stream of people running away, is a cream-colored cowboy hat.

As the smoke clears, the devastation is obvious. Buildings have their windows blown out, right up to the third floor. People lie on the sidewalk on a bed of glass and blood. Some are not moving. Others stare in disbelief at where their legs once were, shin bones exposed, flesh hanging from knee joints. Pools of dark blood spread onto the sidewalk around them, leaving faces ashen gray.

John Odom was four weeks away from retirement and had travelled from California to see his daughter, Nicole, finish her first marathon. Outside the Forum restaurant, the proud father now lies on his right side. The blood spilling from his left leg colors all that is close to him. Looking up, John sees his wife Karen getting to her feet and a chill passes through his body. Nicole is one of thousands of runners the race officials stop a mile before the finish. Unaware of what is happening up ahead, they do not know why their moment of glory has been stolen from them.

A woman running with her phone receives one of the few calls that make it through before the city pulls the cell networks. It's her husband. He is at the finish line and, having witnessed both blasts is worried there will be more. He cries to her over the phone: "Run! Run in the opposite direction! There has been an explosion and there are body parts flying through the air!"

Another runner, a block away, takes a call from his wife. As soon as he answers she blurts, "There's been a bomb and I can't find your mom or our daughter…" The line goes dead.

Chapter 3

Over 3,000 miles away across the Atlantic, the patter of rain plays a break beat on the roof of a small white barn in the middle of Devon, England. The raindrops land among the greens of spring; bouncing, slipping and sliding over the leaves, playing. They fall among the blossom making the flowers dance to their tune.

Dashing out of my door after lunch, I meet my friend Kate for a little run along the banks of the River Dart. Cows in muddy fields shelter under oak trees. The rain makes everything look beautifully green and fills up the river, hastening its flow before being dumped in the sea ten miles away. A brief appearance from the sun conjures up a life-affirming rainbow which arches across the running water in front of us.

Jumping two-footed into the puddles I elicit a frown from Kate but am undeterred as I jump higher for the next one. Kate's dark hair is drenched and flattened to her forehead but her green eyes still shine brightly and she looks pretty, in an aristocratic way. She has a faint scar beneath her right nostril which she maintains was caused by a beetle that burrowed into her face. Kate's husband Steve says it's the result of a skiing accident but Kate insists he's making it up.

Kate is 34, the same age as me. She speaks the Queen's English better than any Royal; something she no doubt honed whilst studying at Oxford University. She's as bright as a button but as streetwise as a fairground goldfish.

Kate likes an adventure and when she's not at work, she can be found flying down muddy hills on her bike, diving into the icy cold waters along the Devon coastline, or running through forests at night following a trail of white flour. She also bakes a yummy cake that Steve and I have been known to fall out over.

Back at the barn, I call my little sister Natalie while Kate goes to get changed. It's Nat's 30th birthday. We laugh about her being old now. She's catching up with me. She tells me how spoilt she's been already and we discuss how I can spoil her even more when she comes to visit the following weekend. I tell Nat I love her just as Kate comes down the stairs and we hang up.

Overhearing the final part of my call, Kate assumes I've got a new love interest and is keen to find out more. But the fact is my love life is as gray and drab as the weather outside. Embarrassed, I steer the conversation towards our favorite pastime, philosophizing about what we should do with our lives and wondering how we can save the world. The old 90's radio-cassette player in my kitchen has been kicking out tunes all day but is drowned out now by the rain outside which adds a throbbing bass line to our animated chatter.

Since leaving university, Kate has jumped from job to job in search of new thrills. She started off in politics then worked as a journalist and film-maker for the BBC, before landing a succession of event management jobs. She says she gets bored easily, but I think she just has a problem with authority. As for me, I gave up a well paid job in the City of London years ago where money came at the expense of my happiness. Now, I'm fighting for a life as a writer/adventurer, where happiness is an ever-present companion but money is scarce.

As we sit at my kitchen table, sipping on mugs of hot tea, I try to educate Kate on the benefits of letting go and living out her dreams. I'm not sure what it is, but there is something holding her back from reaching out to those dizzying heights. I try pressing her on the issue but we're interrupted by my buddy Jamie who walks straight in and makes a beeline for the kettle. Living as I do in the hippy town of Totnes in the south west foot of England, my door is always open day and night. I like it that my friends can wander in and out, as they please. Although it does mean that I sometimes come home to find near strangers hanging out in my lounge. But I wouldn't have it any other way.

Jamie helps himself to a mug of his usual brew, a special blend of instant coffee and mint hot chocolate which I keep in the cupboard just for his visits. I first met Jamie a couple of years ago in London. Walking into a pub, I saw a young lad with maps laid out on the tables in front of him. Intrigued, I wandered over and joined him as he discussed his forthcoming road trip to Europe to film a documentary about the life of AIDS victims. Jamie has a day job but spends all his time and money working the night shift on his own philanthropic projects. He seems to survive by replacing sleep with mint choc mochas.

Jamie is shorter and a little stockier than me. He wears his thick, dark hair short and has black-rimmed glasses that sit above a permanent 5 o'clock shadow. A lot of people say he looks like Vinnie, the sexy pin-up from the US reality TV show *Jersey Shore*. I can see the resemblance but would never admit it to him. Jamie is 23, although you wouldn't know it if you met him. He's already packed a lot into his brief time on the planet and, as I regularly like to remind him, (normally after someone has compared him to Vinnie) he has the well-trodden face of a much older man. He is also a digital genius with the business brain of someone twice his age. Jamie is in many ways different to me but when it comes to music, we are on the same page.

Jamie is a fan of fun pop music and we are never afraid to show our appreciation with a few original dance moves around my kitchen table. Kate enjoys the tunes more than our dancing. As Robin Thicke's *Blurred Lines* comes on the radio with its familiar 'Hey, hey, heys'. Jamie gives me the nod and puts down his mocha. We match each other move for move, trying hard not to trip over Kate's laptop cable as we gyrate around the room. Looking over at Kate, I see she is completely immersed in Facebook.

Macklemore's *Thrift Shop* kicks in and Jamie grabs the broom handle for a microphone, while I use two dinner plates as mixing decks. *Damn! That's a cold-ass honkey.* I'm just pondering what a cold-ass honkey is exactly when Kate gets up suddenly, pushing her chair away from the table. She turns the music off and stares at us. For a second I wonder if the dancing has gotten too much for her. Has she finally snapped? I couldn't blame her. I was close to splitting my pants with that last dance move. But I can see her pupils dilate and she looks confused. Something has happened. This is not normal 'Kate behavior'. I ask what's wrong. Kate replies, "They've bombed the Boston marathon."

*****

I switch the radio back on and spin the dial to find a news station, sure that this is some sick joke playing out over the Internet. There's an irritating crackle as the old radio struggles to tune to the right frequency. But the voice of the BBC reporter is clear to be heard.

"…terrorist attack. Two bombs have exploded at the finish line of the Boston Marathon."

Jamie makes a mocha. The sickly smell of mint chocolate and coffee fills the air. We sit in silence for what seems like hours, listening to the news as it slowly feeds through. We hear the police have no leads, no group has admitted to the atrocity. We use social media to check-in with our running clubs to make sure no-one we know has been affected.

As the news comes in thicker, cloudier and fouler, we sit hunched in the darkness glued to our laptops, the light from their fluorescent screens reflecting on our ashen faces. Over the next few days, we learn that the blasts have claimed three lives. The bubbly Lu Lingzi, aged 23. Born in

China, Lingzi had worked tirelessly to gain acceptance into Boston University. Just a day before the marathon, Lingzi learned she had passed the first half of the major exam required for her statistics degree. Elated, she headed out into the sunshine to celebrate with friends near the Boston Marathon finish line. She never came back.

Another young woman, Krystle Campbell, with a mischievous smile and light freckles, was also at the Boston Marathon finish line when the bombs went off. She had gone down to the finish with her friend Karen to join the euphoric crowd and cheer on the runners. In the aftermath of the bombings, Krystle's family was told she was injured but alive, and that her friend Karen had died. Rushing to the hospital, Krystle's father went to her bedside, only to find Karen and immediately realize that the Doctor's had confused his daughter's identity with her friend. It was Krystle who had lost her life. Interviews with her family afterwards portray Krystle as exactly the kind of girl every runner wants to run past at the end of a marathon. She lived life full of enthusiasm, joy and love. Krystle's grandmother tells one newspaper, "She loved being around people. She was a people lover."

And then there is little Martin Richard, an eight year old who loved playing football and riding his bike, who had been snatched from our world. We learn that Martin's seven year old sister has lost a leg and his mother suffered head injuries in the same blast. Sister and mother remain in a critical condition in hospital. The media find a photo of Martin taken at school during a lesson on the fatal shooting of college student Trayvon Martin. In the photo, he is holding up a colorful handwritten sign which says *No more hurting people. Peace.* The image spreads like wildfire around social networks and soon becomes a symbol of the tragedy worldwide.

Three innocent people living happy, positive lives far removed from conflict and terror have had their futures taken in the most cowardly of attacks. It's clear that many more have also sustained life changing injuries.

Sat around my kitchen table we look at each other in disbelief as the news sinks in. There is a rare silence. Even the rain outside has stopped for the first time in months. Jamie stares out the window as Kate turns to say exactly what I've been thinking.

"We have to do something."

Chapter 4

The impulse to do something in response to the bombings was shared by people all over the world. But few could think of a way to focus their energies. Fired up by the anger they felt towards those responsible for such a cheap shot at a crowd of innocents, many Americans wanted to stand up and fight. But there was nobody to fight. Police confirmed that the two brothers they suspected of carrying out the attack had acted alone. The elder brother was killed in a shoot out with police four days after the bombings. His brother had been captured soon after.

Unable to act, irrational feelings of guilt took over. It's common in the aftermath of such tragedies. Some people felt guilty that Martin Richard's young life was taken and yet theirs were spared. Medics and police officers across the country wished they could have been at the scene saving lives instead of watching the tragedy unfold on TV. Others simply felt guilty that the world they lived in had become so messed up that a sporting event, a running race, had become the target for a terrorist attack. People felt helpless and lost.

Unsurprisingly, the running community was hit hardest. Cell phones rang off the hook and social media were alight with people checking on friends and family. Most people heard the news they were looking for and some fell to their knees with relief finding this place convenient to pray for those that received calls that day who didn't hear the news they were hoping for.

Some runners hung up their shoes and retired from the sport. The mental pain they now associated with running was too much. Some put on their running shoes in an act of defiance and left the house only to break down in tears on the driveway. Others ran and kept running, running further than they ever had before, running through the guilt, the anger, the pain and confusion.

A fund was created by Massachusetts Governor, Deval Patrick and Boston Mayor, Thomas Menino. The One Fund Boston's purpose would be to raise money to help those families most affected by the tragic events that occurred on Marathon Monday. The fund enabled people to show support. Money began pouring in from corporations and individuals all over America, and across the world. But making a donation to the fund still wasn't enough for many people. Writing a check did not quench their desire to give something more of themselves. For them, it seemed there would be no closure.

Yet life had to go on. It is amazing to think that people could go back to work and continue their normal daily routine after what happened. But they did. People went to work, came home, played with the kids, ate, did some chores and went to bed. Outwardly, they got on with their everyday lives. But underneath the surface, the frustration of not being able to do more to show solidarity for the bombing victims gnawed away at them. In some cases it turned to depression. Many people became emotionally color blind. All color in their world had been stolen, bleached by this terrible act.

*****

Struggling to comprehend what had happened, I felt something inside me stir. Ordinarily, I'm a believer that all humans are good. I spend hours preaching to people that humans who do things that upset us do so because of things that that have happened in their past or are happening in the present that they can't control. Why does the woman in the queue snap at you for no reason? Her husband forgot her birthday, again; and the boy on the bus who annoys everyone by playing his music too loud? Maybe he's trying to drown out the soundtrack of his parents fighting that plays on a loop inside his head.

But what about this ... the bombing of a marathon finish line? Sport is the ultimate celebration of the human spirit, where ordinary people can achieve extraordinary things. How could a sporting event be chosen as the target for a terrorist attack? I didn't understand. Unable to get my brain around it, in the pit of my stomach a distain for humanity was growing. All around me I began to notice the darker side of civilization. Instead of smiling at the child who dances at the bus stop, or observing the teenager who helps an old man across the street, I began to notice the teenager tormented by his peers and the child seeking comfort from her parents who is cussed at instead.

I hate negativity; it repels me like opposite ends of a magnet. It makes me want to run away, to buy a boat and sail out into the middle of the ocean. Away from society, I would be oblivious to the cruelty that happens daily in our world. I could cocoon myself within my own world of happiness and fun. But I know this would never work because the happiness and fun I feel comes from the same society that generates the negativity I loathe. People are the source of my energy. Normally I feed on positive interactions and live my life high in the clouds surrounded by love and happiness.

Shortly after the bombings, I found myself watching the tacky British rom-com *Love Actually* to try and rediscover the color in my own life. It's a bit of a favorite, not least because of the minor sub plot of the totally average, slightly nerdy, strawberry-blond English guy who travels to America with the hope that US girls will dig his cute accent and that one girl, *the* girl, will fall for him.

The film begins with a voiceover from David, played by the floppy-haired Hugh Grant. His posh English accent sounds a lot like Kate's. He comments that whenever he gets gloomy with the state of the world, he thinks about the arrivals terminal at Heathrow Airport, and the pure uncomplicated love felt as friends and families welcome their arriving loved ones.

"It seems to me that love is everywhere. Often, it's not particularly dignified or newsworthy, but it's always there - fathers and sons, mothers and daughters, husbands and wives, boyfriends, girlfriends, old friends. When the planes hit the Twin Towers, as far as I know, none of the phone calls from the people on board were messages of hate or revenge - they were all messages of love. If you look for it, I've got a sneaky feeling you'll find that love, actually, is all around."

In this tragedy I'd forgotten how to see love. Maybe I just had to work a little bit harder, open my arms to people and open my eyes to see that *love* is still there for all of us to see.

Chapter 5

The next day, my phone rings early. It's Kate. She tells me she has an idea and is coming over. It is over a week since we sat in my kitchen watching the events of Marathon Monday unfold. As Kate walks in, I feel the atmosphere in the small room change. An air of steely determination hangs over the worktops, wafts through the vegetable rack, and hovers around the pack of colored pens that lie scattered on the table.

Awkward, to begin with and, unusually, a little unsure of herself, Kate begins to tell me her idea. Soon the words are pouring out. She speaks passionately without a pause and I sit listening. Eventually, she takes a breath and asks, "So, what do you think?"

I take a long swig of my coffee. As ever, I've allowed it to go stone cold. I'm not even sure why I drink coffee. I don't particularly like the taste but I love the process of making a proper cup; grinding the beans, waiting for the water to percolate, the earthy smell as it brews. Drinking coffee makes me feel like a grown up. I run a hand through my shaggy, unkempt hair and hear the drips from the tap hitting the unwashed dishes in the sink as I let the idea sit a minute.

The whirr of Kate's antiquated computer seems to hypnotize me. In the absence of a reply, Kate begins to panic that she's made a fool of herself. "Of course it's probably a stupid idea, impossible in America. We'd never be able to make it happen…" She stops, giving me enough time to respond.

"I think it's brilliant." I can feel my blue eyes sparkling. This is it. Kate is a genius.

Kate suggested we could organize a non-stop running relay across the USA, starting on the west coast and finishing in Boston on the east coast. It would be a way for runners across the country to show their solidarity for Boston and those impacted by the blasts.

I pick up my colored pens and start to scribble. The pens are leftovers from my brief stint as a junior school teacher. Marking the kids' work with them, I hoped the bright colors would make my corrections look less negative. After an hour, my notepad looks like it has gone five rounds of The Color Run. But in the midst of all the red, green, pink, orange and blue we're getting somewhere. Just like in the A-Team, a plan starts to come together. There are only a few concerns that are holding us back. We've written them in pink to make them look less intimidating.

Is running really that popular in America? Obviously there are lots of runners in America, but are there enough to make a coast-to-coast relay work? The British media's portrayal of the average American taunts us. It depicts two types of American citizen; the 300lb man who sits on his sofa tossing hotdogs into his mouth, and the ladies who lunch, with their bright nail polish and an inch of makeup scraped across their aging skin. We assume neither enjoys running. This could be a problem.

Will Americans accept us Brits? We fear people may take exception to us, despite our best intentions. Is it possible we could be seen as intruding on a tragedy that's not our own? Will people understand that as runners we feel a strong connection to those the bombers chose to target? Will they be able to comprehend that despite living in another country, three thousand miles away, we felt the impact too?

How do we get started - do we actually know anyone in the US? A friend of mine lives in San Francisco but she's juggling a career as a professional cyclist with post doctoral research at Stanford. Kate thinks she might be able to dig out a few old contacts, but says she hasn't spoken to them in years. They're all people she met while working at a summer camp in Maine in 1998. It seems a long shot. Kate tells me that her one and only trip to the US wasn't the best experience. Riding the Greyhound bus south to New York City at the end of the camp, she'd had her bag snatched at the Port Authority Bus Terminal and was later mugged in Central Park. She takes my pen and adds these details to our list of concerns.

Being completely ignorant of the geography, climate and population density of the United States, we don't think to register these three important factors on our list. It is an oversight we would come to realize in time.

We decide to go for it. We have no idea if what we're attempting will work, but it's important that we try. It's like Steve Jobs once said: You can't connect the dots looking forward. You can only connect them looking back. So you have to trust that the dots will somehow connect in your future. You have to trust in something – your gut, destiny, life, karma, whatever. We trust in our gut and believe we are doing the right thing.

We start playing around with names for the relay, tossing ideas in the air - *The American Relay*, *Relay across America*, *Relay for America*. But none of the names we come up with truly encapsulate what we're doing and why. We think about the nature of a relay with its many parts that combine to form one entity. One run, one purpose, one cause. And so finally One Run For Boston is born.

*****

After that our lives changed. There was no more sitting around drinking tea, philosophizing. We put our other projects on hold and poured all our time and energy into One Run For Boston. We gave ourselves just six weeks before the relay would begin.

We got to work designing a website, planning the route, setting up social media accounts and pitching for sponsorship. We called Dan, a buddy of ours who doesn't just build websites, he brings them to life. We begged him to get cracking on our website right away. He said he couldn't fit anything more into his working week but when we explained the cause he agreed to work the weekend.

Websites are Dan's business and we couldn't expect him to create it for free. But neither Kate nor I had any cash to spare. My bank account was empty and I'd just written an IOU to my landlady promising her a rental check by the end of the month. I did have some money in a separate tax account. But that was money I owed the taxman. There was enough to cover next month's rent, Dan's website fees and a couple of flights to the US. But spending the money on anything but my tax bill meant I would risk penalties, bankruptcy and legal action. Thinking about it for almost 30 seconds, I popped along to the local branch of my bank and told the manager that I would be paying my tax from my current account. He transferred the money and on the way home I stopped off at Dan's house with a check for £3,500. It was all or nothing now.

*****

We knew that the best way to promote the relay would be via social media. Kate and I regularly used Facebook to keep in touch with friends, but that was about the limit of our digital expertise. If we were going to pull this off, we would require a far greater understanding of how the world's largest social network operated. We also needed to embrace Twitter. I have never really quite got Twitter. Left to Kate and me, our social media campaign was going to fall on its arse. In fact there wouldn't even be a campaign to speak of. We needed a young digital dynamo, and I knew just the fellow.

Our friend Jamie had flown to India after the Boston Marathon bombings, to film a short feature starring children orphaned by AIDS. I knew he was due back around now so I gave him a call. It went straight to voicemail and I left a message. Twenty minutes later Jamie called me back.

"Heya, Danny, I got your message!" He shouted cheerily down the phone from the passport control queue at Heathrow Airport. "I can help you out with your social media and marketing, no problem. But you didn't say what you were doing!"

Things had moved so fast that I'd forgotten it was only a couple of weeks since Kate had called round with the idea that would grow into One Run For Boston. I filled Jamie in, as briefly as I could, and asked him to come to my house as soon as possible. I told him to pack some clothes and stay as long as he liked. Mint choc mochas would be on the house. Then I heard the stern voice of a customs officer telling Jamie to turn off his phone. I heard Jamie's unmistakable voice saying, "Oops!" and we were cut off.

*****

Meanwhile, Kate sat at home working out the route in minute detail. Our first thought had been to start the relay in San Francisco, the only city in America where I knew anyone. We'd decided that when the time came, we would travel over to the US to follow the relay by car. If we started in San Francisco, at least we'd have a place to stay when we arrived. We fired up Google maps, entered San Francisco as the start point and Boston as the finish then hit *Get Directions*. It took just a couple of seconds for a blue line linking the two cities to flash up on our screen. It was a journey of 3,100 miles exactly. According to Google, you could drive it in 46 hours. Not bad I thought.

"But how long will it take to run it?" I asked Kate. She started scribbling some sums down on a scrap of paper. "Well, I guess if we allow an average pace of ten minutes per mile, that's 31,000 minutes, roughly 517 hours" she said. "Divide that by 24 and we're looking at about 22 days." Wow, three weeks and one day to run across an entire continent? Awesome! Using MapMyRun, Kate began to painstakingly divide the journey into stages of around ten miles. I left her to it. But the next day she called me up.

"How's it going?" I asked.

"Not great," Kate replied. "So, I've plotted the route out of California and now I'm looking at Nevada and Utah. Danny, did you know there's really not an awful lot there? It's just one big desert."

I thought about this for a minute. "But the people who live there will be used to running in the desert, won't they?" I tried to reason with her. "It's nothing to worry about. Can you see any cacti on the map? It would be cool to see some really big cacti, wouldn't it?" There was a moment's pause.

"Danny, there aren't any cacti just like there aren't any people. This place is beyond barren."

Hmm. That was a bit of a bugger.

"I think we should start in Los Angeles and go via Arizona and New Mexico. That way we can pass through Oklahoma City too"

It would be poignant since Oklahoma City had suffered its own terrorist attack. We'd already decided the route should go via the 9/11 Memorial in New York City. The relay would travel 3,300 miles, through fourteen different states and five different time zones. Little by little, One Run For Boston was beginning to take shape.

Jamie arrived at my house still showing signs of a bout of Delhi belly from his recent trip to India. After assigning him a private bathroom for his exclusive use, we got to work scouring the Web for running clubs along the route and potential sponsors. With less than four weeks to go, I worried we hadn't given ourselves enough time. Ever the optimist, Jamie explained that those four weeks were really more like eight. I didn't quite understand. "Look at it this way," he said. "We're going to be spending eighteen hours a day on this. That's more than double the normal 9-5 day. So we've effectively got double the number of days to get everything sorted. Eight weeks instead of four." You have to admire Jamie's logic.

As we had hoped, Jamie took control of the Facebook and Twitter campaigns.

"Make sure you invite everyone you know to 'like' the page" he told us. Kate and I wondered how getting friends in the UK to follow us was going to help us recruit runners in the US, but we did as we were told. At least our friends were easy 'likes' to get and made our page look popular.

But then, as if out of nowhere, Ian Alden Russell - our first real American - popped up and posted on our wall: "*Providence, RI reporting! Ready to support and spread the word.*" Kate and I went crazy, high fiving and chest bumping around the room. We couldn't believe our luck. How on earth had this happened?

"And that, my friends, is the power of Facebook," said Jamie, barely pausing to look up at us. It turned out that Kate's schoolfriend Jane had indeed liked the page and shared it with a friend in Ireland, who then shared it with a friend in America who turned out to be our real American, Ian. Kate and I were now beginning to understand the power of Facebook. The fact is, we are all connected. Jamie really did know what he was doing.

After the painstaking task of splitting 3,300miles into 10 miles sections Kate's route was ready to rumble. Once the website went public, runners could browse the legs online and sign up to run one in return for a $50 donation to the One Fund Boston. We hoped it would be as simple as it sounded. The website went live on Thursday 16 May. It was 8am in Los Angeles, 11am in Boston and 4pm at home in England.

We waited. No one signed up. Our pages of stages, one for each state, remained empty. We kept refreshing the live feed on the homepage that was supposed to alert us the moment someone signed up. There was nothing. Phoning Dan to check there wasn't a fault with the website he assured us it was working perfectly. We went to bed feeling worn out and dejected.

We woke the next morning and logged on again, nervously. As the screen loaded, a single name appeared, like a lone deer straying from the herd in the middle of the desert plains. Someone called Sandra Lochridge had signed up to run the first leg in California. We leapt out of our chairs and screamed at the top of our voices. We clicked on her name. Up popped a photo of a gorgeous woman with sparkly eyes and beneath it her reason for running:

"I'm running to show my support for Boston and all the people who had to deal with such a tragic event on April 15th. I love to run!"

Thank God for Sandra Lochridge! I raced around the kitchen, fist-pumping the air, then fell back into my chair realizing that we still had a long way to go.

*****

The website averaged two sign-ups a day over the next five days and I began to lose sleep. Unable to prove that our idea was taking off, we'd so far been unable to attract any sponsorship to pay our costs. My tax money was disappearing fast, and so was my waistline. The stress of organizing something with money that technically belonged to Her Majesty's Revenue and Customs was starting to get to me. I lay awake at night grinding my teeth, trying to push the 'what if's?' from my mind.

The fact that we had started to receive emails accusing us of orchestrating an elaborate scam wasn't helping. Some people assumed One Run For Boston was a fraudulent attempt to capitalize on a tragedy. It hadn't occurred to us that people may think we weren't genuine and it felt like a knife stabbing at my heart. We'd been concerned that Americans may take exception to our eagerness to help but we didn't expect they'd take us for fraudsters.

Early on in our planning we had contacted both the One Fund Boston and the Boston Athletics Association, organizers of the marathon, to let them know what we were planning. We had hoped that they would back us and might even share some contacts with us. Presumably up to their eyeballs in administrative work, we heard nothing back from the BAA. We did receive a short reply from the agency that had helped set up the One Fund Boston, but it wasn't what we wanted to hear. "We are gratefully and graciously accepting donations from organizations like yours," they told us. "But we cannot actively endorse specific fundraising initiatives."

For me, the final straw came when I saw a tweet from Fox News anchorman John Pertzborn, asking "Is One Run For Boston Legit?" The tweet, which I interpreted as being less of an innocent question and more of an inflammatory statement, bounced around the whole country before we had a chance to defend ourselves.

I got in my car and drove straight to Kate's house. I was barely through the door before I started telling her that this wasn't working. People didn't trust us. Not enough people had signed up and I was probably going to jail because I'd spent the money I'd been saving to pay off my tax bill. "You're not going to go to jail, Danny!" Kate tried to calm me. But going to jail wasn't even my biggest fear. What I feared most was the alternative; having to return to the City and sell my soul, doing a job I despised so that I could repay the tax man.

"It's going to be alright, Danny," Kate reassured me. "We've got the relay legs online now and people *are* signing up. I'll give that Pertzborn fella a call and sort him out. Just give this a bit more time." But I wasn't listening. As far as I was concerned this had been nothing more than an educational experience. We'd tried our best. But it was over.

Chapter 6

I left Kate's house with my head hung low, dragging my feet, and wondering what I was going to do now. Switching off my phone, I went to see some mates. They asked me how things were going but they could tell, just by looking at me, that things weren't going well. They bought me a few drinks and did their best to cheer me up. By the time I left for home I was feeling better, if a little wobbly, having spent time with the friends I'd mostly neglected since April 15.

Back home I switched on my phone and a flurry of activity filled the screen. Kate had been trying to call me all evening and sent a text message saying: 'Spoken to Pertz. All is cool. We're now best buddies.' I don't know whether it was her eloquence or her accent that won the Fox TV anchorman, John Pertzborn over, but whatever it was it worked. Taking a total about-turn, Pertz was promising to do as much as he could to support the event. He followed up with an email saying the news station would like to feature an interview with two of the St. Louis runners in the morning, adding, "Looks like a fantastic fundraiser." Just a few hours earlier this guy Pertz had come close to pushing me over the edge of a cliff. But right then I just wanted to hug him. What a relief! To have Fox against us would have been seriously bad. But having Fox on our side could be super double acepants.

The next day, we tuned in to watch the breakfast news broadcast live via the station's web stream. Wearing striking blue and yellow 'Boston Stands As One' T-shirts, two of our newly signed-up runners from Saint Louis joined John Pertzborn in the studio. It was so exciting to see these real people - our runners - talking about One Run For Boston so passionately on television.

"I might have known he'd be the type to wear a bow tie," Jamie tutted, as Pertz introduced the item with a clip from the movie Forrest Gump.

"Shhhh!" hissed Kate, shooting him a deadly look. Clearly Jamie had forgotten that Kate and Pertz were now best friends forever. The two runners, Mary Hoatlin and Andrew Koziatek, spoke of how they'd signed up to run in the relay because they wanted to do more than just donate money to show their support for the bombing victims. They couldn't have put it more perfectly.

The tide was turning. An influential tweeter from Boston, a songwriter and producer with over 67,000 followers, picked up the story and tweeted: *Check out @OneRunForBoston and what they're doing for my city #Boston*. It was just the virtual high-five we needed.

News was spreading and we watched as the relay legs were being snapped up from the west to the east coast. People were even signing up to join other runners on the same leg and the total amount of funds raised kept rising. I was waking up 2 or 3 times a night excited to see the new total rise to over $30,000.

We were back on! We sat in my kitchen - the three amigos - watching the live feed on our homepage go crazy as runner after runner signed up to play their part. The emails that had questioned our legitimacy were replaced by emails of support and encouragement, praising what we were doing. Much to our relief, people seemed to have no issue with the fact that we were British; they just thanked us for caring enough to put on this awesome event. I couldn't contain myself and started cheering the positivity that was radiating out across the states.

I was so happy I took to Twitter to declare: "I love positivity so much!!!" Jamie replied with a somewhat less excitable: "I love coffee." The 18 hour days were taking their toll. Jamie had even stopped adding hot chocolate to his coffee for fear it was diluting the caffeine hit.

It was a short-lived high. Gradually I allowed my anxieties to get the better of me again. Now that people were signing up in droves, we were under a different kind of pressure. We still didn't know for sure that the relay would work even if we had all the people lined up to run it. *What if the event simply doesn't live up to the hype?* I wondered. *What if we fail?* Forest fires were raging in Santa Monica, just west of Los Angeles, threatening the area where we planned to start the relay in a little over a week's time. For the first time I realized how precarious this all was. Just about anything could happen, anywhere at any time, and the whole event could be brought to a grinding halt.

Then there was still the ever-present question of our budget, or lack of one. We'd said from the start that we wanted to cover our costs with corporate sponsorship rather than dipping into the runners' sign-up fees. We desperately needed some sponsorship if we were to avoid bankrupting ourselves. Whizzing through another list of companies, I found a guy I used to cycle with in London who now worked for Athletes for a Fit Planet in Boston. They help make events carbon neutral and greener. They were super keen to get behind One Run For Boston and agreed not just to make us carbon neutral, but to cover some of our costs as well. This act of faith was a huge boost and we set to work again with increased vigor. Before long, Poland Spring, a brand of Nestlé Waters, had sent an email saying they were on board for a figure that meant I wasn't going to go to jail for my tax evasion.

The runners seemed to be as addicted to the live feed as I was. They were checking it as they woke up, throughout their working day and last thing before bed. We even had a husband email us, complaining that his wife was spending all night on the ORFB page and he was feeling left out. One such addict was Mary Hoatlin in St

Louis, one of the runners who had been interviewed on TV. Mary said she would do anything she could to help make One Run For Boston a success. Mary and Ian - our man from Rhode Island who had been the first to respond via Facebook - became official ambassadors and set to work trying to find runners to fill the relay legs which were still open. Mary launched a celebrity twitter campaign, in an effort to raise the profile of the event. Although she did spend most of that time tweeting Kevin Spacey on whom she seemed to have quite a crush.

Ian arranged access to the 9/11 Memorial, and attended meetings on our behalf in Boston to try and placate the city's Public Events Committee, who didn't seem keen on us closing Downtown Boston with the hundreds of runners who were signing up for the last leg.

Ian set up a One Run For Boston Facebook group in addition to the main page, so that runners could contact each other and ask any nagging questions about the relay. It was quite quiet to begin with, until Mary put out a post encouraging people to introduce themselves and to say what inspired them to join the relay. After this, the page never stopped.

Runners told stories of how they had been running the marathon, or supporting friends near the bomb sites and had seen the destruction. Others stated that they were running to show that terrorism doesn't limit society - it strengthens those it wishes to break. Some said they wanted to show their children that they will not live in fear. Some simply said they wanted to look back and know they were part of this epic event, to know they had taken part in something bigger than themselves. But one thing on which they all agreed was that they wanted to support the victims and running seemed a great way to do so.

With the ice well and truly broken, people started posting photos of themselves on training runs wearing the One Run For Boston T-shirts donated to each and every runner by Goodwear. These blue shirts, with One Run For

Boston printed in yellow and white beside a signature flame, were now our uniform. We had an identity and people were proud to be a part of it.

Joining Kate and her husband, Steve, at her parents' house for dinner, we talked of little other than the relay. Kate's family was full of questions and concerns.

"Have you taken out insurance for the event?" Kate's dad asked. "America is a highly litigious nation you know and people sue at the drop of the hat."

This had crossed our minds but we knew that getting insurance for such an event would be a costly business and something we simply couldn't afford.

"Everyone has to sign a waiver," Kate said. "I think we'll be fine."

Kate's dad raised an eyebrow.

"Have you sorted out where you'll be staying?" Kate's mum wanted to know. "You're not just going to sleep in the car are you?"

With little funds to spend on accommodation, this was indeed what we proposed to do. But Kate was quick to put her mum's mind at rest. "No, no, Mum. We'll be staying in hotels and maybe even with some of the runners."

Steve mentioned the devastating tornados that had ripped through the southern suburbs of Oklahoma City the previous week, flattening a school and killing dozens of people.

"Would you two know what to do if you saw a tornado coming your way?" Steve asked, concerned for the safety of his beloved wife. Kate and I looked at each other. In England the worst we get is a flood or a bit of sunburn if we're lucky. These sorts of weather conditions just don't exist. Find the nearest house and knock for help perhaps? We had no idea, and sticking to my 'best to not think about worst case scenarios' plan, I never found out.

"And Steve's not going with you?" clarified Kate's mum with a mixture of amazement, confusion and alarm written across her face.

"No," confirmed Kate, squeezing Steve's hand under the table. Someone had to stay at home and pay the bills.

*****

Kate's parents' fretfulness seemed to rub off on her and she began quizzing me on whether I'd got all the various documents I would need for the trip such as passport, travel insurance and driving license. I smiled at her with my best patronizing face and told her of course I had. "And are you sure they're all in date?" she asked. Honestly, what did she take me for? I gave her a withering look and thanked her, in a tone dripping with sarcasm.

We had four days left until the start of the relay and we still hadn't booked any flights. There were still forty-six legs to fill, mostly in Arizona, New Mexico and Texas. Kate and I talked about how many miles we thought we could manage per day. 20 miles each would destroy us, but that was still not enough to close the gaps.

But then it happened. Something occurred that made me decide that I would happily run all the other legs myself if I had to. I would run 80 miles a day through wind, fire and water if that's what it took to get the baton to Boston and into the hand of Miss Massachusetts. She'd just signed up for the last stage and that was it, our flights were booked.

Chapter 7

Two days before our flight was due to leave London for Los Angeles, we were still awaiting the arrival of one very important piece of kit; the relay baton. Designed by a friend of ours, Jon Parlby, a 3D Product Design student down the road at Plymouth University, the relay baton and a spare, had been sent out by the manufacturer Malcolm Nicholls Ltd. earlier in the week. They were now in the hands of the Royal Mail and we just had to hope and pray they arrived at my house in time for me to make the flight. We agreed Kate would go ahead to London and catch the flight regardless, while I stayed at home waiting for the batons to arrive. Although far from ideal, the relay would have to start without the baton if necessary.

Kate rang me from her brother's house, just outside London. She wanted an update on the baton, but took the opportunity to double check I had located and packed all my vital travel documents.

"Promise me you've got your passport and your driving license and they're in your bag, ready to go," Kate said. She was trying to sound light-hearted but I could tell she wanted to add "or else I'll pulverize you," to the end of the sentence.

I gave her my usual response, "Yes, yes, yes. Don't worry, everything's under control." It was a good job she was at the end of the phone a couple of hundred miles away and couldn't see my face contorting under the pressure of keeping up the pretense. I was lying to Kate.

Kate and I are polar opposites. This partially explains why we managed to get One Run For Boston off the ground. We complement each other's weaknesses. My biggest weakness is organization. In fact I can't even call it a weakness. I just don't have any – none at all. Kate on the other hand is the 'Oracle of Organization'. If she could number, file and alphabetically order her friends she would, but she's also good at writing things down and filing things away. It's a process that I simply can't get the hang of.   That's why Kate wouldn't allow me to have anything to do with any of the event logistics, from planning the route to booking the flights.

I blame it on my dyslexia but I think there are bigger forces at work. Some days I forget friends' names; I've arrived at a triathlon race without my bike; I took my sister to Prague to run a half-marathon but, when we tried to check in at the airport, the woman behind the desk kindly pointed out that our flights were booked for the following month. I took a girl to see the West End version of Billy Elliot; a year before it was launched. She didn't take it well. I could go on. I have problems – that's for sure.

The stress of not knowing where my passport was meant I hadn't looked for it. I hid my head in the sand. I knew it was somewhere; but where? My driving license was 4 years out of date. That I knew. I had been receiving notifications to renew it every few months for as long as I could remember. But I filed all these papers neatly in the bin before returning my head to the sand. In my defense, I had gone to the Post Office and requested a license renewal form the week before we were due to fly. But they said it would take at least six weeks to be returned so there wasn't a lot of point. I hate filling in forms, it is so frigging boring. If I was ever a prisoner of war, the enemy could retrieve all my secrets by threatening to put a simple form in front of me. It's at least as effective as blow torching my feet. I have the Myers-Briggs personality type ENFP - Extraversion, Intuition, Feeling, Perception. ENFPs energize and stimulate others through their contagious enthusiasm. We are said to live in the world of exciting possibilities. The details of everyday life are seen as trivial drudgery. ENFPs place no importance on detailed, maintenance-type tasks. 'This is a challenging area of life for most ENFPs and can be frustrating for ENFP's family members and friends,' the publications say. Frustrating indeed! Just ask Kate.

Just as I was finishing the call with Kate I spotted the postman walking up my driveway with a baton-shaped parcel. Thank goodness for that. Not only had the baton arrived, this good news would distract Kate from worrying about my documents, or lack of. I reassured her I would see her at Heathrow airport in the morning and hung up. But as I did so, I realized that not having a valid driving license could potentially ruin the whole trip. Kate surely couldn't drive the whole way across America. And my passport; where the hell was it? I tried my best to focus and concentrate. I asked myself, where I would put something when I wanted to keep it safe. *Think Danny, think. Where could that passport be?* Then it struck me I dashed into the kitchen and reached into the furthest recesses of my spice cupboard. Hiding behind the garam masala and cayenne pepper, I found my passport. It smelled of a nice curry!

*****

Kate meets me at Heathrow airport two hours before our flight is due to leave. It's a weekday morning and the terminal is fairly deserted. Wandering up to the check-in desk, I hand over my fragrant passport. "Mr. Bent, would you mind just waiting over here a minute?" the check-in woman asks me. "I'm going to have to make a call." It seems no sooner has she picked up the phone, than a tall, well-dressed American in his fifties appears out of nowhere. "I'm from the Department of Homeland Security," he says. "Please come with me, Mr. Bent." I turn to look at Kate, her face is a picture. I'd forgotten to tell her that this sometimes happens to me. Having travelled

40

through the republics of the former Soviet Union, Russia, China and Pakistan on a previous cycle ride from London to India, I often get asked a lot of questions at airports. The fact that I'd recently returned from a 24hr trip to Morocco having stolen a friend's passport and whisked them away as a surprise isn't helping. It would seem I'm on some kind of security list and every time my passport is scanned at an airport, an alert flashes up. I then end up having to explain to security staff that I am not a friend of Abu Hamza-al-Masri, the Islamic Fundamentalist with a hook for a hand, who was extradited from the UK charged with plotting to open a training camp for al-Qaeda militants in the United States. Eventually, I manage to persuade Mr. Homeland Security that I pose no threat, and Kate and I continue on to the baggage check.

Having overheard some of my conversation with the security officer Kate keeps reciting excerpts of it to me, whilst giggling. "What was really funny," she tells me, "was when you asked him if you're on some kind of international alert list." She summons up her best American accent to do an impression of the solemn security officer, "The only thing that matters right now Mr. Bent, is that you are on *my* list." We arrive at the X-ray machines laughing and put our hand luggage on the conveyor belt.

I hear a woman asking, "Who does the black bag belong to?" No one answers her. "Whose is the black bag with the coat hanger inside?" she asks again. Oops, someone's in trouble, I think to myself, before realizing that the black bag she is referring to is actually mine.

"It's mine," I say, "but I didn't pack any coat hangers." The woman shows me the x-ray image of my bag on her screen and I see the unmistakable shape of a relay baton. "That is NOT a coat hanger!" I say defensively, taking the baton out of the bag to show her before hugging it close to my chest. Inspired by the shape of a peace lily, the baton was sleek and smooth and beautiful. The woman looks at me, a little surprised by my reaction and I realize I am already beginning to feel a powerful connection with this incredible piece of molded plastic that our friend Jon has designed.

In the departure lounge we collapse into chairs, exhausted from the last few weeks of working round the clock and pleased to have a moment to relax. "Have you had anything to eat yet today?" Kate asks me. I haven't and now she mentions it I'm feeling rather famished. We're just heading off towards one of the cafés when we hear the last call for our flight being announced on the tannoy. We look at each other for a split second then gather up our things and start running.

We race towards a sign for the gates which tells us that the one we need is 15 minutes' walk away. "They'll wait for us, surely!" Kate yells as we rush through the terminal, barging people out of our way. We're still 30 gates away and sweat is beginning to pour through our T-Shirts. I'm beginning to wonder how on earth we're going to cover the relay legs that don't yet have runners if we can't even manage a sprint through an airport. Tearing around the corner to our gate, we see the staff looking at their watches and then at us, with utter contempt. They scan our passports and I hear those words for a second time, "Mr. Bent, would you mind just waiting over here a minute? I'm going to have to make a call."

After another interrogation, by plain-clothed British police officers this time, we are the last people to enter the plane and take our seats in the cabin. As the sweat starts to dry, I am too busy unwrapping my eye mask and headphones to notice the smell at first. But I can hear Kate sniffing and then the pong hits me. We have a fourteen-hour flight ahead of us and there is nothing we can do. Little did we know that sweating and stinking would soon become our standard.

Our TVs don't work so we make our own fun on the plane. There is a group of British soldiers onboard, heading out to California for a rugby tour. We try to recruit them to run the first stage of the relay with us on Friday. It is clear they think we're a bit weird. But it's passing the time and Kate seems to be enjoying hanging out and having conversations with random people we've not met before. This is one of my favorite pastimes but I get the feeling Kate is new to it. Seeming more energized than I've seen her for a long time, she can't sit still. I feel exhausted and hungry. Kate does another tour of the cabin whilst I blag four extra pasties from the flight attendant. Kate returns and settles down for a special edition of Man vs. Food, starring me.

A little later, Kate wangles with a couple of portable DVD players that may or may not have been given to her to stop us bothering other passengers. Time for a bit of *Les Misérables*, I think to myself, loading my DVD. Kate goes for *The Perks of Being a Wallflower*. Unable to concentrate, I drift in and out of sleep for a couple of hours, missing most of my film. When I wake up, Kate is facing away from me, staring out of the window. I give her a tap and she turns round; her face is flushed. It's clear she's been crying.

"What's wrong?" I ask, no longer drowsy but a little bit alarmed.

"Oh, nothing," she says, embarrassed. "Just the film I guess."

"Really?" I say, surprised. I had always thought of Kate as pretty unemotional, I thought I was the crier.

"I don't know," she says. "It just made me think…" before she can finish her sentence she is sobbing uncontrollably.

Kate appears to be having some kind of breakdown and it all feels a bit surreal. I rush to the toilets to get some tissues to wipe away her tears. By the time I come back she's just about managed to compose herself. Having been on such a high just a few hours before, she's suddenly crashed and burned like a kid after a birthday party. With

43

the power of speech regained, she can't stop apologizing and tries to convince me she's OK. "I think I'm just a bit tired and emotional," she says, laughing at herself.

"What was it about the film that triggered all this?" I ask. "I thought *Les Misérables* was meant to be the gloomy film!"

Kate laughs again but then falls silent for a moment. "It just got me thinking about the people in my life who mean the most to me. These past few years I've become so preoccupied with what I've been doing, bouncing from one thing to the next, I haven't made enough time for the people I love." I think back to the conversation about our futures we'd had around my kitchen table just before we heard about the marathon bombings. Now, two months on and 30,000 feet above the Atlantic I sense Kate is finally letting go and re-evaluating what matters most in life.

*****

Worn out by the outpouring of emotion, we fall into a deep sleep. When we wake, we're flying over California, not far from Los Angeles. Craning our necks, we look out of the window. "Blimey, it's quite hilly in California isn't it?" Kate says, sounding surprised.

"Oh yeah, there's mountains everywhere you look along the coast of California," I tell her. "It's because of all that plate activity. Not man vs. food plates – the other ones." That brief spell I'd spent as a junior school teacher had really stood me in good stead for moments like these. "I guess we'll be heading up and over those mountains on day two of the relay."

The color drains from Kate's face as she takes in this information. The silence is broken by the pilot announcing that we'll shortly be beginning our descent. He tells us that southern California is experiencing a bit of a heat wave at the moment. "It's a comfortable 78°F / 25°C in Los Angeles right now," he says, "but for those of you heading east, watch out for top temperatures around the 118°F / 47°C mark." Kate looks at me with a 'WTF?' expression.

Even with her exceptional planning and eye for detail, she has overlooked a couple of important matters.

"Danny, this is a disaster," she tells me. "I didn't allow any extra time for mountains or heat waves. How the hell are the runners going to stick to ten-minute mile pace if they're scaling mountains in that kind of heat?"

"Don't worry," I say, "they'll smash it. No issue." Kate looks unconvinced.

Reaching passport control, I'm once again dragged off to a special unit for the usual search and questioning. I tell Kate to go on to Arrivals without me and see if she can book us a hotel for a couple of nights. Reunited 30 minutes later, without me having to experience any rubber glove treatment, Kate tells me we're booked into the cheapest motel she could find, a couple of miles from Venice Beach, the starting point for the relay. It sounds perfect.

Risking extortionate international roaming charges, I check what's happening online. The One Run For Boston Facebook feed is going wild. While we've been in the air, three Ultra runners from the east coast have offered to run a number of the empty stages. They just needed to find flights. As Ultra runners, they spend most of their time running, and most of their hard-earned cash is spent fueling and clothing them for their epic workouts. They asked the group if anyone had any spare Air Miles they could donate to the cause. Will Allender and John Kohler, saw the post and within a few hours Stephen Bender, Gary Allen and Ty Thurlow had their flights taken care of and we had 10 fewer stages to worry about running.

This was the first of many acts of generosity and kindness that the group, and particularly Will Allender, would become famous for over the coming weeks. At the airport, we were left awestruck by the incredible acts of generosity that One Run For Boston had inspired.

Gary Allen wrote a post thanking John and Will on Facebook ending, *'Not All Superheroes Wear Capes.'*

Chapter 8

Standing in the back of the biggest pickup I have ever seen in my life, I couldn't stop myself from grinning. A beautiful navy blue, with shiny silver alloys, the truck exuded power and testosterone. I loved it! It was perfect.

"This is perfect, Kate!"

Lucky for me, the girl at the rental car desk hadn't seemed to notice my license was out of date. She just pointed out the window and told us to take any of the SUVs parked in lot C. We had made our way outside with Kate stopping to get her glasses out of her bag. By the time she looked up, I had disappeared.

"Isn't this just perfect, Kate?" I repeat, towering over Kate from the back of the truck.

Five minutes later, I'm driving away from the parking lot, with Kate beside me and all our gear thrown in the back of a very sensible, and grey, Ford Escape. Kate's practicality has won out over my testosterone-fuelled impulse in the dispute over the car. I put on my best grumpy face but it doesn't last long. As we leave the airport, we drive under a sign saying *Welcome to California*. We stop the car in the middle of the road and jump out, handing the camera to a passer-by. I lie across the bonnet and pose for the camera, like the over-excited British tourist that I am. The childish smile is back.

*****

We head straight to Venice Beach to check out the first stage of the relay. It is grey and surprisingly cold. A misty haze hangs in the air. So much for this heat wave! We pass a couple of tramps, pushing trolleys full of their belongings along the strip, past herbal medicine shops and tattoo parlors offering to ink your body, or pierce any extremity. It isn't quite what we were expecting but it is frigging cool! Artists adorn the streets pulsing with carnival beats that fashion icons bop along to.

Passing Muscle Beach I see a man with a stomach more ripped than the washboard, kitchen sink and toaster put together. He has deltoids the incredible hulk would be jealous of. I simply can't help myself. Gesturing to Kate to get the camera ready, I jump the fence and land beside the hunk. He looks a little shocked. Noticing the bar he's been lifting is twice as heavy as me, I begin to wonder whether I should have given him some warning. I hope he doesn't consider my leap over the fence to be an act of aggression. That would not end well for me. "Hey man!" I say, trying my best to sound cool and relaxed. "That's some heavy shit you're lifting." I thought if I got in quick with a bit of flattery he'd be less likely to hurt me. "Can we take a photo?" I ask quickly. He looks at me and I flash him a smile. "Please?" I add, as a bit of an afterthought. His pal swaggers over. Oh no. It's two against one now. At least Kate's got the camera to capture my last moments.

"Ten dollars," says his pal.

Ten dollars for a photo? Now that's taking the piss. "That's a bit steep," I say, suddenly unafraid. I hate being ripped off.

"Ten dollars" he repeats.

"Really?"

"Just a quick snap for the album" Kate pleads. The hunk nods and tells his friend to move aside. Moving in on him super fast, I put my arm around his solid waist. Kate reminds us to say "Cheese!" and leaving him with a slap on the back and a quick "Cheers mate!" I jump over the fence as fast as my lily white ass will allow.

I'm feeling pumped with adrenaline and run excitedly back to Kate, snatching the camera out of her hand to see how the photo turned out.

"Did you get a close look at that man's face?" she asks me in a whisper as we walk away. "He had tear-shaped tattoos on his cheeks. What is that all about?" I have no idea but neither of us thinks it's a good idea to go back and ask him.

It starts to get dark. We wander back to the car and I ask Kate what she thinks of California so far.

"It's really weird," she says. "I've spent hours on Google maps, looking at street views of Venice Beach and Santa Monica. In some ways it's all really familiar. But to be honest it's not exactly the warm and welcoming place I thought it would be." She turns to look out to the ocean. "It all feels a bit lonely." I know what she means. As soon as she's said it I realize I am feeling the same.

But in the pit of our stomachs, battling for space amid the nerves and self-doubt there are balls of excitement. We just hadn't had time to properly imagine what this moment would be like. About to embark on the most extraordinary journey we feel weird knowing that no-one around us has the faintest idea about why we have come here. Kate says she feels we stick out like sore thumbs, and yet at the same time she has never felt more anonymous.

Was this really happening? Were we really about to embark on a running relay across an entire continent? A moment's reflection on why we were doing it brought us both back to reality.

*****

We get back in the car and I realize how late it is. 7pm in California is 3am back home. I feel wrecked. I throw some trail mix into my mouth to refuel me and accidentally spill some. It's messy stuff, trail mix. Kate watches as the nuts and seeds fall between the seats and into the foot well. It prompts the first of Kate's rules of the road.

Kate's Rules #1: There will be no eating or drinking in the car.

Stressed and close to breaking point after the rollercoaster weeks we'd just come through, Kate was completely wired and becoming a little irrational. She worried incessantly. As her words and deeds exposed how stressed she was, I retreated further and further into myself. A little voice inside my head was telling me this trip could be harder than I thought.

Leaving Venice Beach, Kate takes the wheel for the first time. When it comes to driving, America has the rules all wrong. The driver sits in the wrong side of the car for starters. What is more, Americans drive on the wrong side of the road entirely and don't have any roundabouts. Kate's first attempt at driving in America is not a great success. Within minutes of starting the engine, she takes us the wrong way up a one-way street, into the path of an oncoming car. Eyeballing the driver of the car in front of us who frankly can't believe what he is seeing, we're going to have to reverse. Kate is getting stressed and starts swearing at the car as she tries to fathom out the stick of this automatic. "Take your time, Kate" I say. "Just be calm. Don't worry about the other cars." But I don't think she's listening. Having grown up in the countryside in England, where most of the roads are no wider than one car, Kate is bloody good at reversing. She manages to extract us from the one way street no trouble, but then parks up and gets out. "Maybe you should drive us back to the motel" she says, walking round to let me out the passenger door. "Sure" I say, a little relieved. "Perhaps your driving will be more suited to those nice long, straight desert roads?"

Back at the motel we park the car next to the Reception and go to check-in.

"Lock the car, Danny," Kate orders. I'm a bit taken aback.

"I thought we were just going to Reception to grab the keys to the room. We'll only be a few minutes."

"Yes, but you never know what can happen. We're in America, Danny. We need to lock the car at all times."

Kate's Rules 2: The car will be locked as soon as we remove our booties from it.

Kate had an idea that America was, on the whole, an unsafe place to be. I guessed this was probably a result of her experiences in 1998, when she was mugged in New York. In contrast, I like to assume that all people are the same and equal and that all can be trusted. I tell Kate that if someone is desperate enough to rob our car, I'd prefer that they just open the door rather than smash the window or get the keys from us at gun point. She thinks about it, but is not convinced of my logic.

I could see Kate's world was falling to pieces under the pressure she was feeling. The rules she was coming up with were just her way of trying to exert some control on her surroundings. This wasn't the real Kate. Locking the car was just one click. No issue.

Picking up the room key I head up to our room, stopping to collect my toothbrush from the car. In the room, Kate struggles through the door with all her bags. She's carried everything she's brought with her, up two flights of metal stairs to our room. "We can't leave anything in the car overnight," she tells me. "People may see it as an opportunity and steal it."

Kate's Rules 3: Nothing will be left in the car overnight.

Fumbling for the keys while balancing everything I own in my arms, I press the button and make sure I hear the click of the central locking system. I return to the room, drop my bags on the floor and fall face first onto one of the beds. Jet lag has completely smashed me. It is the early hours of the morning back in England and before my head even hits the pillow I fall asleep, leaving Kate organizing her belongings into neat and tidy piles.

The crazy thing about jet lag is that it makes you absolutely exhausted, but almost as soon as you fall asleep it wakes you up at ridiculous o'clock telling you it's time to get up again. I lie in bed unable to sleep, then decide to take my laptop into the bathroom trying not to wake Kate who is sleeping soundly. Sitting on the toilet, I fire off some emails. At 6am I go down to Reception in search of breakfast and I am on my second donut when Kate arrives, looking bleary-eyed. We smash back some highly-sugared coffee and make a plan for the day. We have 24hrs to sort ourselves out. Top priority is to get a US SIM card and some maps … and more coffee. We are going to amass quite a collection of Starbucks loyalty stamps.

We head out in search of a phone shop and are told to "Just go and knock on the door by the yellow Porsche." We do exactly that, passing the inappropriately named Morning Glory nursery school on our way. The door is made of metal bars and we peer through them into a dark and dingy store room. It doesn't feel entirely legit but we don't have a lot of options. "Hello!" I call out through the bars. "Is anybody there?" We hear a bit of chatter between a man and a woman in Spanish and eventually the woman opens the door to let us in. She gestures to us to go through the store room. We feel our way through the darkness, open a door and are surprised to find ourselves inside an actual shop with a front door looking out onto the main street. Blinking, our eyes adjust to the sunlight blazing in through the window. Our entrance may have been a bit unconventional but the man behind the counter is happy to help if he can. He takes our phones and begins trying various SIM cards.

While we wait, we get chatting to a couple of guys in the shop. One is English and has been living in LA since he moved over in the 1980s. He looks a lot like Ronnie Wood from the Rolling Stones but I don't mention it. It's not exactly much of a compliment. His friend is a potato farmer called Kenny. As we tell them about the relay, Kenny invites us to swing by the Venice Farmers' Market next morning on our way to the beach. "Just wait until you taste the cherries!" Kenny is clearly quite excited – it's the way his dirty beard is wavering. The man behind the counter tells us it's a no go with our phones. He can't unlock them, which means we have no choice but to buy a US phone. Kate's already heading out the door on her way to the T-Mobile store when I turn back to the man behind the counter and ask, "I don't suppose *you* have any cheap phones for sale?" Pausing, he explains, "I'm really just a repair business. I don't sell phones." But I can't help noticing a battered looking handset in a cabinet under the counter which appears to have a price tag on it. "What about that one?" I ask. "That one?" he says, looking surprised. "The owner dropped it and brought it in for me to replace the screen. They never came back for it." I thought about this for a moment. "Is it for sale?" I asked. "Sure, if you want it, it's for sale." And that is the story of how I scored an absolute bargain on the phone that we hoped would be our point of contact, our internet, our email and our GPS navigation system rolled into one. High hopes indeed for the price.

Our next stop is Barnes and Noble bookshop. We head straight for the map section and are surprised to find that all of the road atlases containing complete maps of the USA have next to no detail other than the major highways. I'd forgotten just how big America is. "I guess we could buy more detailed maps for each of the states that we're going through?" Kate suggests. "Don't be silly, that would cost an absolute fortune," I said. "And anyway, it won't be necessary. We've got the phone now and that's supposed to have some kind of 'sat nav' app. on it. And we've got your brother's Tom Tom. If we can get the maps loaded up on that, we'll be laughing."

I head to the checkout, armed with a $12 Rand McNally atlas under my arm and, at Kate's insistence, a fold-out city map of New York, just in case. As the cashier rings through our goods, I can't stop myself from asking if the store has *You've Gone Too Far This Time, Sir* in stock. I never tire of hearing, nor do I ever quite believe, that stores stock and sell copies of my book. "No, never heard of it," replies the cashier. Ego deflated, we leave quickly.

Once outside, I put more money in the parking meter while Kate fields a call from a documentary maker based down the road in Santa Monica. I look around me and observe the typical American high street, with each lane of traffic twice the size of the average city center road back home. No wonder the Americans go wild about the English cities which still have cobbled walkways. I pick up the gist of Kate's phone call – the film maker is cancelling our dinner date. He obviously has bigger fish to fry. Missing this eleventh-hour opportunity to get someone onboard to document the One Run For Boston story is a major blow. But I'm surprised by how little I'm bothered by the news. I guess it's one less thing to worry about. I'm motioning to Kate to cut the call - it really doesn't sound like we should be wasting any more of our time on this guy – when a group of runners comes past. There's something a little bit different about them, so I stop and ask them what they're up to. It turns out they are taking part in a race organized by a local running shop to celebrate the launch of their new store. Out of the blue, one of the women asks me to marry her whilst her friend snaps a photo. Was this the effect of my English accent? Was it true that hot American girls fall for nerdy-looking British guys? I could feel the love of my life edging closer. The women explain that to win the race they have to complete certain tasks and get photo evidence. The marriage proposal was just one of a list of tasks. Damn it.

Undeterred, I tell them about One Run For Boston and encourage them down to the start the next day. Still worried that no-one will show up, I have visions of Kate and me standing alone on Venice Beach with just the tramps and hippies for company. The women suggest I go back to the running store with them and recruit some more runners there. Waving at Kate, who is still on the

53

phone, I point across the road to where we're heading and she nods, gesturing she'll see me in there.

I walk into the running store to rapturous applause. They assume I am part of the race and congratulate me on being the first runner back. I'm quick to put them right and, as Kate arrives at my side, we begin to tell them about the relay. Perhaps seeking an opportunity to get some good exposure for their brand, the store owners offer to kit us out in their finest running gear. They give us a tour of what is honestly the biggest sports shop I have ever seen and soon we're trying everything on. I take some shorts, a cap (which soon becomes my savior in the desert) and socks. I frigging love socks. I rarely wear them as I like to be barefoot, but I collect socks in the way a lot of women collect shoes. You don't have to wear them. They're just nice to have.

Kate and I are enjoying the attention way too much and we've lost track of time. Looking at my watch, I tell Kate we have to get going. We thank everyone profusely and hope we'll see at least a few of them at Venice Beach in the morning. We throw our swag bags in the car and race off to Encino and the Fleet Feet store that we've been using as a mailing address. We arrive to find half a dozen large boxes waiting for us. Amongst other things, there are One Run For Boston T-shirts sent by Goodwear and a pair of running shoes for each of us in the Boston Marathon colors, courtesy of New Balance. We put them on and immediately look and feel fantastic!

We make one last stop in Santa Monica to double check the handoff location at the end of the first group stage. I can't contain my excitement. Touching the ground, I tell Kate that this is where Evy, the runner signed up to run the second relay leg, will take the baton tomorrow. But Kate isn't listening. As darkness falls, she's getting jittery, so we make our way back to our empty, clean and locked car.

Leaving Santa Monica to head back to our motel is a right royal pain. The traffic is terrible. There seems to be a lot of road closures and diversions in place and we worry about how this might affect the relay. If nothing else, it's going to make following the runners by car tricky. We sit in a traffic jam listening to the radio and learn that President Obama is flying into Santa Monica in the morning. It sounds as if the situation on the roads is going to be even worse by the morning. "Get ready for an almighty Obamajama!" jokes the radio DJ.

Eventually, we get back to the motel and get all our stuff packed up ready for an early start. Just before we go to sleep I decide to call Evy, the runner of our second stage. Wanting to make sure she is ready to rock and roll, I also want to share my excitement. After three rings she picks up.

"Hi Evy, it's Danny from One Run For Boston," I gush, "I'm just checking you're all groovy for tomorrow."

"Oh, hi Danny," she says, a little awkwardly. "Listen, about that. I've been meaning to call you. I have another appointment. I'm not going to make it."

Chapter 9

A grey, overcast sky reminds me of home. I do a double take as a rusty tractor chugs past our parked car. We really could be back in rural Devon. Then a boy with sun-bleached hair and a dark surfer's tan skates past our car, towed along by his dog, and I realize that the tractor is not plowing a field but manicuring the soft, white sands that lead down to the crashing waves of the Pacific Ocean.

Killing the ignition, Kate and I sit in silence, staring out to sea. We keep the car doors closed as long as possible. We'd been here two days before, but this was different. The same doors now opened on a different world, like portals to a strange new reality, a gateway to a new us. We did not know if the journey of a lifetime lay before us, where footfalls would be our heartbeat, or if we'd be running to catch the first plane home, tails between our legs, embarrassed to have ever thought it possible.

Taking the plunge, I open the door and salty sea air engulfs us. Gulping it down in a series of deep breaths, I try to relax. Squawking seagulls follow as we walk the mile or so to Venice Beach Pier, the starting point of the relay. The tension across my shoulders rounds my back. My jaw is locked and the tightness of my diaphragm is obvious in my voice as I shakily ask Kate if she thinks people will really show up. "I hope so," she replies quietly, for she has no more of a clue than me.

My phone call to Evy the night before had shaken me. If one person could let us down without blinking an eyelid, who was to say that others wouldn't too? The gap left by Evy had been filled easily enough after an emergency appeal posted on Facebook, but we didn't want to make a habit of it. Seeing my post, One Run For Boston ambassador Mary Hoatlin, the woman who puts the Staint in St. Louis, had replied offering to contact all runners the day before their stages, asking them to confirm they were ready to go. Continuing along the beach in silence, I feel our new phone vibrate in my pocket, alerting me to a new email. It's from Mary. "All runners confirmed for today and tomorrow ☺." Mary was turning out to be a bit of a legend.

As we walk the last half-mile, Kate and I discuss how we should behave around the runners. It's not something we'd normally think about. In fact it seems crazy to even mention it, but it suddenly occurs to us that given the serious purpose of the relay, it might be seen as disrespectful if we appear too jovial. Yet, we want One Run For Boston to be a positive experience, proof that good things can come from bad. We solve the dilemma by agreeing to wait and see how the runners behave, then simply follow their lead. Until we know better, we will play on the safe side and greet everyone with a solemn shake of the hand and some polite chit-chat. If they know that we're British, they'll surely expect nothing more anyway.

The parking lot at Venice Beach, just short of the pier, is dominated by a large truck with a twenty meter aerial sticking out of it, like a giant cocktail stick. It can only be a television truck. I spot a woman wearing leggings, a sun visor and a purple T-shirt with the words Running for Boston written in white. She looks like she's a runner. Clocking my yellow and blue T-shirt, she smiles. She's one of us! The relief that we have a runner completely overrides any thoughts I might have had of how to act. I let out a whoop and run towards her. Stopping in her tracks, she wonders whether to start running prematurely in the opposite direction, but before she has a chance to react, I am upon her with my arms wrapped tightly round her in a tight hug. Recognizing that her life is not in danger, she relaxes into my arms and whispers in my ear, "thank you for doing this."

*****

It seems fitting that the first person we meet is Sandra Lochridge. Sandra was the very first person to sign up to run when the website went live just three weeks ago. Unable to sleep, Sandra has already been at the parking lot for over an hour when we arrive. She tells me that the van with the big antennae is from KTLA Channel 5. "The cameraman has been here since 6.30am," she explains. "He says he's been sent to film the start of the relay but I told him that he's way too early, that nothing is really happening until 10am." We wander over to the truck and join Kate. "They want to go live at 9am," she tells us, "but there's no one here yet!" The cameraman is on his phone to the studio. He must be wondering why on earth he's been sent here. This isn't going to feature in his top ten list of red hot assignments for sure. As soon as he gets off the phone, the cameraman slaps his camera on top of a tripod and starts filming. "Do you not want to wait a little while for more runners to show up?" Kate asks him, a little desperately. "Not possible," he replies panning the camera round as scenes of an empty parking lot with not much happening are beamed into people's living rooms across Los Angeles.

I shrug my shoulders. "At least they made the effort to get down here," I reason, convincing myself that making the breakfast news with panoramas of an empty car park was better than not making it at all. But Sandra is less-forgiving. "I contacted every news outlet in Los Angeles to get them to come down here this morning," she says. "It's just typical that the only station that actually bothers to show up gets here so damn early that they miss what they came here to film!" Kate and I didn't expect a big media send off but Sandra is adamant that it's what One Run For Boston deserves. "The reporters are probably out there chasing down the latest bad news story as we speak," she goes on. "They're not interested in the good news stories." She has a point but I wonder if that's because as a society *we're* not interested in the good news stories. Why is it that negativity sells papers and lifts viewing figures? Surely that's all wrong? What if the media were to stop feeding us stories of calamity and devastation and give us more good news? Might this inspire us to live more positively and bring about some good news stories of our own?

I file that thought away as more people begin to arrive. Standing modestly among the growing crowd is Holly Miller, a woman who models sports clothing for good reason. Having already signed up to run this first stage and two more in Arizona, it is Holly who 12 hours earlier responded to my emergency appeal on Facebook, and signed up to fill the runner-less stage two.

With thirty minutes to go, laughter fills the air and rows of straight white teeth fill every American smile around me. I can't help but return my own wonky-toothed English smile. "Where are all the men?" I ask. I am assured that it is normal to see more women than men at running events in the US. This comes as a surprise to me because back home in the UK men outnumber women 5-1 at most races. If ever there was a reason for men to start running in America, this was it.

I know of many couples who have met through running. Running clubs can be hotbeds for romance and my running club in London, the Serpentine Running Club, is no exception. It's the best dating agency in London. I am slightly taken aback to learn that one of the club's romantic success stories is joining us for this first stage of the relay. Ruth Jackson is English, her husband is American, and they met through the Serpentine Running Club in 1998. They live in Los Angeles and Ruth had heard about One Run For Boston via a post I'd made on the Serpentine e-group. She has brought her dog, Tess,

59

along to run with us. "Tess has her own survival story," she tells me. "I went to the animal shelter and asked for a dog I could take running with me. She was scared of everything at first, especially men. It took her a week to stop barking at my husband." She leans down to give Tess a reassuring rub. "However, she loves to run, especially in a pack. Running with people seems to give her confidence and, with time and care, she is slowly beginning to trust."

It strikes me that Tess's story is one that many humans share. People often say that running has given them confidence, taught them self-respect and restored their faith in humanity, through the simple act of putting one foot in front of the other.

Jumping up at me, Tess seems very keen to hold the baton. I haven't yet let go of it and have no intention of doing so before 10am, especially not to a mouth full of sharp teeth. It is then that I remember that we've forgotten to do one extremely important thing. We haven't yet turned on the GPS tracking device inside the baton. Kate gives Jamie a call, back in England, while I struggle to unscrew the baton cover to get at the tracker. The tracking device is linked to an online map of the USA embedded in our website. All being well, the tracker will automatically plot the baton's journey on the map in real time, allowing anyone with a computer or phone to follow its progress across the country, twenty-four hours a day. I can hear Kate chatting away to Jamie, filling him in on how things are going. She asks if he's got his computer turned on. I have to laugh. I don't think Jamie ever turns it off.

"Fire up the tracker map, and tell me if you see anything," Kate says down the phone. The tracker is flashing its little light at me, which I think is a good sign. I resist the urge to press any more buttons. "Can you see us yet, Jamie?" Kate asks. I hold my breath. God knows what we'll do if this doesn't work. "It's working, it's working!" Kate cries out. "We're on the map!" The crowd of runners, which by now has swelled to over thirty, give a cheer. Five minutes to go.

With the energy mounting, I find myself bouncing between runners who repeat the same sentiments over and over again.

"I didn't believe this was possible," they say. "This is so awesome. It's restored my faith in humanity."

I smile but can't help thinking, "We're not there yet."

As 10am approaches, people start to gather around us. We've prepared a few things we want to say and written them on our hands in case we dry up, but the words come naturally. I thank everyone for coming and find out how far people have travelled to be here today. Kevin Fitzpatrick, a Senior Product Manager from New Balance, has come all the way from Boston to run. He intends to top and tail the relay and so will run the final stage when, *if*, we reach Boston in three weeks' time.

"No matter where we're all from," Kate continues, "we're all here for the same reason; to honor those whose lives were lost in Boston on April 15th and in solidarity with those whose lives will never be the same again." No one makes a sound. "Today is an historic occasion. It's the beginning of a journey that we hope will unite the running community and that you will all be able to look back proudly and say 'I was there at the start.'"

The runners start to cheer and shout in agreement. I wait for quiet.

"When we had the idea for this relay, we had no clue how you, the runners of America, would respond," I tell them. "It's beyond what we could have imagined or hoped for. You guys have made this happen." I sense a smile cross my face that feels more sincere than any other in my lifetime. Then, looking around at all the runners standing in front of us, I wonder if I'm having some kind of out of body experience. I can see everything so clearly – it's like the world is fitting into place - and yet I still can't believe I'm actually here. Everything is silent and I realize I've stopped speaking. Kate is smiling at me and gesturing towards the baton. I pass it into the hands of the runner with the biggest smile. A back of the pack runner, Angela Arunarsirakul, had been hesitant to sign up for the relay at first, fearing she would be too slow. She didn't imagine that she would become the first runner to carry the baton at the start of its epic journey. "Run strong for Boston!" I cry, as we set off down the strip cheering each other on in the absence of any spectators. "Boston Strong!"

*****

As we run past the quirky shop fronts of Venice Beach, I am suddenly aware that we are being stared at by a host of giggling onlookers. A man, dressed in a sheer lace dress with a bra and knickers clearly visible underneath, points to our group and chuckles. A scantily-clad inline skater almost falls over as she cranes her neck to get a better look. A group of tattooed men in denim shorts stop and stare, laughing.

"What does everyone find so funny?" I ask one of the runners beside me, bemused. "I don't get it."

She doesn't beat about the bush. "Danny, it's your red shorts. They are *very* short."

Having started running in the 1980's when I was two years old, I've never worn anything other than *old school* running shorts. Some people may think they show a little too much leg but they're just running shorts, they're normal to me. Made of a nice wicking material with a split either side that runs up to the crease in my hips, they allow my legs to move freely without any material drag. They are my favorite shorts. I never go anywhere without them. They have been to World Championships and broken World Records (of the bog snorkeling variety). I have never felt more proud than when wearing my *Northern Runner* red shorts. If the residents of Venice Beach would only try a pair, they would know exactly what I mean.

Starting at the back, I run through the group making sure everyone has a go at carrying the baton. I want everyone to touch it, knowing that if we get to Boston, the baton will have been held by hundreds, perhaps thousands, of runners and each of them will have left a little bit of their energy, their story, on it. I have an idea that the baton could become a powerful symbol of hope and love.

Kate runs at the back to make sure no one is left behind. But as we near Santa Monica Pier and the end of the first stage, we all stop to allow the group which has playfully named itself 'the turtles' to catch up. We want to finish together. I announce an impromptu photo call and line everyone up on the wall with the ocean behind us. I am hoping for a picture that will persuade everyone who has signed up to run other stages to keep their promise and show up. I want to capture the smiles and enthusiasm with a beautiful backdrop. As I'm snapping away at the group, in a fashion Austin Powers would be proud of, I hear Kate yell out behind me, "Everyone shout, 'We love Danny's shorts!" I get the perfect picture of everyone laughing, heads thrown back and eyes twinkling. But unbeknownst to me, Kate is filming everything. She later posts a short video on Facebook of thirty excitable runners, mostly women but among them some men, shouting back "We love your shorts, Danny!" at the top of their voices. This is the first of many posts that would help make the red shorts become a symbol of the relay itself.

*****

It seems like only moments have passed since we set off from Venice Beach, but already we're at Santa Monica and it's time to pass the baton to Holly. We cheer as she sets off down Ocean Avenue. A Reporter from CBS has come to film the handover and she asks Kate and me a few questions as Holly heads off into the distance. We talk excitedly in front of the microphone about how we came up with the idea for the relay, why we are doing it and how exciting it is to see it finally starting here in California. But the Reporter seems disinterested, bored even. At least, it seems that way to us. We realize that this is just another story for her, and are reminded of how fortunate we are. While we are feeling energized by being part of something meaningful, this woman's spirits are slowly being crushed by the daily grind.

Jumping in the car, we spend the afternoon driving through Los Angeles, hanging out the window, cheering wildly at the runners who are carrying the baton on the next stages of its journey. At the end of each stage there is no balloon arch, no crowd of spectators and no bananas or bagels to welcome them across the finish. It's just Kate and me, ready with a sweaty hug and a warm bottle of Nestle Water, waiting with the next runner.

John Sanders and Dianna Torrez are another couple who met through running.

"Were it not for running I would not have met the love of my life," John says of Dianna. They have signed up to run stage 5, an 8.5 mile route from El Monte City Hall to Covina Park, east of Los Angeles. Shortly after the Boston bombings happened, John learned that a family member of a high school classmate had been badly injured in the explosion outside the Forum restaurant. Richard Coleman, an Immigration and Customs Enforcement official, was off duty and standing at the finish line with friends when the second bomb went off. He was knocked to the ground, but immediately got up and rushed into the restaurant where he started helping others. He was wearing his work jacket with '*Police*' on the back and people began to look to him for direction. As he stood in the restaurant, instructing others how to get to safety, a woman came up to him and told him he was bleeding to death. Looking down at his feet, he saw that he was standing in a 2-foot pool of his own blood. A piece of the bomb had ripped into his foot and torn an artery in his leg. Coleman had been walking around helping others without realizing the shrapnel had torn out some of his tendons and muscles.

Thankfully, he got help and survived. Three days later, Coleman's unit was involved in the shootout that resulted in the death of one of the bombing suspects.

"I would have been there had I not been injured in the blast," said Coleman. "I felt helpless watching the images on TV."

As they wait for the baton to arrive outside El Monte City Hall, John takes a photo of Dianna next to a statue with the inscription, 'In memory of those who served that the world might live in peace'. "That explains perfectly why we're running," John says.

Kate and I speed ahead to a Starbucks for much needed coffee and an internet connection. We have photos to upload and share and we're excited to tell the world we're up and running. Nothing can stop us now. Kate sends out a news release and we hop back into the car as the phone starts ringing. It's a blocked number. "Ooh, ooh, ooh, I think it could be a reporter," Kate says, gesturing to me to turn the music down. "Bring on the interviews!" I shout, prompting Kate to spin round and 'shush' me with an evil glare.

But on the other end of the phone is Jamie. It is 4am in the UK and he is tirelessly working away like the machine that he is, monitoring the social media feeds.

"What?" Kate suddenly exclaims, eyes wild. It is clear that Jamie has decided to bypass the usual polite chit-chat and cut straight to the chase. "Stop the car, Danny! Stop the car!" Kate's sounding panicky. Her stress levels rocket through the roof and I can feel myself melting next to the pressure cooker that she's become. Has someone stolen the baton, I wonder? Worse still, has someone been hit by a car or attacked? "There's been a no-show, turn around," Kate explains ...and what's worse it's the runner carrying the baton. Without hesitating, I make a U-turn in the street – perfectly legal in the UK, not so legal in the US - and speed off in the opposite direction on a search and rescue mission.

Soon Kate is on the phone to Mark Goddard, the runner who has been stood up. Mark's been at the handoff point for over an hour. Kate is double-checking his location when I hear a male voice shouting on the other end of the line, "Here he comes!" Armughan Syed's belated arrival at the handoff is greeted with loud cheers. It turns out he got lost less than 400 yards away and has spent the last hour running round in circles searching for Mark. It is going to be tough to make up the lost time. But we both realize it could have been a lot worse.

We catch up with the baton halfway through Mark's stage and follow it late into the night, barely letting it out of our sight. My eyes start to feel tired. The lack of sleep, the jet lag, and the fact I've been driving all day are beginning to take their toll. I wonder if it's time to dig in to our stash of Energy Bits. These small green pills made of algae are supposed to be the latest super fuel. They're designed to be swallowed whole with water before and after racing, or any time you need a pick me up. I am tempted to give them a try until I hear Thomas Popp, a handsome bearded chap, waiting to run his stage, say he chewed on a few earlier without realizing they were meant to go down whole. "Now I know what it's like to have a seal shit in your mouth," he tells us. So, leaving the little green delicacies for emergencies, I opt for a burrito instead.

One of the many great things I love about America is that you get unlimited soda at restaurants. Back home you have to pay for these drinks by the glass. I also like the fact that Mexican restaurants in the US give you unlimited chips (or crisps as we prefer to call them) while you wait for your take-out. Being less accustomed to American ways, Kate's not convinced I'm right on this last point. So, as I tuck into the chips on the counter with the hunger of a man who hasn't eaten all day, Kate stares up at the TV pretending to understand the news in Spanish and making out that she is not with me.

I wash down the salty chips with my first root beer of the trip. We don't have root beer in the UK, which after tasting it, seems completely insane and unfair. I stomach as many refills as I possibly can before falling into a sugary, caffeinated coma. It's time we found a spot to stop for the night.

We park up outside a Dunkin' Donuts and I jump out to watch Thomas Popp handoff to Michael Than. Replying to a few urgent emails on the phone, Kate doesn't get out and misses the baton exchange. This is lucky, as the parking lot is being used as a super highway for cockroaches. I'm not sure how happy Kate will feel about that, so I decide to keep our creepy-crawly neighbors a secret from her. I get back in the car and we agree it's time for sleep. We recline our seats and I put my feet up on the dashboard with a big smile on my face. Donut shops and cockroaches; this is the authentic America I had been craving.

Kate is already asleep when I shut my eyes and think about the runners who will be running through the night for every second of our slumber, each stride taking the baton one step closer to Boston.

Chapter 10

An eerie horn sounds and in my dreams I'm struggling against the ropes that hold me to the railway track. Suddenly awake, it takes me a few seconds to realize that the train that I hear is not heading for me; we have parked up next to a freight line. Looking over at the track, twenty meters away, I see a train passing through. It looks infinitely long. It heads towards the horizon, into the rising sun ahead of us. Behind us, the line of wagons is still visible, emerging out of the darkness of another horizon in the west.

The look on Kate's face tells me that this is one of many trains that have kept her awake for most of the night. "I was surprised by how cold it got last night," she says, piling on a couple of layers of clothing to warm up. "I could murder a nice hot cup of tea." Kate has yet to realize that Americans don't do tea. At least, not the way we do, with boiling water, a tea bag and some milk. "We'll see what we can do," I say, trying to postpone as long as possible the moment when Kate must inevitably find out the bitter, disappointing truth.

Without a proper internet connection, the bargain phone isn't quite cutting the mustard on the internet front, we have no way of knowing where the relay has got to, or if the runners have managed to make up any of the time lost yesterday. Although we don't realize it at the time, we are quite possibly the least well-informed of anyone, anywhere. It's less than 24 hours since the live tracker map flickered into life as the baton left Venice Beach, but already the runners awaiting their turn to run have become obsessed with it. Right now, all Kate and I know is that, barring incident overnight, we're probably not more than 30 miles away from the baton. And yet there are people sitting 3000 miles away on the east coast who are tracking its every move over breakfast and know exactly where it is. Across the Atlantic, Jamie is also monitoring the baton's progress and can see that it is five miles from Banning, the end of stage 12. But it doesn't occur to us to give him a call.

The fact that no one has called *us* is reassuring. Surely we'd know if there had been any more problems?

We hazard a guess at where the baton would be if it was still running an hour behind and head for Banning. We are relieved to find Ryan Rodriguez and Mark Villalovos waiting beside the railway track with their partners. Standing together in the cold and windy pre-dawn darkness, we hear the baton before we see it. Over the din of the freeway overpass, we hear chants and singing from a group of runners organized by the LA Chinatown Firecracker run. Then across the railway track we see them, a group of fifteen or more runners, escorted by bicycle outriders and a large pick-up truck full of cheering supporters. They wait at the level crossing as another freight train rumbles by. Among them is Jenny Chen, who spent two years in Boston studying for her MBA. Until now she has never run at night, never run more than six miles and had been worried she wouldn't keep up.

"I planned to run four miles, rest, then finish up at the end with the other runners," she tells us. "I haven't been to sleep for the whole night. It's amazing seeing people up in the middle of the night with me." She explains how she ran most of the stage at the back of the group, with one of the bikers for company, offering her water when she needed it. "There were times, I was going to give up and wanted to hop on the van, but the van was way behind and the bikers just kept telling me that I could do it," she says.

"So with a bit of power walking and mostly running, I finished eight miles. My new milestone! My first time running through the night and the first time running with a group of people – eight miles!" she gushes, beaming with happiness.

The Firecrackers live up to their name, handing over the baton to Ryan and Mark before opening a crate of beers in the back of the pick-up to celebrate bringing the relay from night into day.

"We've been running," one says, clinking his bottle of beer against another's. "It doesn't matter if it's 6am or not." I liked their style.

Dragged away from the party, we head east into the Mojave Desert. Dry, parched lands surround us as far as the eye can see with little growing from the ground other than the odd railway pylon, a rusted, red, water-pumping windmill and a couple of giant dinosaurs. If you drive along Interstate 10 near Cabazon you will see them too; a one hundred and fifty ton Apatosaurus named Dinny and a smaller, 100 ton T-Rex known simply as Mr. Rex. Starting in 1964, Dinny was created over eleven years by Claude K. Bell who wanted to attract customers to his nearby café. Bell is said to have persuaded a friend to paint the finished structure, which stands 14 meters high and 46 meters long, in exchange for one dollar and a case of Dr. Pepper. Mr. Rex was constructed some years later, in 1981. Presumably it took Mr. Bell all those years to find another friend willing to be paid in Dr. Pepper. I might have considered helping out if Bell's preferred currency had been root beer.

At the next handoff we meet Lindsey and Adam. With her long blond hair, pristine skin and full pink lips, Lindsey has the beauty of the all-star American cheerleader that British kids grow up believing only exists in films. Adam has rock star looks and twice the charm. They live in Los Angeles and had driven out to 29 Palms separately the day before to stay with Adam's mum. All three are signed up to run a different stage of the relay today. Adam explains how Lindsey called him just after he'd arrived at his mum's house saying her car was stuck in a sandy wash. She had gone to scope out her relay route and, not realizing it was mostly off-road, got stuck. She had managed to get a tow truck to get her out but by the time she eventually arrived at 29 Palms it hadn't left much time for sleep. More alarmingly for Kate and me, we learn that Lindsey never did get to properly recce her route.

With the wind at their backs, Ryan and Mark had cut through the desert like a knife and are soon upon us with the baton. We wave Lindsey off and she quickly disappears down a sandy track. Adam jumps in his car to follow her while we hang around chatting for a while. It comes as a surprise to learn that Ryan and Mark did not know each other before they met a couple of hours earlier by the railway crossing. They seem like old friends. We pose for photos and they wish us luck.

"May the adrenaline continue to fuel your passion and may you experience life changing memories along the way," Mark says, as we exchange hugs before leaving.

When she signed up to run stage 14, Lindsey had unwittingly chosen a stage that cuts through the foothills of California's coastal mountain range. She now finds herself running off road on unmarked trails, over hilly terrain in the scorching heat. It may be only 8am but the sun is blazing and even though she's not running, even Kate is rapidly shedding the extra layers she put on earlier. We worry that Lindsey may not know where she's going but Adam remains calm and keeps in contact with her by phone to check she's OK. As Lindsey discovered to her cost yesterday, it is not possible to take a car down these paths. We must simply wait patiently at the other end. In the middle of a massive windmill farm, I kill the time by taking a few photos of these impressive giant structures. Then Adam's phone rings and it's Lindsey. She says she's come to a fork and doesn't know which path to take.

"Hold on a minute, Adam tells her. I'll call my mom." Kate and I look at each other, doubtful that someone sitting thirty miles away up the road is going to be able to help here. "I guarantee you that my mom will be at home following the GPS tracker online," Adam explains. "She'll know exactly where Lindsey is and tell us which direction she needs to head." Genius. Adam gets through to his mom and keeps her on the line while we call up Lindsey on our phone. With a phone in each hand, Adam then proceeds to relay his mom's directions to Lindsey. He makes sure she is safely on her way again then throws our phone back to us. "What's that? You're excited? Oh, you're excited *and* sweaty?" The other phone is still pinned to his ear as Adam turns to smile at us. "You're right, mom. It *is* exciting. Absolutely, we *are* on a mission."

When Lindsey eventually appears, she looks done in. "Oh my God, that was like a trail hike!" she tells us. "I was trying to use those Boston songs for inspiration but they weren't working anymore, so I was just praying to God that I would get through this." Adam asks if I fancy running a stretch to give Lindsey a chance to cool down in the air con for a few minutes. I jump at the chance, literally. Jumping over a barbed wire fence to get to where she is, I slip and fall, catching my hand and shoulder on the wire.

It's probably worth making a second confession here to Kate: that travel insurance I told you I had. I didn't. Of course I told her I had. But it involved more form filling, so I hadn't. By contrast, Kate had bought the most comprehensive travel insurance policy known to man which covered every eventuality imaginable, including a range of natural disasters.

The barbs lacerated my fingers and tore deep into my shoulder. As blood poured from my wounds, the baton became streaked in red, adding to the dirt and sweat marks left by the previous runners. Later in the day, this beautiful baton, this symbol of hope and positivity, would also receive a coating of Adam's vomit. But before that could happen, the baton still needed to climb up the mountain and onto the plateau where Adam's excited, sweaty mother on a mission was waiting to complete her stage.

*****

Kate waits up the road with Molly Thorpe, a 58 year old public school teacher who has chosen the stage with the toughest elevation climb in all of California. With Lindsey back running again, Adam gives me a lift to join them at the handoff point. Seeing the blood on both the baton and me, Kate goes straight to the boot of the car and rummages around to find our first aid kit. The size of a pac-a-mac, the kit is woefully inadequate for this kind of adventure. For a start, it contains only one small antiseptic wipe. We use it on my fingers and clean the baton with a wet wipe. There isn't another antiseptic wipe for my shoulder so we use a wet wipe on that too. Kate is embarrassed by the crappy kit, and makes sure Molly and Adam don't see it. She doesn't want them knowing how unprepared and ill-equipped we really are.

Up the road waits Jen Mihalcin, a mum of four with the body of a twenty-one year-old. She runs to bring order to an otherwise chaotic life and to set an example to her kids.

"Running has been my health, mental and physical, my release, my accomplishments, my 'me time'," she later tells us.

It is to be an emotional day for Jen and, as we arrive on the scene, she is already a little tearful. "I think I just got chills in the desert!" she jokes. It is 110°F. I put a towel over my head to protect my pale freckled skin from the sun. It's a Saturday morning and there's already a party atmosphere. Jen and friends have invited a fine selection of their lean, mean Marine husbands to join them and they've brought along a huge support team that includes at least twenty kids. The kids have made hand held signs which cry "Ooh rah, Boston!" and the support vehicles have been

73

painted with heartfelt sentiments such as, "We run for you Boston." It's the first time Kate and I have ever seen cars painted up in this way. Compared to our unmarked car, these guys look way more official than us. It's also the first time I've ever tasted peanut butter pretzels. The support team has stocked up on drinks and snacks to help the runners through their stage, but don't mind me tucking in. These pretzels are a taste sensation, a complete revelation!

Chatting with Jen and her friends, I begin to feel the blazing sun turn my skin a shade of lobster red. Looking around at the barren desert, it's easy to see why the US Marines are stationed out here. If a human being can survive here, they can surely survive anywhere – the altitude, the heat, the desert landscape. The Marines aren't the only tough cookies living out here, as we soon discover.

When Molly Thorpe signed up to run in One Run For Boston she could have chosen any stage. She could have chosen a short stage, but she didn't. She could have chosen a flat stage, but she didn't. Instead, Molly chose a 10-mile route which was mostly off-road and uphill all the way. In the first three miles alone she would climb 2000ft.

"I knew that dealing with the desert heat, the steady increase of elevation and the solitude of this trail route would be a personal challenge," she said. "Every footfall would be a tribute to those who died or were injured on marathon day. My progress would pale in comparison to the tough road that the survivors had ahead of them." As a public school teacher, Molly mentors a group of youngsters to set goals by running and raising money for worthy causes by putting on local community races. "I knew that participating in One Run For Boston would model the spirit of community, the strength of unity and the empathy and compassion for those who had been stricken by the devastation of April 15," she said. "I recognized that running would satisfy my need to do something and set an important example to my students."

Jen was supposed to receive the baton from Molly at 9:50am, but with the hour delay from yesterday and the fact that our ignorance of the topography meant we hadn't factored in any extra time for Molly's mountain, it is already approaching midday. I can feel the nervous energy mounting amongst Jen and her friends. They keep looking to the horizon, waiting to catch sight of Molly with the baton. But still there is no sign. Every now and again, they head back to their cars, take a sip of water, make sure the kids are behaving in the little section of desert they have made their camp, then return to the road and wait.

We get chatting with Michelle, a friend of Jen's who has recently had an operation on her nose and is disappointed not to be running.

"We were all so excited when we found out about the relay," she tells us. "Not a lot of things happen round here, apart from earthquakes." We talk about the route we'll be taking through the next couple of states once we leave California. "You were wise to keep north through Texas," she says. "This desert is like Beverley Hills compared to southern Texas." We all laugh but only Kate and I know that our fortunate route choice is really a matter of luck rather than our own good judgment.

While we wait, I get the whole gang together for some photos. One of the kids gets everyone laughing by flexing his muscles for the camera and shouting, "cheesecake!" instead of "cheese". I take a team photo of the men and another of the women. They laugh and poke fun at each other but every so often, they glance at the mountain pass in the hope of spotting Molly.

Suddenly, a speck appears on the horizon but no-one says a word for fear it's just a mirage. We watch as the speck grows larger and larger and eventually we hear Jen gasp,

"She's coming." Choked with emotion, her voice is barely audible. She turns to two man mountains, the finest American Marines, and says, "Go and make sure she's alright." They do as they're told and run half a mile back to help Molly finish. Out of respect for their fellow runner, they don't offer to take over; they simply run behind Molly in silent support. Standing in the road watching, Jen's tears start to flow.

As Molly reaches Jen she relinquishes the baton. Strangers until a week ago, these two strong, determined women look deep into each other's eyes and embrace, as tears roll down their cheeks. Breaking the embrace, Jen turns to her troops and says, "Ready?" Before we know it they are gone.

Kate and I linger a while with Molly and her husband. She describes the incredible adventure she's just had through dirt, rocks and tunnels.

"With every step, I could feel the solidarity of all the runners and each stride brought me closer to the realization that we are one," she tells us. A few days later Molly wrote to us, thanking us for giving her the opportunity to run. "My students were awestruck as I told them of my adventure that day," she wrote. "Although the pictures captured the terrain, they had to see into my heart to truly understand how inspiring, satisfying and humbling that experience was for me."

*****

Jen's team of nine runners set off up the hill, with a citizen patrol vehicle tucked in behind them for safety. I was shocked to see the patrol unit there, giving up their time to keep a bunch of sweaty runners safe. When planning the relay, Kate and I had decided it was best not to contact any of the police along the route fearing they might try to stop us. But Jen had managed to get the whole community behind her.

For the first couple of miles, Jen's pack of nine stick together, taking it in turns to run with the baton. But the heat and the elevation soon cause their pace to slow. The heat wave hitting California is certainly not aiding the baton's passage through the state. It is hotter than we've ever known. The wind blows in my face like a hairdryer and Kate burns her knees on the tarmac. Inside the car, the steering wheel is too hot to handle and our skin sticks to the plastic seats with pools of sweat gathering between our legs. The relief as the air conditioning kicks in is comparable to a ship-wrecked sailor finding a land of plenty.

We catch up with the runners. Jen is out in front with two of the Marines. Behind them the group is beginning to get strung out. The baton is being carried by one of the runners at the back, slipping further and further behind. "It's a shame the baton's not up with Jen," Kate says, reading my mind. We're both aware that time is ticking and we can't afford any more delays. We wonder if we should pull in and say something, but neither of us has the heart. These guys are flogging themselves to get this done. Who are we to intervene? Then, an unexpected thing happens. We see the runner with the baton sprint ahead using every last bit of strength that he can muster. He catches up with Jen and hands her the baton. Exhausted from his sprint and unable to speak, he silently conveys the hopes and wishes of the group. It is a sign for Jen and the two Marines to go on, to run with all they've got and make up as much time as possible.

Proudly carrying the baton, Jen runs the last six miles fast, hot and inspired. Marines that look as fit as a butcher's dog can't keep up with her. Sweat trickles over the shaven head and tattooed torso of the last Marine to keep her pace. His face grimaces in pain as the sun's scorching rays lash down on him. Incredibly, Jen looks as fresh as when we first met her. We speed ahead to make sure the next runner is present and correct; it's the turn of Adam's mum, Laurel.

"The red shorts!" she shouts, as I get out of the car.

Days after the Boston Marathon, Laurel found out that her boss's wife had grown up with Kevin Corcoran, the husband and father of Celeste and Sydney Corcoran, both seriously injured by the first bomb.'

"Hearing that made the bombing so real," she tells us. "It was no longer just a news story." Blown off her feet, Celeste looked down to see blood and bone. She never lost consciousness through the nightmare. Lying on the pavement with grit in her mouth and in her hair, Celeste believed her eighteen-year-old daughter, Sydney, was somewhere safe watching the race with friends. In reality she was lying a few meters away with a large piece of shrapnel in her leg and bleeding heavily.

Laurel tells us that a month before the Boston Marathon, she had gone to cheer on her son at the finish line of the Los Angeles Marathon. "We celebrated with him at the finish for over an hour," she says. "So when my friend texted me on April 15 to inform me of the bombing, it hit so close to home. We were the mirror image of Boston. Some of us were there to run the marathon, some of us there to cheer on our loved ones and friends. It was chilling to know it could have been any of us. We were, and are, so fortunate." Then, when Adam called his mum to tell her that a relay to support those impacted by the Boston bombings was going to be coming through her town, she immediately got on the website and signed up. "One Run For Boston has taken over my life like a virus," she laughs. "I've been obsessively checking the website to see which legs are filling up and sending out press releases. Now I'm on the website every free moment, tracking the baton."

Despite the conditions, when Jen arrives to hand off to Laurel, we realize she has caught up ten minutes of lost time. "I honestly don't think I will ever have a run produce the energy, inspiration, pride, humility or emotion that One Run For Boston has," Jen tells us. She has run the race of her life. Laurel sets off like a rocket while we wait for every member of Jen's group to finish. It's an emotional reunion for everyone involved.

Laurel is joined by her friend Brenda partway through the stage. We notice how they've both customized their One Run For Boston t-shirts by cutting off the sleeves and adding slits in the back to act as air vents inspiring us to take the scissors to our own t-shirts. Feeling the effects of the heat, Laurel and Brenda switch on and off the last few miles. "We improvised and got it done!" Laurel says, passing the baton to her son, as she finishes her stage.

Adam is a trooper and keeps on running, even after he throws up at the top of the hill into 29 Palms. Concerned for her son, Laurel runs the last couple of miles with him. The bond these two share, through their mutual love of running, is something special to behold. It is clear that Laurel is a big inspiration for Adam, just as my mum is for me. I've trained for marathons with my mum and the last time we raced together she beat me by a minute. In fact my whole family ran in that marathon. My two amazingly talented sisters, Alison and Natalie, came in soon after me and my Dad brought up the rear, race-walking it in four and a half hours at the age of 61.

*****

Having slept in our car overnight and sweated all day, Kate and I are starting to pong a little, even at this early stage, and we're not the only ones beginning to notice the stink. We are overwhelmed by the generosity of people we have never met before who step up and offer us keys to their house or hotel room so we can take a shower and sleep if we want to. To us, it is the ultimate expression of love and trust.

Nicole Cook has travelled from the coast with her husband and two kids to run a stage of the relay in the desert. They have booked into a hotel and as they go to grab some lunch they invite us to use their facilities. I take the opportunity to wash my red shorts in the shower, stomping them beneath my feet with shampoo washing over them. Back in the car I decide to make use of the oven hot temperatures outside to dry them. Winding down the window just a fraction, I trap the shorts between the glass and the doorframe, and we drive off with them flapping in the wind like a tiny flag.

Stephen Hefner, a courteous young Marine, who calls me "Sir" and calls Kate "Ma'am", knocks out a stage, seemingly with no effort. But it's early afternoon, the mercury is rising and all other mortals are bound to suffer. Once past 29 Palms, the desert either side of Route 62 is virtually uninhabited. The runners who have signed up to run this stretch have travelled from their homes on the west coast. Like Kate and me, they certainly aren't desert dwellers and conditions are tough to say the least.

We watch as the gutsy Sean Laird does battle with his stage but eventually slows to a walk. I offer to run every other mile with him to keep the baton moving. Sucking in the dry, dusty air, my lungs soon begin to burn. I cough, and with each cough, a pain shoots through my body. To paraphrase the rock group ACDC, Route 62 is turning out to be nothing less than a highway *through* hell.

The wonderfully named Clay Lindberg Van Batenburg has driven 500 miles from San Francisco, with his friend Todd, to be part of the relay. They turn up hours before they are due to run, to support the runners ahead of them. They plan on overseeing the night shift for us so we can drive ahead and get some sleep, before they turn around and drive the 500+ miles back home to San Francisco. They seemed like great fellows, and not just because Clay bears the name of Kate's favorite marzipan cake.

Busting a gut, trying my best to put some extra miles in for Sean, I feel like I am about to crumple. Meanwhile, fresh on the scene and as yet unaware of the hardships we're enduring, Clay seems delighted by it all. As I'm hacking up my dusty guts and cursing the rotten road I'm running on, Kate explains to Clay that I am helping Sean out with a couple of miles.

"That's Danny running?" Clay asks astonished. "What a riot!" Yep, that is the sound of a carefree man who knows he won't be tying his shoelaces until the sun has set and the temperatures plummet. Kate takes an instant liking to Clay, not just, because his name reminds her of English teatimes, but because he lightens the mood and epitomizes the sunny, carefree attitude that she associates with Californians.

Passing the baton back to Sean, I collapse into the car, lungs burning from the dry air and legs sore from the long shorts I'm not used to wearing which have begun to chafe. I am soaked in sweat from head to toe. At least my freshly washed red shorts will be dry by now and ready for another day of action tomorrow. With Kate behind the steering wheel, I slink down into the passenger seat and begin to close my eyes. I'm thinking about a cool glass of iced root beer when I glance out the window and realize something's not quite right. Expecting to see the shorts still flapping in the wind, cleverly trapped in the window frame I jolt upright as I realize that there is no flapping. There is no streak of bright red cloth lighting up the dusky sky outside the car. The shorts have disappeared.

Chapter 11

My heart sinks as the reality of what has happened dawns on me. Somewhere along the Highway Through Hell, between 29 Palms and Sheep Hole Mountain, I have lost my shorts. They must have found their freedom as I wound down the window to holler at one of the runners.

"Get over it, it's just a pair of shorts!" I can hear you say. But these shorts weren't just any old shorts. They were different. They had personality. In just two short days they'd already built up a following. Someone had even gone to the trouble of giving them a Facebook profile. How would we break the news that they were no longer with us? We question whether we should go back and look for my shorts in the dark, but decide to leave them. Instead, we imagine that a Marine from the 29 Palms barracks might one day come across a ragged pair of faded short shorts, bleached white by the sun, and wonder how they got there.

Mourning their loss, we drive on in silence, barely able to appreciate the fantastic sunset that appears in our rear-view mirror as we head east. The difference that a change in light makes to the appearance of a desert landscape is quite incredible. As the monotone blue of the sky is replaced by a palette of pastels, shadows begin to appear on the rocky ranges ahead of us. The stark, ugly and inhospitable daytime look is replaced by something much more appealing. The stars begin to glimmer above the silhouette of the hills in the distance. For the first time since entering the desert, I am perhaps starting to appreciate its beauty.

Beauty before me, beauty behind me, beauty to my left, beauty to my right, beauty above me, beauty below me, beauty within me. With sleep creeping up on her, Patty Hurtado begins to repeat her mantra, a Navajo prayer, and tries to stay focused. As she repeats these words, she looks for something beautiful in each direction. Deep within the Californian desert, she finds beauty everywhere she looks. Running with eight others beside her, Patty stops every mile for a sip of water to rehydrate her body and to steal a run-through kiss from her fiancé, to keep her soul hydrated. Nearing the end of her stage, someone asks Patty about the cool design on the back of her shirt. Wearing a plain tank top she has no idea what they are talking about until she sees a picture they have taken. There for all to see is a perfect heart shaped sweat spot. Unable to explain it, she puts it down to the magic of the energy that was coming from this powerful experience. The heart must have been formed, she tells her group, by the streams of love flowing from all of their hearts, pouring into this run for Boston, for peace, for humankind.

*****

I can't remember how the conversation started, or what exactly we said on our long drive that night. But driving through the desert at dusk, quite literally seeing our surroundings in a different light, prompted the first conversation that Kate and I had had since arriving in the States that wasn't about the present. It was the first time we'd talked about anything other than the mechanics of the relay and the details of the here and now. I'd like to say that Kate was beginning to relax. But she wasn't. All that was happening, as the sun set on that second day, was that her minute-to-minute anxieties about the relay were being replaced by other concerns on a much grander scale. There's nothing like being out in the middle of nowhere to make you evaluate your life.

Having a conversation in the car when you're looking straight ahead and are able to avoid eye contact allows you to explore and communicate with freedom. More so at night, when it's dark and you can barely even make out the form of the person sitting next to you. What I lament as being my childish, nerdy, slightly annoying side, Kate saw as the carefree, lover of life, generous with time and fun to be around. Happy to have the cover of darkness to disguise my blushing, Kate goes on. This is who she'd always been until growing-up got in the way. It's a view shared by many adults when they experience childish fun again. Surprisingly to me, spending time with me wasn't annoying the hell out of Kate, it was making her realize how unhappy with herself she had become. She was simply no longer who she wanted to be. Bouncing from one demanding job to the other, sometimes juggling two at the same time, taking on new challenge after new challenge, unable to say no to anything, had made her addicted to stress and, she admitted that night under a blanket of stars, an absolute nightmare to be around. She said she needed a break.

These sorts of conversations are sometimes painful, but I love them. It's like seeing a beautiful butterfly fighting to free itself from its chrysalis. You want to help and offer words to ease the butterfly, but sometimes those words aren't what the butterfly wants to hear. I was trying to get to the bottom of why Kate had let life become this way. Having poured so much out she suddenly clammed up, not wishing to say anything more for fear she'd regret it. She was surprised at herself for being so open. Frank conversations are what I live by, but this was totally new for Kate. I don't think she knew how to handle it. She didn't want to talk any more. She didn't want to face her demons. She wanted to go back to pretending that everything was alright. She turned the radio back on to signal the end of the conversation.

It's pitch black outside, not a streetlight to be seen, and the desert is making us feel uncomfortable again. We are still 30 miles from Parker, our destination for the night, when in our headlights we catch sight of a long wooden fence with shoes and other clothing tied to it. We've heard about the enormous pile of running shoes that had been created in Boston's Copley Square as a monument to those who lost their lives in the bombings. But this is completely different. We pull in a few hundred yards up the road and walk back with our head torches. It's friggin' creepy. A fence, strewn with hundreds of pairs of shoes and other clothing, all faded to white by the sun. A few odd shoes are scattered across the road and clothes litter the ground. Behind the fence are the foot high remains of some small buildings. The earth is scorched by fire and littered with glass bottles. What the hell had gone on here? It is all a bit cultish for my liking. Perhaps the fence is a shrine? But to whom or to what? We have no idea. Spooked out, Kate is keen to leave before we discover any human remains. I try to get some photographs but Kate is getting jittery and insists we move on. It is a relief to get to Parker and find the Crossroads Inn just about open.

Kate goes in to check whether the Inn is still serving food and I turn the car upside down in search of my shorts. Maybe they didn't fly away and are just jumbled up with our belongings on the back seat? I am only persuaded to abandon my search with the promise of a beer inside. We take a seat in the empty bar and the cheery waitress comes to take our order. I ask what beers she's got. She rattles off a long list but we are so exhausted it's hard to concentrate. We both look at her blankly, barely able to communicate. Kate is willing to take pot luck.

"I'll have the first one, please," she says wearily. "Whatever it was." I ask the waitress what beer she'd recommend, and we engage in a pleasant conversation about the pros and cons of the various beers she sells. Kate is tired and looks irritated. I can see in her eyes that she's thinking, "It's a friggin' beer for goodness' sake. They all taste the same. Hurry up!" The waitress recommends a local Arizonan brew so I decide to go for that. When she returns with our beers a few minutes later, Kate and I clink bottles and each take a long, cool slug.

"How's yours?" Kate asks.

"Heaven," I reply, "How's yours?" I ask, and Kate thinks for a second.

"Tastes like rat's piss" she says, wrinkling up her face and sending us both into fits of laughter. We toast the red shorts and then we remember we're in Arizona – the baton would arrive tomorrow morning! So we toast that too. One state down, thirteen to go.

"Cheers!"

*****

On July 7th 2005, four bombs detonated in London in the morning rush hour. Three Underground trains and a red double-decker bus were attacked by suicide bombers, killing 52 people. Working in London at the time, every day on my bus ride to work I passed close to the rail stations that were hit. On July 7th, at work, my attention was grabbed by the TV in my office that showed BBC News 24 throughout the day. I saw dust and debris in the air. People were saying it was a power surge, just like many had assumed immediately after the Boston attacks. Realizing later that bombs had gone off, I tried to get in touch with my Mum; I knew she would be panicking. Cell service went down so I couldn't get through to her mobile and she wasn't in her office. Going through the same frustration as many of the people in Boston did that day, I tried time and again.

It finally rang and I ran to one of the glass office rooms surrounding my desk. When Mum answered I couldn't say a word. I managed 'Hi Mum' then I just cried down the phone. On the other end she was crying with relief that I wasn't part of this horrendous attack.

People walking by saw my tears and assumed the worst. Forcing a smile, I gave them a 'thumbs up' to let them know I wasn't one of the unlucky ones who'd had a family member taken from their lives.

*****

When the bombs exploded at the Boston Marathon finish line and the cell coverage was cut, it left people unable to contact their loved ones. As they waited for news, hundreds of thousands of friends and relatives entered a living hell, tormented by a succession of 'What Ifs?'

Mel Pugliese's daughter was a quarter of a mile from the finish line in Boston when the bombs went off. Six weeks later when he signed up to run stage 29 of the relay, the leg that would bring the baton over the border into Arizona, Mel explained, "I run because she was lucky."

If she had been just five minutes faster, Mel's daughter would have been at the finish when the bombs exploded. Hearing this made me think about all the races I have run where I've been disappointed to finish just behind the time I've been aiming for. I guess every runner has finished races wishing they'd been five minutes faster. Mel's words will stay with me forever. Those days of wishing I had run faster times are now behind me. I run because I can. I run because *I* am lucky.

Waking in Parker, time is very much on Kate's mind. She wonders if the people running overnight have been able to make up any of the time lost in the days before. With the cooler night-time temperatures, we'd both been banking on it. Parked outside the Inn, we have access to Wi-Fi, but it isn't helping since the live tracker map on the website appears to have stopped working. The problem seems to be that while the satellite tracker does indeed use satellites to receive information on its location, it relies on the cellular network to relay this data to our website. Out in the desert, where there is little or no cell coverage, we're screwed. The gossip on Facebook suggests the relay is still almost two hours behind. This is seriously bad news. With the temperatures rising already, it is inevitable there will be more delays to come today.

"Shit, shit, shit," Kate is demonstrating her unique ability to go from zero to Blind Panic in less than three seconds. She flings the car into reverse and speeds out of the parking lot onto the wrong side of the road. "Get over!" I shriek as a 10-ton truck heads our way, deafening us with its horn. "Fuuuuuck!" screams Kate, yanking the wheel hard right. It's normally quite funny hearing Kate curse; those kinds of words just don't sound right in her posh accent. But this morning, there is absolutely nothing funny about Kate's mood.

"You nearly killed us!" I shout, stating the obvious.

"It's fine," screams Kate, "everything's fine!" before adding, without the slightest hint of irony, "just stop panicking, will you?" We drive back in the direction we've come from the day before, scouring the road ahead for any sign of runners.

"Where *are* they?" says Kate, her voice sounding strangled. "Where the hell *are* they?" She is angry. Telling her she shouldn't be angry at the runners, I remind her they're surely doing their absolute best.

"I know," she snaps back "It's me. I've screwed up, haven't I? I should have given them more time. I should have known how hot it would be out here. I haven't allowed enough time." There's not much we can do about it now and there's certainly not any point in getting all het up over it.

"Just calm down. It is what it is," I say.

"It's all gone to rat shit," Kate answers back. "We're never going to make the time up and what happens then? We'll just keep getting later and later and if we're lucky we'll arrive in Boston in time for Christmas!" I shudder at the thought of being stuck in this car with Kate in her current state for the next 6 months.

"Look, that's not going to happen," I say. "We'll step in and run some miles to share the load if we have to. That will speed things up." But Kate isn't listening.

"We're just going to get later and later and people are going to start dropping out, saying they can no longer run their stages because it's all got so delayed they've got other stuff they need to do. It's OK now, it's the weekend. But it's Monday tomorrow and people have got jobs. What if you signed up thinking you were going to run at 6am and then found out that the relay was delayed and you wouldn't be running till 9am when you should be at work?"

I think about it for a second. "I'd skive off work and run anyway" I say.

"Well, maybe *you* would, but Americans aren't like you. They're hard - working and they won't skive for anything or anyone, least of all us!" Kate retorts, turning to look at me to reinforce her point.

"Watch it!" I shout as this time Kate's erratic driving nearly lands us in a ditch. I have had enough.

"Pull in" I say.

"What?"

"Look, there's a gas station up ahead, just pull in. We need some fuel."

Trying to work out how to get the petrol from the nozzle, I end up pushing what little manliness I have aside and ask the guy behind the counter how it works.

"You have to pay first, before you can take the gas," he tells me, speaking very slowly and deliberately. I think he assumes I must be a couple of sandwiches short of a picnic.

"It's just that in England you take the petrol, I mean the gas, and then you pay," I explain. "Well, you folks are a lot more trusting over there in England," he replies. Kate gets us both a coffee and then goes to jump back in the driver's side.

"No way," I say, shaking my head. "I'm driving." Without saying a word, she slams the door shut and walks round to the passenger side.

With my eyes on the road, I start another frank conversation that has been brewing since we arrived in LA. I explain to Kate that her levels of stress are not just endangering our lives, but they're endangering the whole relay. Unless things change, I'm not sure I can continue on this journey with her. Not used to this level of honesty, I sense Kate thinks I'm being a bit brutal. In some ways I am. I don't hold any punches, I say exactly how I feel and decide I will have to live with the result. Yes, we are tired, and at times it is stressful, but we are doing something so awesome and meeting so many amazing people who, rightly or wrongly, all appear to have an overwhelming faith in us. Why should we be stressed?

We keep driving. Kate's first instinct is to defend herself. But she decides against it. Instead she goes quiet. I assume she is reflecting on what I've just said but she later confesses to having had a little sulk. There's no time for sulking though, because here in front of us is Mel Pugliese! We have finally tracked him down, and what's more, the relay isn't half as delayed as the Facebook gossip made out. We put all that we've said in the car behind us, and get out to cheer Mel on.

Mel is 75 years old. He has survived prostate cancer but continues to suffer with his heart and is fitted with a pacemaker. According to Mel, if it wasn't for running, he might well be dead. He's certainly a tough cookie. Mel has enlisted a couple of friends to run the stage with him, sharing the mileage between them as they carry the baton over the state border from California into Arizona. As we wait for Mel and his team to hand-off to Pablo Sandoval, it's not quite 10am but it's hot enough already. The local Sheriff pulls up in his car to find out what is going on.

"Rather you than me," he says. "It's gonna be 120 degrees by noon." Our hearts sink.

Trying to lighten the atmosphere, I ask the Sherriff if I can wear his hat.

With a look like I'd just asked to borrow his left kidney, he says, "No."

Undeterred, and hoping Kate's English charm will seduce him, I ask if *she* can wear it. With a shake of his head, his response is unchanged.

"Can I take a picture of *you* in your hat?" I persist in desperation, but with a delicate side order of sarcasm on the side. It yields no return. The best we can manage is a photo of Kate, hat-less, crouched beside the door of the Sheriff's car. I was desperate for some authentic interaction with a US cop. Little did I know that before too long my wish would be granted.

On the outskirts of Lake Havasu City, we see a sign for London Bridge and hit a hard left at speed. When the gravel and dust settles we see we are in a weird looking mock-English town oddly located in the middle of the desert. It may not have stood out as the finest piece of engineering when it spanned the River Thames, but London Bridge is a marvelous sight in the middle of the Arizonan desert. The bridge was originally constructed in London in the 1830s, replacing a series of dodgy bridges dating back to medieval times which inspired the children's rhyme, "London Bridge Is Falling Down." By the 1960s the bridge was no longer able to handle the demands of London's increased traffic. A modern bridge was built and the granite stones of the old bridge were put up for sale.

Robert McCulloch, the founder of Lake Havasu City, bought the 10,246 blocks of stone for $2.4 million and had them shipped out and reassembled in Arizona at a cost of another $3 million. Rumor has it that McCulloch bought London Bridge thinking he was buying the far more recognizable Tower Bridge. But this was ardently denied by McCulloch. London Bridge is now the centerpiece of a development designed to attract tourists to the area. The bridge's finely carved stonework stands in permanent rebuke to the tacky mock-Tudor buildings, which have seen better days that stand in front of the bridge. Stumbling upon a traditional red English phone box in amongst the stucco, we monkey around for photos and do our best to ignore the tension still present between us.

*****

Lake Havasu City brings us back onto Route 66 for the first time since leaving Santa Monica. Built in 1926, Route 66 was one of the original US highways and it was a major route for those migrating west. Every year, hoards of Brits come to the USA simply to drive stretches of the iconic route which runs between Chicago, Illinois, and Santa Monica, California. We Brits like to drive along the road in large open-top cars, with the sun turning our pale skin red, as Bobby Troup's song blasts from the stereo:

If you ever plan to motor west
Travel my way, the highway that's the best.
Get your kicks on Route 66!

If you're looking for great displays of neon signs, rusty middle-of-nowhere truck stops, or kitschy Americana, Route 66 is the place to be, and although we had to make do with a sensible Ford Escape as our wheels, I was excited about getting to see this side of America.

*****

We spend the early afternoon following three hardcore Ragnar Relay runners who have signed up to run three consecutive stages. The guys are doing a great job banging out the miles, but it's obvious that the novelty of running a relay in an oven is wearing off rapidly. I feel like our presence is becoming a hindrance. I guess that when you're running in 120°F and you're suffering more than a little, it's not everyone's cup of tea to have two slightly oddball Brits jump out of their car every 2 miles telling you to "Keep going!" or, worse still, blatantly lying to you that, "You're nearly there!" The heat of the day is simply taking the edge off everything and we retreat to the nearest Starbucks to send some emails.

We emerge from the air-conditioned café a couple of hours later, as the sun is beginning to set. We pick up some dinner at a supermarket then proceed to leave our roast chicken on the roof of the car as we drive off. By the time we realize our mistake, we're ten miles down the road and there is no sign of the chicken. We truck on, with rumbling stomachs, to the hand-off location for stage 35, where we sense a change in the air. Here, on a service road beside the I-40, wearing a skimpy pair of shorts and a tight-fitting top, we meet Robyn. She has travelled all the way from Seattle to share two stages with her friend William. He is altogether quieter and more sensible, but equally likeable. That said, even Lady Gaga would seem sensible next to Robyn. I am instantly captivated.

Robyn tells us she has always been a runner but became serious after dating a runner six years back.

"The running lasted, the relationship didn't," she grins, eyes twinkling. She is playful, provocative and sexy; a natural born poser with a love of performing in front of the camera even greater than my own. In the five minutes I've known her she has totally made my day.

Robyn and William plan to rotate every few miles. They arrived early to scope out their 20-mile route, but found that the road they'd expected to run on simply doesn't exist.

Holding a crumpled map in her hand Robyn tells us: "To be honest, until you guys showed up, I was beginning to wonder if this whole thing was an elaborate hoax." We laugh. But of course, it wasn't the first time that had been said. The Americans were turning out to be more cynical than we Brits give them credit for.

The only alternative to the highway is a trail which is rocky, hilly and, with the sun dipping beneath the horizon, is now getting very dark. Imagining that Robyn would be up for the adventure, I'm surprised when she tells us they've opted to run on the highway, with William's wife driving behind to protect them from the crazy truckers who frequent this route. But I'm also relieved. We're still running behind and can't afford any more delays. At least running on the highway should help us make up some time... so long as they don't get hit by a truck.

Whilst I've been giving Robyn my full attention, Kate's eyes are on William's wife's car. 'One Run For Boston' has been splashed across the back windscreen of their SUV in yellow and blue paint. On the side window they've daubed, 'LA to Boston' and added an arrow pointing the way. Kate seems to have forgotten we've seen this before, on the vehicles used by Jen's supporters back in Yucca Valley.

"Danny! How cool is this?" she gushes, eyes shining, arms waving in the direction of the car. I look over. On the streets of London teenagers get arrested for this. In America, however, it is perfectly normal to graffiti your own car in honor of all sorts of events and occasions; coast-to-coast running relays included. "We need to pimp our ride!" Kate announces, gesturing at the drab, grey chunk of metal we are currently calling home ...and she is right. A do-it-yourself decal is exactly what is needed. Amateur yet awesome – it seems to sum up the whole relay.

*****

While we wait for the baton to appear, William's wife digs out their leftover paint and we set to work. Taking a back window each, we really go for it. Kate attempts a yellow outline map of the USA with a blue line depicting our route.

"Does that look like America to you?" Kate asks, standing back to admire her artwork. "I guess it'll probably wash off as soon as it rains anyway. Won't it?" Her face drops. "Shit! This stuff does wash off, doesn't it?! We've got to return this car when we get to Boston." She turns round to look at us, starting to panic.

The others look at me, as if to say, "Is this girl for real?" Typical Kate behavior.

Kate's shame is cut short by the arrival of Dillon Jenkins and the baton. With the baton in her hands, Robyn begins striking poses for the camera, then I watch her disappear down the road, unable to take my eyes off her.

"Get in the car, Romeo," says Kate, breaking my trance. Robyn's energy is infectious and addictive. It is just what I need.

One mile down the road, I get Kate to pull in so I can give some encouragement, not that Robin needs it.

With a leap and a dance, shaking her butt in those oh-so-short shorts, Robyn runs past shouting, "7.24 bitches!" She is smashing it, shaving 2.5 minutes off the 10- minute mile target pace over the first mile. If she and William can do this for every one of their twenty miles we'll claw back 50 minutes of time, no problem. Awesome!

Robyn is flying along, waving at the truckers, pointing at the baton, trying to share how important, how cool this is. She holds the baton above her mouth, pretending to drink from it. Now, there's an idea. She runs past us again, and calls out that she's broken a finger nail. When Kate asks me to pass her the phone I assume she's getting bored of The Robyn Show. Not a bit of it. "Man down! Man down! We've got a broken finger nail on Stage 35" she posts to our Facebook wall. Is Kate finally starting to relax?

The lift in energy is contagious and Kate and I are the ones reaping the benefit. I pick up my camera with renewed vigor. Lying in the middle of the highway in an awkward position I try to capture a picture of Will, lit up by the lights of his wife's truck. Barefoot as ever, I have to pull some nasty thorns from my foot afterwards, but it is worth it.

We stop in a rest area for a bathroom break and overhear a group of truckers saying, "Hey, aren't they the relay guys from England?"

Cool! But I wonder if we're more recognizable by our smell than our looks. We've not had a wash in a while and I'm sure we must stink. Our own noses have probably become immune to the pong. Popping into the bathroom, I strip off beside a tiny sink. Unfortunately, one of the truckers who recognized us just minutes before enters the bathroom as I stand stark naked splashing myself in cold water. But he doesn't bat an eyelid and gets on with his business ... loudly.

Feeling refreshed, I drive us ahead to the next handoff which takes place over a barbed wire fence, on a remote dust track in the pitch black. Joe Tedesco, an obstetrician from Kingman, is up next and looks like he knows what he's doing. I'm glad it's him and not me running off down the lonely desert track. We stay a while in the dark, chatting to Robyn and William across the wire. Robyn is heading back to Las Vegas before flying home to Seattle. I'd been to Vegas the year before, stopping for a night on a rock-climbing trip during a mammoth hitchhike. That one night was pretty terrible. I expected noise, laughter and excitement, flirting and camaraderie. But the reality was very different. Standing beside me around the roulette wheel were people with serious gambling habits who looked thoroughly miserable. They didn't even cheer when they won, let alone when my infrequent wins came around.

The hotel lighting in Vegas is deliberately set to a permanent dusk, making it easy to lose track of time; and that is the point. The casinos want you to stay up all night placing more bets and lining their pockets. I tell Robyn and William how, as I'd left the hotel, I passed two people selling at the top of their voices. One was encouraging me to take the way of the lord; the stairway to heaven. The other was encouraging me to take the dark and dingy staircase down to a brothel. It was the stairway to his heaven, perhaps, but not mine.

"Vegas," I say, shaking my head with regret. "It's the only place I know where pimps and preachers work side by side."

"They're probably working for the same agency," quips William. Vegas: my least favorite place on earth.

Piercing our chests on the barbed wire fence we share a goodbye hug. "You know, when I signed up to run this relay, I didn't really know what to expect." William tells us. "I have to say, congratulations guys. I think this must be the most grassroots event ever."

Chapter 12

We wake at 5:30 am to a bug-splattered windscreen. We're parked up just outside Kingman and, all being well, the relay should have passed through town overnight as we slept, heading north to Hackberry on Route 66 again. We munch on some leftover biltong that we are delighted to discover in the pocket of the side door and set off in search of runners. But half an hour later, they are still nowhere to be seen.

We scour the roadside for any signs of runners or support vehicles but see nothing. Suppressing our innermost concerns that maybe the relay hasn't even got as far as Kingman yet, we do our best to keep chipper.

"At least there's a nice shoulder on this road," Kate says, "it should make things a bit safer for the runners." I agree the shoulder is unusually wide. "You could drive a car down that shoulder," I observe. We chatter away, me at the wheel and Kate with her head in the map, trying to work out where Hackberry could be exactly. Unsurprisingly, it isn't marked on our map. Not many places with a population below 50,000 are.

"It's funny that Americans give the same stretch of road more than one route number, isn't it?" I say.

Kate was thinking the exact same thing, "I know what you mean. Yesterday we were following Route 66 along State Highway 95. Today we're on Route 66 and I keep seeing signs saying I-40. It's the sort of thing that could really confuse stupid people." Pointing out a single-track road running parallel to the one we're on, I suggest they took the frontage road. Another I-40 sign whizzes past us.

Navigating onto the frontage road, we hypothesize about what could have happened to the runners. Most scenarios don't end well for the runners. Back on the highway Kate looks up at the signs and starts rifling through her papers.

"Did that say Seligman?" she asks, confused. "The relay isn't due to pass through there until late this afternoon." Kate looks down at the map on her lap and turns to me. "Oh Danny, you'll never guess what…" Yep you guessed it. We have in fact spent an hour and a half driving up and down the interstate. We are very definitely not on Route 66. The good news is that both routes converge in the town of Seligman. So we get off the I-40, and make our way easily enough onto Route 66, westbound – 80 miles to Kingman. Oops! I put my foot down.

Cars in the US are hugely more powerful than cars in the UK. The average American vehicle has a V6 3.4 liter engine. Compare this to the average UK car at 1.7 liters. The first car I owned was an 800cc Daewoo Matiz. An American wouldn't put that engine in their bike, let alone a car.

We're making good progress when a police car approaches, flashing its lights.

"Maybe there's something up ahead they're trying to warn us about?" Kate says, reasonably enough, as the cop car disappears from view. "Should we slow down, just in case?"

I let off the gas a bit but have to laugh. We're on one of those long, straight Arizonan roads through the desert where you can see for miles and miles. There is definitely nothing up ahead. Then we see the flashing lights again. Another cop car, but this time they're behind us and signaling for us to pull over. I can't believe my luck! Finally, the authentic bit of cop interaction I've been dreaming of since I'd arrived in America. This is exciting! We sit together in the car facing forward, watching the cop in our rear view mirrors as he puts on his hat and walks towards us.

"Shit Danny, how fast were you going?" Kate asks.

"I dunno, but this time I'm definitely getting a photo," I whisper out the side of mouth. Kate looks at me with genuine fear in her eyes. "No, please. Don't do that Danny. He doesn't look in the mood for photos." We put our hands on the dashboard to allow the cop to see that we aren't armed, just like they do in the movies. He swaggers up to Kate's window and asks me if I know how fast we were travelling. I tell him I'm not exactly sure but I can tell from the way the conversation is going that I might have been doing a little over the limit.

"We clocked you doing 102 miles per hour," the police officer says in a serious tone.

"No, really?" I say, feigning shock and horror. "I am *so* sorry." I'm entirely confident that a heartfelt apology will be sufficient and soon we'll be on our way again, perhaps with a picture of me wearing the cop's hat. But the officer retrieves a ticket book from his pocket and asks for my driving license and passport.

"You do know that in Arizona the state law automatically requires anyone found speeding in excess of 100mph to spend a night in jail, don't you?" the officer asks.

My jaw drops into the foot well. Part of me is excited by this news. I imagine myself being cuffed and bundled into the police car, then interviewed and fingerprints taken. They'll throw me into a cell where I have no option but to sit or lie in the excrement and urine of past occupants, whilst cockroaches explore my body and my boss-eyed jail mate digs with a spoon, speaking manically about tunneling out of the cell by morning. I might even lend him a hand if we get there before nightfall. What a story to write home about. And O to the M to the G, a full night's sleep! That isn't punishment – even if I am rolling around in someone else's shit.

I look over at Kate. She's pretty quiet. I suddenly feel guilty. I think about her and the relay. She will have to carry on alone while I spend a night in the cells. Oh goodness. This is actually really bad. I try to catch her eye but she doesn't look at me. She sits facing straight ahead with her cap pulled down over her face, as the police officer and I conduct our conversation over her lap. I could swear her shoulders are shaking. Oh please no, please don't cry. Her husband will never forgive me if I have to abandon Kate in the middle of the Arizonan desert.

As much as I want to spend a night in the cells, I decide I should at least try and fight this out and explain in my best English accent what we are doing. I tell the officer that we are trying to help the victims of the Boston bombings. I tell him that we have runners to support and that we've been searching the wrong road for over an hour. He doesn't have an awful lot of sympathy.

"Don't you have speeding limits in the UK?" he asks. I have to admit that yes, he is right on that point, we do indeed have speeding limits in the UK. Kate's shoulders are shuddering even worse now. I want to tell her to pull herself together, that this is nothing to cry about. It's just another experience which makes life all the more colorful. Even if I have to spend a night in the slammer it will be a story we can both dine out on when we get home.

The police officer informs me that the speed limit here on Route 66 is 60mph. I can't help thinking why on earth do they make car engines so big over here if that's the limit? My little 800cc car could smash 60mph. I guess that's why we see so many great car chases taking place in America on the police camera action shows in the UK. Americans just want to find out what their cars can do.

Leaning into the car the officer tells me that we have just entered the Navajo nation and he has the option to invoke Tribal Law. Without a clue whether this is a good thing or a bad thing I pathetically answer, "Yes?"

"I can just fine you for your offence and let you off your night in jail."

The smell of urine in my hair and the dirt under my finger nails from digging my way out of my cell evaporates into the desert air. "Thank you, sir. Thank you, officer. Thank you."

Slapped with a fine of $5 for every mile we were over the speed limit, I hold a $185 fine in my hand. As the policeman walks away from the car, Kate pulls her cap back off her face revealing tears of laughter. "Oh my god! That was so funny!" she says. "It was all I could do to keep myself from laughing out loud!"

"What?! I thought you were crying!" I say.

"No way! Really? Seriously, it was hilarious!"

"But I could have gone to jail!"

"I know, how funny would that have been?"

"Not for me it wouldn't."

"OK, I'm sorry. I just can't help it. I'm like those people who laugh at funerals."

"What? Those people really exist?!"

"Yeah, of course they do. I saw a documentary on it once. They don't want to laugh, in fact they're really, really sad, but they just can't stop themselves. It was the same for me when I was a kid. When my mum and dad would tell me off, I used to laugh right in their faces. It used to really piss my mum off. Maybe I'm just wired-up differently?"

"You're certainly different," I say, starting the engine.

"Hang on a minute," Kate says, clambering over into the back seat with the camera. I don't believe it. The police officer is still behind us, standing outside his car chatting with his colleague. "One for the album," Kate says as she takes a cheeky photo out of the back window then hops back in the front. Exchanging a quick high five, I set the cruise control to 64 mph and we continue westwards, laughing till our faces ache.

Three hours later than we'd originally planned, we meet up with the Kingman Runners team. Between them they've carried the baton all through the night, gaining time bit by bit on every stage. Supported by their friends and family, sharing hugs, tears, sweat and stories all night long, the Kingman Runners have done a supreme job.

We are greeted by Diane Stokes. Diane had run her own 13 mile leg out of Kingman in the early hours and, after she finished, she continued in her car, supporting the runners that followed. She looks as fresh as a daisy, parked up by the roadside with the best-stocked trunk we've ever seen. It is practically a cafeteria. Next to the energy drinks and chocolate bars there is a cooler filled with sandwiches, individually wrapped in plastic bags, each with their own sachet of mayonnaise or salad cream. Diane is my kind of woman. I think of the strip of jerky we'd had for breakfast, some three hours earlier.

"Help yourself!" Diane says enthusiastically. She must have heard our stomachs growling. While Kate holds back, embarrassed that we should be tucking into food intended for the runners, I have no such reservations and start making a serious dent in the mountain of sandwiches. It isn't long before Kate joins me. As we munch, Diane tells us how hard everyone has worked in an effort to get the baton back on schedule.

"When we started, the relay was 90 minutes behind," she says. We glance at our watches. "Look!" she says."Now we're only 20 minutes behind!" Words tumble out of her mouth as she fills us in on what has happened overnight.

"We had a police officer and a doctor out there running, before the baton even reached our city limits! Then Shanna led her group through some unmarked trail paths and the Department of Public Safety gave us an escort through the city, to make sure nothing bad happened to Shirley."

Diane pauses a second, as if waiting for us to say something but our mouths are too full of sandwich.

"Then, I was out there running in the wee hours of the morning with this silly song stuck in my head that goes something like this... 'On a dark desert highway, cool wind in my hair...' You may know it?"

Hotel California. Classic.

"It was hilly this morning and the heat was rising, but Anna never slowed. We were all filled with determination and purpose!"

It is so wonderful to hear Diane talk about the relay with such passion. But before we can even begin to thank her for all she has done, two more members of the Kingman Runners team run up to us beaming, carrying the baton aloft. Diane shuts the trunk and gets each runner to sign their name on a 2 meter long vinyl banner attached to the back windscreen. Diane has had the banner specially made up, printed with the One Run For Boston logo and the map showing our route across America. Every member of the Kingman team has signed it.

"Will you take the banner with you?" Diane asks. "We'd like to donate it to the cause so that every runner can get the chance to sign it."

We are bowled over by such an extraordinary gesture and vow to fill the banner with all the signatures we can possibly get.

"I look forward to keeping up with the baton as it travels across the country," Diane says, as we pack the banner into our car, together with at least half the leftover contents of her trunk. "As this story unfolds, hearts will open and we will all forever be united in One Run For Boston," she says, as we say our goodbyes.

*****

In all the excitement, we don't notice that we're running out of fuel until the dial is close to empty. Passing through Peach Springs, we spot a gas station only to get out and discover that it shut down a long, long time ago. If we want gas, we must head back to Truxton.

"How far back is that?" Kate asks.

"Seven miles, according to the sign," I tell her.

"That's alright then. According to the dashboard we've got nine miles of fuel left." Talk about cutting it fine! So we turn off the air conditioning to conserve what little fuel remains and gasp our way back to Truxton. Fuelled-up and heading east again, we realize that we're also low on water.

"You know what would be really good to have," I say to Kate, "is one of those coolers that everyone seems to carry in the back of their cars packed with ice to keep their water cold." Kate nods in agreement. "Absolutely, but I don't hold out much hope of getting one out here though." She's right. The best we can muster is a polystyrene box from the only store in Peach Springs. They've run out bottled water so we wait half an hour for their delivery to arrive and then scrounge some ice from the hotel over the road. We must learn to plan ahead a bit better.

Twelve miles up the road, at a mock 50s diner with a larger than life Betty Boop at the till and a cabinet of Muppet Pez dispensers at the door, Van Patterson waits. He has travelled up from Phoenix, camped in a forest overrun with ants and cycled 25 miles to get to the diner which marks the start of his leg. In the absence of a support crew, Van has left his car at the finish in Seligman and is planning to drive back to pick up his bike after he's finished his run. At 25 miles, Van's leg of the relay, stage 45, is unusually long, more than twice the distance of the average leg so far. The reason for this is simple. In the middle of the Arizonan desert between Grand Canyon Caverns and Seligman there is nothing, absolutely nothing, barring the odd bundle of tumbleweed. There are no houses, no gas stations, no intersections with minor roads, not even a dirt track leading off the main route.

Back home in England a few weeks earlier, when Kate was plotting the route, she had scoured the landscape using Google maps but failed to find anything recognizable along this stretch of Route 66 that she could use to identify a baton handoff point. She had reassured herself that a 25-mile stretch through the desert in the early afternoon would be OK. A group of friends would probably sign up to run it together, taking it in turns to run and drive a support vehicle laden with water. But Van is running on his own, with no back up; he is planning to carry all the water he needs on his back and around his waist. He seems comfortable with this, but is happy enough when we put his bike in the back of our car to save him the extra journey later and offer to carry his extra water for him. All he has to do now is run the 25-miles back to his car.

The irony of running such a large chunk of what is arguably the most iconic path in America's obsession with the automobile, is not lost on Van. Likewise, the irony of meeting a long distance runner named after a type of automobile was not lost on Kate. Van lamented America's reliance on the automobile, which he said had helped form a spiraling epidemic of obesity and urban sprawl. The man was lyrical to say the least.

As he exits the Route 66 diner, proudly wearing his running attire, Betty Boop shakes her giant head in contempt and Pez Head Kermit farts in his general direction.

Van is dressed for the job with almost every inch of skin covered in an attempt to protect him from the sun and heat. He wears a long white t-shirt, a cap with neck protection, sunglasses and compression socks. The socks are more to protect his calves from the sun's rays than to give his muscles relief. On his back is his Camelbak hydration rucksack, full of water. It's a long straight road to Seligman. Wild horses prance in the scrub to Van's left and every now and again, to his right, a freight train rumbles past. Strong winds blow tumbleweed across his path, accompanied by sharp stinging pieces of sand. Barring this there is nothing but an empty stretch of highway.

Every couple of miles we stop and make the most of our new cooler. Kate dishes out ice water sponge downs as if she's Van's mother, and fills his cap with ice, a tip we'd picked up from the Californian desert runners. Van asks Kate if she's beginning to wonder what the hell went wrong with her life. But from the smile on her face she looks like she's starting to enjoy herself. She scoops ice into Van's cap, pops it on his head and tells him to get back out there; he is halfway through and doing fabulously. As Van runs, the ice melts, releasing a cooling river down his scalp and neck.

Van loves the desert and the heat. He says he was born in the desert and will die in the desert. In fact when he dies he's instructed his wife to cut his body into quarters and feed one each to the vultures, the lizards, the coyotes and the ants. But he tells us he doesn't run well in hot conditions. After so many miles without an inch of shade, his mind starts to wander and he retreats into his own head. Elite runners warn of the dangers of letting the mind stray. Proper cogitation during a run apparently involves either an intense focus on the immediacy of each step or a kind of bipedal, Nirvanic emptying of the brain. Van says he is not an elite runner. His brain concocts intricate, tangled fantasies of a better world, usually one with dragons, or Congress members able to tie their own shoes. It doesn't seem to hamper Van's progress today though. He is smashing it, knocking time off every mile and then some. By far the fastest person we've seen in this heat, he is managing to maintain the same quick pace past 15 miles. He is getting us back on time.

The tracker is still down and we do our best to keep everyone updated via social media. "I'm beginning to think Van is an actual van," someone tweets. Kate takes a photo of Van and posts it in our Facebook group with the caption: "The actual Van, 7 miles from Seligman. #ReallyMotoring"

107

The group goes wild. "If Van Patterson were a corvette, I'd be a jalopy! Go Van Go!" posts Katherine Shea. Martha Munoz uploads a 'We're Not Worthy' clip from Wayne's World.

With two miles to go, it is clear that by Van's standards, he is suffering. We pull up alongside him to give him encouragement. His face is caked in salt from the sweat he is losing. As we tell him how awesome he is doing, he replies, "I'm sorry I'm not going faster. I ran an ultra marathon at the weekend and am a little tired." I look round at Kate. Did we just hear this right? The weekend was only two days ago. This guy is a legend amongst men. If there were dragons out here, he'd be running them down and making pets of them.

Pulling into Seligman, we position the car so that the open windows face the road. We crank up the sound system and give Van a blast of *You're the Best Around*, the theme tune from Karate Kid. This attracts the attention of Frank, the owner of the Route 66 souvenir shop. He starts taking photos of us all for his blog.

"Kate and I don't look our best after three days on the road," I say, pretending to flick my hair.

"Oh, I dunno, you look pretty good for Route 66!" Frank replies.

With the Karate Kid theme blaring in the background, we witness one of the most surreal hand-offs yet. It isn't the fact that two men who have never met are sharing a lingering hug as Van hands the baton to Mark Meury. It's more the fact that Seligman is one of the weirdest places I've ever seen. It is chock-full of wackiness. There's a store decorated with scantily-clad mannequins seated on its roof, another with a garden full of decorated Christmas trees, and memorabilia shops galore with brightly painted exteriors, selling everything from the weird to the wonderful.

Mark and Andrea told us they ran for their health, mental and physical, and to set an example to their beautiful children. The children had been persuaded to come along to Seligman to see 'Radiator Springs'. It is full

108

of unusual automobiles and was the inspiration for the Disney / Pixar film *Cars*.

Then there's the famous Roadkill Café, and an old Territorial Jail House that once housed such notorious outlaws as Seligman Slim, Carl "Curly" Bane, and Four-Fingered Frank. It's OK, I've never heard of them either, which is a shame, because it sounds like they would have brightened up our history lessons.

Mark and Andrea have left a $20 bill for Van at the bar across the way. They tell the barman to look out for a hot, sweaty guy who'll be coming in later; they want to make sure his first beers are taken care of. As Mark runs off, leaving this strange town behind him, Andrea tells us she wasn't just supporting Mark but supporting her community, her fellow runners and all of Boston. She said she realized something epic was going on.

"Every heel strike represents a step closer to ensuring our children can live in a world without fear."

Van signs our banner and thanks us for our enthusiasm.

"You turned a grueling, sweaty chafe-fest into a leisurely jaunt, filled with appropriately motivating music, a glamour photo shoot and perfectly chilled water," he says. Van has hopes of qualifying for Boston in 2014. "And on the run, I will think of you both," he tells us, "and possibly vampires and leprechauns too."

We unload Van's bike from the car as Andrea gets ready to follow her husband. She checks on the kids who have fallen asleep in the back of the car, unaware they have just witnessed history in the making and that they themselves have just become part of that history.

Whilst we laugh and load Van's bike into his car, Andrea puts her car into drive and begins to follow her husband into the emptiness. She looks back at us then at her children, asleep in the back of her car. Smiling, she thinks how unaware they are that they'd witnessed history and repeats to herself, "We will not allow our children to grow up in fear…"

Chapter 13

Throughout the night, runners report sightings of bobcats and deer on the forest roads approaching Flagstaff. Pairs of eyes appear between the trees, lit up by the runners' headlamps. I'm jealous. We don't have bobcats in England and I would love to see one. They are about twice the size of a domestic cat with black-tufted ears and a stubby tail which gives them their name. Bobcats hunt by stealth, but deliver a deathblow with a leaping pounce that can cover three meters. Now, that's something I would like to see, albeit from the safety of the car.

The scenery has changed dramatically. In the space of a few hours, we've left the desert behind and have climbed into an Alpine world where the air is cool and fir trees stretch as far as the eye can see. At 7000 feet, Flagstaff sits just south of the highest mountain range in Arizona. It may be mid-June, but we can see snow-covered peaks in the distance, overlooking the city. Flagstaff is one of the best spots for altitude training and elite athletes from all over the world base themselves here for months at a time. It's a pretty cool place in all senses of the word.

During the long climb up to Flagstaff the baton has fallen behind again, and Kate and I sit in the car, nervously munching our way through a bag of trail mix, trying to keep our minds off the fact that the relay is running over two hours late. I hand Kate the bag and she starts throwing handfuls of mix into her mouth. Nuts and seeds cascade into every crevice of her car seat. But she doesn't even notice. Or if she does, she doesn't care. I want to ask

110

about Rule 1: *Thou shalt not eat or drink in the car,* but decide we're past that now and join Kate in a trail mix bonanza breakfast.

We are excited to be reunited with Holly Miller, from stages 1 and 2. Today she is running another two stages back-to-back, with her mum Dee in support. We meet up in a parking lot in the center of Flagstaff and are delighted to discover that Dee is just as gorgeous as her daughter. She is like the sun, radiating warmth and positivity towards us. We rename her Sunny Dee, less orange but just as sweet as her namesake. Looking absolutely shattered from their night spent out in the wilds, Brady Dohrmann and James Gamache arrive in the parking lot and hand-off the baton. They seem relieved it's over. I ask if I can join Holly for some of her stage and we set off towards the Navajo Nation.

As we run and chat, Amy Horton is up ahead, scouting out her stage in the car with her husband, Shawn. Kate leaves Holly and me to it and drives on to meet them. Amy had woken up on April 15 and wished her husband a 'Happy Boston Marathon Day!' before skipping off to work imagining what it would be like when she had her chance to run Boston the following year. She downloaded an app so she could follow her favorite elite runners while at work and went about her normal day. That afternoon she watched the news coverage from Boston in disbelief and horror. She thought of something Shawn had told her before one of her marathons. "I don't like to wait for you by the finish line. I like to watch a few blocks before the finish. I love seeing the joy on the runners' faces when they see the finish line for the first time." Amy realized that this would have put Shawn right in the firing line of the second explosion. It was Shawn who first found out about One Run For Boston, via a friend on Facebook, and he encouraged Amy to sign up. She immediately knew it was something she wanted to do.

When I catch up with them, my first words to Amy are, "Wow, you look strong! I bet you're a fast runner."

Shyly she replies, "I'm pretty good. I should have no problems staying on pace." There is no hint of arrogance in her voice. Amy knows what she is capable of; it is just a simple, truthful statement.

Watching as Dee and Holly run the last two miles together, Shawn tells us, "The only running I've done in the last 15 years is running a tab at the local brewery. But you guys make me feel like I could grab that baton and go!"

Shawn has watched many marathons from the sidelines and fully expected that One Run For Boston would have less impact on him than on the people who were actually putting in the miles. Leading up to the relay, his wife's levels of anticipation were much higher than his. But now he's actually here, Shawn is also excited. He knows he isn't just here for water stops and moral support. He may not be running but he stills feels like a part of something big. As his wife takes the baton from Holly to begin her journey and support the victims of the Boston bombings in the only way she knows how, Shawn swells up with pride. "Now I realize we're involved in something so much bigger than the both of us," he says.

Amy sets off like a lightning bolt. I pop my head out of the window as we drive by and shout, "I wasn't wrong, you *are* strong! You are flying! Keep it up!"

Shawn stops every mile to offer water and cheer Amy on. It's a pretty desolate highway and he has an ulterior motive for stopping so often. "Somehow I married a pretty one," explains Shawn. "Anyone who knows me knows that my chances of landing a wife of this caliber twice in a row are pretty slim," he confesses, and keeps a close eye on her until the end of her stage.

I suddenly need a pee and dive into the bushes just as the local Sheriff's car drives by.

"Did you know urinating in public is a sex offence in Arizona?" asks Shawn, with a twinkle in his eye. Lucky for me, the Sheriff continues on his way, oblivious to the sexual deviant in the bushes. Shawn is right though. According to the Arizonan Civil Code, if you get caught peeing in public three times, then you will automatically be branded a sex offender. If there's anyone under the age of 15 in the area at the time, you don't get a third chance; it is two strikes and you're out.

"You'd better be careful Danny," laughs Kate, looking at my reserve pair of shorter than short shorts. "I bet wearing those in public is a sex offence here too."

I run up the road, water in one hand, camera in the other, taking pictures of Amy as she traverses the high desert highway.

"He is so full of energy, always smiling and laughing," Shawn says to Kate. "If we could figure out how to harvest the energy from him we could eliminate our dependence on fossil fuels immediately!" Then, quoting one of my favorite lines from a Tim Minchin comedy sketch, Shawn says, "He is certainly a ginger on the go! I can say that though, because only a ginger can call a ginger a ginger." This guy is a class act.

Shawn looks down the road in Amy's direction and sees a car appear out of the heat haze, slowing down alongside his wife. On high alert, Shawn is ready to jump in his car and shoot to the rescue. "Damn it, I knew I shouldn't have married a pretty one," he says, convinced that the occupants of the car are trying to make a move on his wife. But the mystery car speeds up, leaving Amy to it. In the car are Cicely and Nancy who are running the next couple of legs. They pull up beside us and as they chat to Shawn they discover Amy will be running the San Francisco Marathon the following weekend. They are running it too and suggest meeting up for lunch after the race. Shawn politely declines, telling them it is his wedding anniversary. The race entry is Shawn's gift to his wife.

I smile at Shawn. "If you go out for lunch afterwards, Amy will probably eat a massive plate of food, fall asleep and be out cold for the night."

Shawn looks at me and says, "Same as last year then."

*****

We have entered the Navajo Nation. This semi-autonomous, Native American governed territory occupies 27,425 square miles of Arizona and western New Mexico, touching Utah and Colorado to the north. It is the largest land area assigned primarily to a Native American jurisdiction within the United States.

Until the late 1500's, the Navajo people lived a mainly peaceful life. Then as we Europeans came along, their peaceful world was turned upside-down. Initially, it was the turn of the Spanish in the late 1500's. The Navajo people were killed, burnt and taken as slaves. Then came the Americans, who arrived in Santa Fe in August 1846 with the intent to make the territory home. Navajo leaders met with American soldiers that November, and concluded the Bear Springs Treaty. However, raids, hostilities and out-and-out fighting continued.

Eventually, following a peace treaty with the United States, the Navajo even allowed the United States to capture the South West. This was not a debt the United States would honor or repay.

In 1863, "Kit" Carson ruthlessly attacked the Navajo People, burning their homes and killing their sheep. U.S. forces starved them into submission. Later, in 1864, the Navajo people were marched 300 miles across New Mexico, to a prison camp in Bosque Redondo where they were fed rations of rancid bacon and insect-infested flour. The march eastwards across New Mexico is known as the Long Walk, and took a similar route to that of One Run For Boston. On route, the Navajos were beaten and killed arbitrarily for 'sport' by Cavalry troops and their Indian allies. Finally, in 1868 they were allowed to return to the four corners area, the land that they love, and still call their home now.

*****

Native Americans have long understood the positive benefits of running. They believe running creates a healthy and strong body, increases life energy and drives away feelings of unhappiness. These are definitely beliefs most runners around the world will identify with. Before the Europeans arrived, Native Americans relied on running to hunt and gather food. Man's ability to run for 20 miles at a constant pace will exhaust prey like deer and elk. These animals are only able to outsprint us over much shorter distances. Running was also a way to communicate with neighboring tribes. The top runners would earn respect and admiration. They still do today. Running is still very much part of the Navajo way of life with entire communities turning out to run in frequent local races that are highly competitive at the sharp end.

Thomas Hatathli is the first Navajo we meet. He is tall, wiry and super anxious to get started on his run. Like many of the Navajo, Thomas' manner is quiet and reserved. He tells us that he first ran the Boston Marathon in 1997. "When I arrived in Boston, the person who picked me up at the airport said 'Your dad passed away today.' On the day of his funeral service I was unable to attend because I toed the line for my first Boston Marathon." It's what his Dad would have wanted. After that the Boston Marathon became a very special marathon for Thomas. "I go back every year to connect with that special feeling. Not a feeling of grief, but a feeling of peace, tranquility, calmness and inspiration," he explains.

On April 15 2013, Thomas ran his twelfth Boston Marathon, finishing in 3:37. He had waited a while at the finish hoping to see some fellow Native Americans cross the line. He didn't see any so he made his way to the nearest subway. His legs were sore, so he grabbed the side rail and started walking backwards to make use of a different set of muscles. It was as he was walking backwards down the steps into the subway that he heard an explosion.

"It sounded like a heavy piece of metal falling from a sky scraper. I had no idea it was a bomb explosion until I got off the subway and walked into an ice cream place. I sat down to enjoy my ice cream and watch the marathon on the TV. But all I saw were chaotic scenes at the finish line." Thomas flew home to Arizona feeling discouraged and unsure of whether he would ever want to go back to Boston for another marathon.

Then he read a quote, "If the terrorists are trying to defeat the human spirit, marathon runners are the wrong group to target." He processed the words and with a sense of renewed motivation, he told himself, "Damn right. I *am* going back next year."

As Thomas starts his run, baton in hand, the temperature is 100°F.

"How wonderful," thinks Thomas, "I am going to be blessed from the heat radiating from our god, The Sun." Kate and I have a lot to learn from Thomas when it comes to positive thinking. Thomas started running at a young age. At ten, he ran away from his boarding-school in Tuba City, back home to his family in Coalmine Mesa. It was a distance of exactly 26 miles and Thomas' first unofficial marathon.

Thomas has deliberately chosen the longest stage of the relay, another 26-mile stretch, along Indian Route 15 to Dilkon. He runs alone, barely stopping for a sip of water. Twelve miles in, Thomas' daughters arrive to cheer him on.

"I love running," Thomas calls out to us, "no matter how bad you look, people always cheer."

We are keen to find out more about life in the Navajo Nation and Thomas' daughters chat freely. Until fairly recently, they tell us, Navajo children were forced to attend boarding schools as the American authorities attempted to eliminate traditional Native customs and language. Thomas had himself been sent to boarding-school as a young boy, against his parents' will. The boarding-schools were full of unhappiness and children were punished for speaking the Navajo tongue. The complex language was used by the Americans in World War II as the basis of a secret military code which the Japanese were unable to crack. And yet the Government was hell bent on eradicating Navajo in the communities where it originated. They have done a pretty good job. Thomas' daughters explain that they do not speak any Navajo and as a result have never spoken a sentence that their grandparents, who only speak Navajo, could understand. This strikes me as incredibly sad. I think of my own grandparents with whom I love to sit talking, joking and playing word games. Granddad and I always team up to pitch our dyslexic minds against the women of the family – the games often breakdown into fits of laughter as our dyslexic spellings are sometimes harder to understand than the Navajo language.

The two girls run with their dad for the last few miles and they are joined by members of the high school cross country team that Thomas coaches. By the time they reach Dilkon, Thomas has been running for almost four hours. It's been an absolute honor and a privilege to watch every step.

Bill Orman is a white American who has lived and worked on the Navajo Reservation for twenty years. He has persuaded his son Billy, and Billy's friend Dennis, to join him for a little nighttime adventure which involves running 42.5 miles from Dilkon to Burnside. Another friend was due to join them but has had to pull out due to injury. He is worried about letting them down, but Billy and Dennis agree to split his miles between them, on top of the miles that they are already down to run. They are excited to do their part. In his professional life, Bill is a pediatrician. He promotes running as a simple, easily accessible, low-cost form of exercise to his patients, many of whom struggle with their weight or with drink and drug addictions. Being a runner himself, Bill feels it gives him a lot of credibility with both his patients and their families.

Bill takes the baton from his good friend, Thomas, and is soon alone in the darkness. Running in silence with a blanket of stars overhead, he watches meteors fall through the sky and hears the occasional coyote singing in the distance. There is a mystical quality in the air tonight as Bill becomes the latest link in a chain of compassion, dedication, pride and strength that is building from west to east. Bill runs to honor those whose lives have been impacted by the Boston Marathon bombings and to honor the Navajo Nation which has accepted him as their own.

At 2am, Billy takes the baton from his father with the relay running two hours behind schedule. Billy is a talented collegiate runner and holds the Arizonan record for the mile distance; four minutes and six seconds. When we met him at the finish of Thomas' run, Billy told us that between him and Dennis, an equally gifted runner, they hope to get the baton back on track overnight. He kicks things up a couple of gears and launches himself into the night, his curly mop of hair bouncing up and down with the rise and fall of his long stride.

Billy has just returned home from Harvard and the sudden change of scenery, coupled with not having eaten enough before the run, is disorientating him. He hears rustles in the bushes and sees dark shadows flit across the road. Before he set off, Billy had entertained romantic notions that running these back roads of his childhood, beneath starry skies and in complete solitude would be a calm and meditative experience. But instead, with the starlight washed out by the cone of light cast by his headlamp, Billy's morbid imagination takes over. He pictures ghosts following him in the dark, and begins to get spooked. It's certainly an incentive to keep the fast pace going. He hands-off to Dennis then tucks into a very, very early breakfast of chocolate chip cookies.

Dennis is a member of the Hopi tribe, a sovereign nation surrounded entirely by the Navajo Nation. In Hopi culture, it is felt that by running, the runner brings positive energy not just to the Hopi people, but to the entire world. Running is especially valued by Hopi desert farmers because it is thought to bring rain. When running events take place on the Hopi reservation, which is often, villagers looking on call out, "KwatKwe" which means "Thank You" as the runners pass by.

As Dennis takes his turn, cries of "Nahongvita!" fill the air. It means, "Run Strong!" And Dennis does just that, making up minute after minute of lost time. When he finishes, the relay is ahead of schedule for the first time in five days.

*****

Sitting on the border of Arizona and New Mexico, the city of Window Rock, with a population of just 2,712, is the capital of the Navajo Nation. It gets its name from the hole in the 200ft high sandstone hill that overlooks the area. This natural window is sacred to the Navajo as one of four sites where the Navajo medicine men collect water for the Water Way ceremony, held to ensure abundant rainfall.

We don't get a chance to go and see the sandstone window and I regret it. Two days earlier we'd passed within miles of the Grand Canyon and had not seen that either. But neither of us had been too bothered about missing that at the time, realizing that what we were witnessing every hour on the road in front of us, was far more remarkable, beautiful and humbling than any gorge, no matter how grand. But now that we are beginning to learn a little about the sacred significance that the Navajo and Hopi tribes give to different features of their landscape, I want to explore every bump and every hollow.

But following the baton's uninterrupted journey, there simply isn't time.

As we continue our travels through the vast Reservation, word is spreading among the different communities. Groups of people are turning out to run and many more to support at every stage. It is a real community affair.

"If we'd had more notice," one woman tells us, "everyone would be out to support. The roads would be lined with people handing out food and water." Judging by what we are seeing, we don't doubt it. "We could have got the casinos to sponsor it," she goes on. This strikes us as an odd thing to say. Casinos and running don't go together in our minds. Kate and I had passed a few casinos on our route and had been surprised to see them out here in one of the poorest and least densely populated parts of the country. It didn't seem a very good idea to me.

We found out that the Navajo Nation was one of the last few remaining tribes in America's Southwest to resist the temptation of gaming. Then in 2008, nearly two decades after the first casinos began opening on American Indian lands, the first Navajo casino opened in Gallup, New Mexico. By attracting wealthy gamblers from outside the reservations, casinos are seen as ways to generate billions of dollars for destitute tribes where high percentages of the population are unemployed and live below the poverty line. They offer employment opportunities and benefit surrounding communities through sizeable charitable contributions. This is what the woman must have been referring to when she said the casinos might have sponsored their communities' participation in the relay. But alas, there is a downside to casinos. They are perceived as a threat to Navajo culture and tradition and can compound economic and social problems by encouraging gambling addiction and crime. I suspected they were probably doing more harm than good.

As we leave Window Rock, we pull in for fuel and a woman introduces herself saying she is a sports coach from a local school. She knows others who will be running in the afternoon and is keen to show her support.

"Let me pay for your fuel," she says and before we can answer, she is handing over her credit card to the cashier at the kiosk and pointing back to our pump. Not quite believing that this woman is for real, we cautiously lift the gas nozzle out of its holder and slide it into the tank. Giving the trigger a slight squeeze, the gas starts flowing and we look over at the woman uncomprehending. She gives us a thumbs up, jumps back in her car and drives off without even giving us a chance to thank her.

*****

The Saturday following the Boston Marathon bombings, the Boston Red Sox returned to Fenway Park for a game against the Kansas City Royals. The game coincided with the return of David 'Big Papi' Ortiz to the line-up after an Achilles injury. Taking to the microphone at an emotional pre-game ceremony to honor the victims of the bombing attacks, Papi addressed the crowd,

"This jersey that we're wearing today, it doesn't say 'Red Sox.' It says, 'Boston.' We want to thank you, Mayor Menino, Governor Patrick, the whole police department, for the great job that they did this past week," Ortiz began. "This is our fucking city. And nobody is going to dictate our freedom. Stay strong." The stadium erupted and, in the days and weeks that followed, Papi's expression, 'This is our fucking city' was recited and adopted by hundreds of thousands of people across the city of Boston and beyond. Living in the UK and therefore not massively into baseball, Kate and I were unaware of this phrase and how it had recently entered public consciousness. We hadn't even heard of David Ortiz. So when we cruise into Ya Ta Hey and spot two young women standing on the curbside wearing bright red T-shirts with the words, 'This is my f*cking city' on the front, we just assume we've come across two of Ya Ta Hey's proudest, most aggressively possessive, residents. On further inspection, the women turn out to be Katie Jacques and Carm Upshaw, and they are waiting to begin stage 68. While they wait, they post a photo of themselves to Facebook saying, "Leg 68 is ready!"

The GPS is still up the spout and the post is intended to let everyone know that the relay is on track. But the response they get doesn't see past the T-shirts. Our followers in Boston are blown away by the support that they and their city are receiving from so many, so far away.

Vern Jaques is waiting at the start of stage 70, wondering whether his car will be OK parked up in the tiny village of Brimhall Nizoni, while he completes his 16-mile run. His wife will give him a lift back to collect it later. To relieve him of the worry, I offer to drive it to the end of his stage, to save him going back for it. Two other men, Mario and Mike, have signed up to run the stage with Vern, and Kate has already offered to give Mike's mum a lift in our car. My offer to shuttle Vern's car for him isn't purely selfless. Leaving Kate to make conversation with Mike's mum, Maryann, for the next three hours, I drive ahead in Vern's car, park up, then curl up and go to sleep.

Maryann looks as though she's in her seventies and can't be more than five feet high. She has lived on the Reservation all her life. She sits beside Kate clutching her handbag, half a bottle of water and a packet of peach-flavored chewing-gum. She was not expecting today to turn out like this and says little. Mike has signed up at the last minute, only two hours ago. He and Maryann skipped lunch to ensure they made it to the hand-off point on time and didn't think to pick up any food or drink on route. The back of our car is full of empty bottles and wrappers; evidence of our dwindling supplies. Mike is running 16 miles and Kate calculates they're going to run into trouble. She considers doing a forty-mile round trip back to Ya Ta

Hey to resupply, but Maryann reckons there is a little van parked up ahead where they can pick up what they need. Kate is skeptical. She wonders whether she's heard Maryann correctly, her accent is quite thick. But Kate really doesn't want to drive any more miles than she has to and, hoping Maryann is right, drives on. Sure enough, on the roadside up ahead, beside the only couple of houses visible for miles, there is a battered white van with its tailgate down. Kate jumps out and wanders over to take a look. The van appears to specialize in just the one thing; snow cones served in dusty paper cups. Aware that small cups of ice smothered in lurid sugar syrup aren't going to be the most ideal food source for the miles ahead, let alone the most easily portable, Kate turns to cross the road, empty-handed. Her mind is occupied with whether there are enough bottles of water floating around in the ice box to see them through. And if not, would it be wrong she wonders, to drink the liquid contents of the ice box itself? It's only melted ice from three days ago after all. Pondering this last point, she heads back to the car. In full view of Maryann, who might have fancied a snow cone herself, Kate steps out onto the road in front of the only moving car for miles. The remote roads we've been travelling on for the past couple of days have been so quiet that we've both unconsciously given up looking out for traffic before we cross. This, plus the fact that Kate is exhausted and is still having difficulty remembering that cars travel on the right hand side of the road over here, means she is an accident waiting to happen. Frozen in the middle of the road, not knowing whether to run forwards or backwards to avoid the oncoming car, she shuts her eyes and leaps. The car swerves around her, beeping its horn until it has disappeared from view. Taking a deep breath, and thanking her lucky stars, Kate opens the car door and jumps back into the driver's seat. Maryann sits shaken, having had a ringside seat to view Kate's brush with death.

"Crikey, that was a close one," Kate says, breaking the silence. Maryann relaxes and begins to giggle. This sets Kate off too and soon they're laughing like a pair of schoolgirls.

I wake up in an unfamiliar car with Vern's wife, Lena, staring through the window at me. She has driven out to meet Vern at the end of his stage and recognizes his car, if not the dirty hobo asleep in the front of it. I introduce myself and soon we find ourselves talking about her childhood. After an accident at home, the authorities took Lena from her family and sent her to Utah to live with a Mormon family. The Church of Jesus Christ of Latter-day Saints, as Lena prefers to call them, is a predominantly white Church and so growing up as a dark-skinned girl in a white area was a tough experience for Lena. All I knew about the Mormon Church is that they haven't exactly embraced feminism yet.

"Don't they still believe that a woman's place is in the home?" I ask Lena.

"They do," she says. "But that place is highly regarded and women are well-respected by Church members." I was surprised by her response. Lena had embraced the religion of her adoptive family and as a young woman had spent time serving on a Mormon mission in Canada. But she had always held her Navajo beliefs close to her heart and, though still a practicing Mormon, had returned to her native land to set up home with her husband.

When Kate rocks up, I turf Maryann out of my seat and we begin a long, late-night drive to get ahead of the relay. This has become our routine at the end of the day. We need to stick on Indian Route 9 for fifty miles, until we hit a tiny settlement called Pueblo Pintado. The road is known locally as the Superstition Highway. We've been told by one of the runners, due to run their stage along it later, that there are stories of skin-walkers and other scary things along this route. The term 'skin-walker' is new to us and I wonder if it is in any way similar to a skinny dipper.

Images of naked people roaming the highway looking for water go swirling round my head. Come to think of it, I haven't been wearing much clothing myself in the heat. I hope I haven't been mistaken for a skin-walker? But I'm barking up the wrong tree. The true definition is much creepier, if pretty awesome. According to Navajo legend, a *skin-walker* is a person with the supernatural ability to turn into any animal he or she desires. Skin-walkers tend to be witches on a mission to deliver a poison curse. The ability to shape-shift into an animal form allows them to travel surreptitiously and unhindered. As we drive along with our eyes peeled, we feel an even deeper respect for the courageous guys and girls who have signed up to run alone along this infamous stretch of road tonight. Safely in the passenger seat, I shut my eyes and try to turn myself into a tiger.

We make sure we leave Superstition Highway safely behind us before pulling up for the night. We have decided to stretch out in our bivvy bags under the stars, rather than sleep another night cooped up in the car. Earlier, Kate had asked Maryann if sleeping outside was a good idea and she had assured her we'd be perfectly safe. The odd coyote might come up to take a sniff, but other than that, we should be fine. Finding a good spot to settle down, we browse through the list of people who will be running in the early hours. We see the familiar name of Steve Bender, due to run at 3:35am and can't recall why this name rings a bell. And then it dawns on us. He is flying in from Pennsylvania, on a flight paid for by another runner, John Kohler, and we had offered to pick him up from the airport. Shit. We've had no phone signal all day and so haven't been able to receive his calls. But luckily, we've got some signal now and so, imagining him stranded at Albuquerque airport some 80 miles away, I get on the phone to him right away. A cheery voice picks up the other end, it sounds like Steve may have had a few beers.

"Where are you?" I ask, "Are you still at the airport?"

Steve laughs. "Don't worry guys, I'm sorted. I figured you'd be too busy to provide an airport shuttle so I got another runner to pick me up."

Relief floods over me. "Who are you with?" I ask, inquisitively.

Steve replies, "Will Allender."

Of course! Who else could it have possibly been?

Chapter 14

We sleep soundly in our bivvies and wake at 6am. Carefully rolling out of our sleeping bags, we take care to check we've not acquired any unwanted bedmates overnight; a rattle snake perhaps, or a deadly Apache Brown spider. Applying my usual slathering of 'factor ginger' sun screen, we hit the road. Surrounded by hills in all directions, the air is so hot and dry that our throats rasp as we speak. Today is the day we've put our names down to run a 16.5-mile stage starting at midday. Well, we are English after all, and mad. Thoughts of our impending doom fade a little when we remember that Steve Bender is signed up to run 30 miles today. In fact, he should be finishing his first stage round about now.

We meet up with Will Allender as he waits to take over from Steve. Will is tall and lean with a black sun visor on top of his sandy red hair and a long nose that leads from his sparkling eyes to a wide smile. The smile is a constant fixture on his face and lights up our morning. Will has driven down from Fort Collins, Colorado, collecting Steve from the airport on his way. He is signed up to run a second stage the next day and Kate and I work out that by the time he gets back home he will have completed a round trip of well over a thousand miles. Waiting with Will is Ronald Parks. Ron is a bit more straight-laced and immediately makes it known that he is not comfortable posing for photos with my half-naked sun-screened body draped all over him. I assume it's just a little early, but Ron is uncomfortable with it, full stop.

"How do I know you won't use them to blackmail me?" he asks, genuinely concerned. Posing for photos with Kate is much more Ron's cup of tea. Like Will, Ron has also signed up to run a stage tomorrow, but he has offered to split this morning's stage with Will.

There's a third person with them who doesn't look dressed for running. USA Today, America's best selling newspaper, has only gone and sent a photographer along! This is friggin' awesome news! His name is Craig. At least, we think it's Craig. In England we pronounce Craig with a long 'a' as in Cr-ay-g. But from the way he introduces himself, it sounds more like 'Creg', which I'm pretty sure isn't a proper name. Maybe it's a nickname? Or maybe it's Greg? Whatever he's called it's a mystery to me, so I decide to just try and mimic the sound he makes, adding a bit of a mumble to cover myself. I think I just about get away with it.

As Craig's camera comes out, Will jokes about our disheveled appearance. I actually don't remember the last time we showered, and I still have bed hair. I give Will a hug and let it linger a tiny bit, just enough to get Ron worried that I'm coming for him next. I quietly thank Will for everything he's done to help One Run For Boston, from the frequent flyer points he donated to book Gary Allen's flight to Texas, to the detour he took to pick Steve up from the airport, to stepping in to run more than one leg himself. It is obvious he doesn't want a song and dance about how much he has given and done; he would be embarrassed if we did.

Steve arrives, brandishing the baton, and Will bounces out of my arms to take over. A touch more cavalier than Will, Steve has signed up to run every other stage of the relay between 4am and noon at which point Kate and I will run our stage. It's only 6.30am, and already it's so hot that sweat is pouring from his neatly shaven head, down his face and dripping onto his soaking wet T-shirt. His first stage of 12.5 miles has been hilly, hot and at an elevation of 7000 feet, much harder than Steve was expecting.

"Now I see why no-one wanted to run these stages," he pants, gulping in the thin air, with a big grin on his face. I have no idea why, but I get emotional at this hand-off. Something special is happening today, I can feel it. It's there in the jokes, the smiles and the hugs.

"There's magic in the air," I whisper to Kate.

Will sets off down the road taking giant strides. He looks a little like Roald Dahl's BFG, only he is armed with a baton instead of a dream blower. Craig, the photographer is busy contorting himself into crazy positions to get the best possible shots of Will's silhouette against the rising sun. I ask Craig if he wants us to stage anything for him. Does he want us to do the baton hand-off again or get Will to run a little in the opposite direction so he can get a better shot of the sunrise? Craig is appalled by my suggestions and says he would never fake anything. He says his integrity is at stake here. He simply wants to tell the real story as it happens. Craig clearly knows what he is doing and without the need for any kind of jiggery-pokery at all, he takes some incredible photographs that capture the spirit of the entire relay in a few single frames.

Six miles in, Will hands over to Ron, just as they have planned. We continue stopping every mile to offer him water. Some local ranchers drive by and ask what we are up to in broken English. From the looks on their faces when we tell them, it's obvious they think that we are all stark raving bonkers. While Ron runs, I ask Will what running he has done in the past. He is one of the most passionate runners we've met and pretty fast to boot. His response knocks me for six. "Oh I don't run," he replies, "I ride motorbikes."

I look at him quizzically, "Sure, you ride bikes as well, but what races have you run?" I ask him.

"Actually, I only started running two months ago," Will says. I am absolutely flabbergasted. The Boston Marathon bombings just eight weeks earlier had been the catalyst that got Will into running. "I sat there watching the TV coverage and thought, why do all these people hate us so much? They hate our government? I could understand that. Join the club. But why kill innocent people? Anger, hatred, sadness, determination; I went through all of the emotions. Then, by the end of the week, I had decided that I wanted to run a marathon."

One Run For Boston was the first running event Will had ever signed up for. He'd been concerned he may not be able to keep to the ten-minute mile pace required, so had done a couple of time trials around his neighborhood at 3am, the time of day he was due to run his second stage, just to be sure he could do it. Any neighbors who caught sight of him out of their windows, as they got up to use the bathroom in the night, must have wondered what on earth he was up to.

By the time Ron gets to the end of his half of the stage, it is so hot that even after a quick five minutes supporting by the roadside, we are begging to get back inside our air conditioned cars. Steve hasn't had enough recovery time and isn't relishing the prospect of his next eight-mile stage. So Will suggests that we all share the running from here on in, taking it in turns to run a couple of miles each until we get the next forty miles done. The temperatures are only going to get hotter and with five of us rotating instead of three, things are going to be a lot more tolerable. Plus, the last 24hrs have seen the baton slip behind again by over an hour, so Will's idea is an opportunity for us to get it back on track. Ron is due to head home to Albuquerque straight after his stage but has no intention of leaving now. We're all in this together. It's lucky for Craig he's already left to file his photos, otherwise we would probably have dragged him in too. Steve seems relieved by our group decision and sets off again with a spring in his step. After a couple of miles, he passes to Will who passes to Ron who passes to me. I pass to Kate who passes back to Steve and the cycle repeats. We take no notice of where the proper hand-off points should be. Instead, we opt for arbitrary changeovers at frequent spots along the endless road that leads us towards the shimmering heat haze in the far, far distance. We keep our spirits high with some light-hearted banter and Will observes that I am getting all the downhill miles. "We'll have to call you Downhill Danny," he jokes, and the name sticks.

Fighting for his turn with the baton, Ron's sense of humor is beginning to shine through. "Hey, I'm the oldest one here, give me some respect! I want to run, give me the baton!" he chides us.

It has always amazed me how quickly runners are able to bond with each other. There is obviously the shared interest in putting one step in front of the other for exercise, but there's something more to it than that. Runners share a special spirit. There's something in their soul that connects them. When a runner moves to a new town, city or country, they can make a beeline for the nearest running club and find friends immediately. Running along next to another person, watching each other's foot falls, encourages people to talk. The adrenaline pumping around your body makes you more open and honest. You can find yourself finishing a run and being surprised at the inner secrets you have divulged to a perfect stranger along the way. Plus, runners know the physical pain and mental tricks that must be overcome in order to finish a run or a race. Shared moments of adversity help form bonds that can blossom in to true friendships. One Run For Boston was nothing different. These people I was running with were fast becoming people I wanted to hang out with for life, not just for a few legs of the relay.

As we swap on and off, each time exchanging the baton for a mock-insult or some other form of friendly abuse, we have no idea that the symbol of peace and positivity we are carrying in our hands is being given an identity.

A couple of days ago, one of our followers in Boston, Sandra Gitten, posted on Facebook, "Should the baton get a name? Like the kids have Flat Stanley that they take different places and take pictures?" Jamie reposted the message asking people for suggestions and the post attracted five thousand views and a hundred different comments. All of a sudden, Sandra's idea to give the baton a name took off. I'm not sure what name Steve Bender would have put forward if he'd been asked for his opinion at the time. It would probably have been unprintable. Steve was finding the baton awkward to hold and said it was bruising his fingers. Slightly top heavy owing to the GPS tracking device inside, some runners had taken to carrying it upside down, others carried it tucked under their arm like an (American) football. When we weren't looking, some even carried it in their backpacks. People's responses to what the baton should be named ranged from the simple, 'Stumpy,' to the fancy, 'Phidippides,' to the meaningful, 'Faith,' or 'Hope.' But far and away the most popular suggestion was made by Michele Winkler-Gettings, and from that day on, the baton was forever known as 'Miles.'

The baton wasn't the only thing to get named that day. We hadn't been doing a very good job of keeping the inside of our car clean, and a combination of sweaty plastic seats, dirty clothes and an ice box full of rotting vegetables, floating around in a pool of tepid water was creating quite an aroma. Kate and I were vaguely aware that something didn't smell quite right but having lived in the car for a week our noses weren't as sensitive as they might normally be. Steve had driven ahead in Will's car and after handing off to Ron, Will grabbed a lift with us. It was the first time we'd carried a passenger in the back seat and we apologized profusely, as we swept away bits of food and sweaty items of clothing to make room for Will. He didn't mention the pong at all and we assumed we'd got away with it, until we rejoined Steve and Will made a break for freedom, exiting the car quicker than anyone we'd ever seen before. "That's the last time I hitch a ride in the Stink Mobile," he said, wafting his hand in front of his nose. "Seriously, guys. Your car smells as though something has crawled inside and died!" Perhaps it had? We couldn't be 100% sure. But we were delighted to have a name for our wheels and the Stink Mobile was perfect.

Just outside Torreon, Harry Barnes arrives on the scene. His name isn't on the outdated list of runners we have with us and so we've not realized he is down to run a stage. A local man, he has sensibly chosen a 9-mile stretch that is all downhill. It's not long before Harry finishes his stage and hands Miles back to Steve. He leaves as he arrived, with the minimum of fuss.

By this time, we've been joined by Frank Cherne, who is due to run in two stages time. In our impromptu relay within a relay. Frank is not your typical runner's build. He is slightly heavier set, with a cheeky face that exudes happiness. He sizes up our motley crew and can see that we are showing some of the warning signs of dehydration. Knowing that he is fully hydrated, has fresh legs and is used to the elevation, he decides to jump right in and help out with our intervals. We agree to keep the mini-relay going through his stage too. It's a deal. At this point, Ron says his goodbyes and heads home to Albuquerque. He has another fifteen mile stage to run in two days' time and needs to get some rest. Smoke lingers in the air from forest fires that have been raging throughout large swathes of New Mexico, and as Frank charges up the road with the baton, he soon finds himself wheezing uncontrollably. Waiting for him a mile further on, we have no idea that Frank is having an asthma attack. He slows his pace to catch his breath and is somehow able to make it to our car. In spite of his asthma attack, Frank says this first mile run has made him feel alive.

"Running for the cause, running with people who care about strangers, all of this brings back a childlike joy I thought I'd lost," he tells us.

Creeping ever closer to our finish, we continue to trade British-American jabs to keep up our morale. I can hardly believe how our 'non-runner' Will is faring. He says he is cooked to a crisp and that he's just about "done", but every time I ask, "You good for one more, Will?" he doesn't say no. I've lost track of how many miles he must have run today.

As we approach the town of Cuba, the scenery starts to change. Green trees appear, as do clouds and even a little rain. The rain feels almost as good as the thought of the cold beers in Will's cooler that Steve keeps going on about. We're gonna have a sup of them for sure when we're done and that's all the encouragement we need to see us to the finish.

Eighty miles on from where we'd first met up with Steve and Will twelve hours ago, we reach Regina and it feels weird to give Miles up at last. Marisa Snyder and Hilary Lorenz are ready and waiting to receive him. We tell them it's been a very, very long day. But I think they know that just by looking at us. It has also been one of the most special days that I can remember for a long time. This shared experience has meant a lot to everyone involved, but most especially to Frank. Eight months before, Frank's wife had left him. Frank was heartbroken. But he tells us that the warmth and caring that has surrounded him today has filled the vacuum in his heart with love. Frank had not expected this would be the outcome of hanging out with four very sweaty runners for an afternoon.

We stand together and clink our bottles of beer. I can only manage a few mouthfuls before it goes straight to my head. Kate doesn't even dare open her bottle. As the sun dips below the horizon, a shaking noise catches my attention. I creep closer. It is a baby snake. A baby rattlesnake. Cool! I have been keeping my eyes peeled for snakes all day and had given up hope of ever seeing one. We don't get proper snakes in the UK, not ones that can kill you, anyway. This is another item on my list of authentic American experiences that I can now happily tick off. I creep closer and closer with my camera, inch by inch until I get a full frontal. The snake's tail is going mental and I decide to pull back. Steve, who has watched me getting too close, breathes a sigh of relief. He asks me what I am playing at.

"It's only a baby one!" I say.

"But it's the babies that are the most dangerous," Will explains. "If an adult rattler bites you they don't necessarily release their venom. They'll save it for a more threatening adversary. The first bite is usually just a warning bite. But a baby, on the other hand, has no control over its venom. When they bite, they inject all their venom at once. Only when they get older do they learn to control their venom." I've had another lucky escape.

*****

Before she leaves, Hilary writes her address down and says we are very welcome to go to her home to shower, eat and sleep. She has assembled a team from the Santa Fe Striders to carry Miles through the night and her house is being used as party HQ. She seems completely unaware of how good this all sounds to us and tries to sell the idea further. "And we've got the most enormous box of homemade cookies to get through," she says. We are in the car with the engine on before she's even finished her sentence. A friend had brought the cookies round to a film night at Hilary's the night before, but left them on the side and never handed them over to be opened. Luckily, the friend didn't take them away with her when she went home and so a giant box of cookies now sat on Hilary's fridge, out of the reach of her dogs, ready to refuel any running friends or English vagabonds that happened to drop by.

Frank drives in front of us, using his sat nav to direct us to Hilary's house. But we arrive at the final destination and there appears to have been some kind of mistake. We are in the middle of an empty, desolate area with no houses and no cookies. A few dogs run wild but nothing else is visible. We are about to turn around when we notice within the landscape there is a barely visible staircase, leading down below ground level. The stairs open out into a garden with flowers and trees and built within the dry sandy cliff at one end we see Hilary's house. It is just like a little hobbit-hole.

We are greeted by the smiling faces of Carina and Mike, two young artists who are staying with Hilary for the summer. And then there is their friend, Chris, a crazy Texan who is 'just passing through' so decided to stop off for a few days. A couple of black Labradors jump up and lick our salty bodies, their warm rough tongues like sandpaper on our aching legs. Inside Hilary's home, it is like a very homely cave. The air is naturally cool and fresh without the need for air conditioning. To the right is a shower that we are invited to use, instead of the 'dog wash' we are currently receiving. To the left is a box of three hundred or so cookies. I am struck dumb for a second, and wonder whether to turn left or right first. Diving to the left, I grab a handful of cookies then lock the shower door. My body turns the water brown and I watch as it swirls down the plug hole. I stand mesmerized, thinking about the random stranger who has just told us to go to her house, use her amenities, and while I do just that she is running through the night with a baton called Miles that has travelled over one thousand miles on foot in the past week. It didn't seem real.

Carina and Mike serve up a delicious meal and we fill our bellies with healthy vegetables and salad that we have been craving all week. Throughout the evening, members of Hilary's running club call in as they prepare to run their stages later. Among them are Vinny, who is 66 years old and has run the Boston Marathon every year since he was 15. Then there's Diane and Vince, both Crossfitters like me, and we immediately hit it off. They have parked a big RV outside which they plan to sleep in while they wait their turn. From what these guys are saying, it sounds like feral dogs rather than skin-walkers will be the main concern on the roads tonight.

When Hilary returns, we gratefully take her up on her offer to stay over. She apologizes that there is only the living room to sleep in, but we are more than happy with that and roll out our sleeping mats next to the dogs' baskets. The lights go out and all is silent barring the shallow breathing of the two Labradors lying on the floor beside us, one next to Kate and one next to me, enjoying this new company and friendship.

*****

Kate's alarm goes off early and wakes the whole cave up. She scrabbles around in the dark trying to silence it, adding to the disturbance as she panics.

'Shit! Sorry! Shit! Shit! Sorry!'"

Hilary brews a fresh pot of coffee and leaves us to help ourselves. We search in vain for some milk in her fridge, but there's not a whiff of any dairy to be seen. As Unsophisticated, latte-drinking British softies, we can't face the rich brew without a generous splash of cow juice so we wonder what to do. I'm all for tipping the coffee down the sink and pretending we've drunk it but instead Kate pours it into mugs and takes it outside to give to Hilary and Chris. Hilary is a bit puzzled but doesn't say anything.

As we leave Hilary's hobbit home, Steve Bender is in the skies above us, making his way home to Pennsylvania. Walking down the aisle to stretch his legs, he passes a gentleman reading a copy of USA Today and can't resist peering over the top of the paper. As his eyes hit the page, he realizes that the man is reading an article on page three about One Run For Boston. Above the article is a photo of a pale white English man running downhill, appropriately enough, in his backup pair of skimpy shorts. Immediately Steve recognizes that this must be one of the photos that Craig took yesterday.

"Man, that was a very hot day, but a great event," Steve says. The man looks at him with a puzzled expression on his face and Steve walks back to his seat without saying much more than that.

We drive past miles of impressive scenery, following the Rio Grande, as we make our way to meet Phil Blong at Shadybrook Village. Phil is a member of the United States Air Force and had seen how his home state of New Mexico was caught off guard when One Run For Boston was launched. The stages just weren't filling, so Phil signed up to run as many stages as his work restrictions would allow. He ended up with three stages, over three separate days. We had missed his first stage, a romantic midnight trek through an exquisitely remote stretch of beauty near Chaco Canyon, two nights before. This next stage would be a steady uphill climb of 1000ft, taking Phil up to the hand-off at Palo Flechado Pass. At 9101ft, this marked the highest point on the relay. From there it would be downhill all the way to Boston! Kevin O'Brien joins us just before Ronnie Archuletta appears with Miles. Ronnie tells us he had got his dates wrong and turned up a day early to run his stage. Lucky for us, he returned 24 hours later to give it another go, but unfortunately, his support crew had not been able to. So Kevin and his wife Nora had stayed on to crew for Ronnie after Kevin had finished his stage. Kevin says what I have been thinking pretty much non-stop for the last week.

"Only in a relay such as this do you meet friends for the first time, yet feel as if you've known them for years," he tells us. "We all run because it brings us joy and we run to share that joy. When the darker side of human nature attempts to tarnish or diminish this spirit, runners may be knocked off-balance and stumble, but we're not down for long. We get up and keep going. It is our way." Tears are forming in his eyes as he takes Kate and me by the hands and says to us, "Thank you. This experience has been so healing."

The landscape is beautiful and I can now see why New Mexico is given the nickname 'The Land of Enchantment." Shrouded in pine forests, everywhere we look is green and some of the views stretch out into the distance for miles and miles, as far as the eye can see.

At the top of the pass, we are reunited with Frank Cherne. He had studied the maps when he signed up to run this stage and knew it would be all downhill. Clever Frank. He has brought his friend Bill to run with him today and has dropped Bill off on the hill to run with Phil. I think Frank is trying to tire Bill out. Even cleverer of Frank. Frank has brought with him some proper magnetic signs for the sides of our car, advertising one of our sponsors Nestle Water. He has picked them up in Santa Fe, on his way out here this morning, saving us the journey. From the outside, the car now looks awesome and a lot more professional. But on the inside, it still stinks.

*****

We drive in search of a Laundromat, hoping that washing our clothes will lessen the stink. The weather is much cooler now, the relay is running on time and we've just polished off a delicious hamburger and fries. Everything is going swimmingly. But the beautiful day is soon soured by an online spat between Mary Hoatlin, our Saint in St. Louis, and Gary Allen, the Maine-iac runner who will shortly be flying into Texas to run three stages back-to-back.

Mary was doing a super awesome job looking after the Facebook group, making everyone feel welcome and keeping an eye out for any inappropriate posts. Gary had rightly received much praise and flattery after stepping up

139

to fill the gaps in the Texan Panhandle, his flight paid for by Will Allender's frequent flyer miles. But perhaps all the acclaim had gone to his head because he now appeared to be using the group only to promote his already fairly large ego. Gary was posting a constant stream of photos and videos of himself doing lots of awesome things but with no relevance at all to One Run For Boston. This did not sit well with Mary, the mother of the group, who had emailed Gary to warn him off a little. There was an immediate clash of personalities over email and I became stuck in the middle with both asking me to back them up. I can see Gary is being a bit of a plonker and is posting some egotistical crap. I also don't like a lot of the stuff he has written to Mary in emails when she asked him to stop. I am simultaneously trying to calm them both down over email when Kate and I hear cheering coming from the other end of Cimarron's main street. We realize we've missed the hand-off between Loretta Giglia and Kathy Dobesh. I am annoyed that a petty squabble could have distracted my attention from the relay and jump in the car to find Loretta, hoping she hasn't disappeared already.

Kate fires up the engine and we speed up the street in the direction of the cheers. Kate is breaking the speed limit and honking the horn as though she's possessed. She drives without a seatbelt while swigging coffee from a polystyrene cup. It's amazing how much more you can do when you're not driving a manual shift. We catch sight of a large group of runners at around the same time that we clap eyes on two policemen standing by their patrol cars, staring in our direction. Concerned she could get arrested for any one of the four offences she is guilty of right now, Kate quits the honking and hits the brake, throwing her coffee cup over her shoulder as she buckles up her belt. It's a master class in multi-tasking. Coming to a screeching halt in front of the group sends me lunging forward and back in my seat. Turning my head to check I've not got whiplash, I see the contents of Kate's coffee cup spilling out over the back seat behind me. I am shocked, but quietly impressed by how relaxed Kate has become in this department. We get out of the car under the watchful eye of the policemen who have been the runners' escorts and go to meet the group. Loretta is joined by her husband and a group of kids from the local high school where they both coach. They have all been running the stage together. The runners have written the names of some of the bombing victims on their arms and legs as a way of paying tribute to those people. Loretta has chosen the name of Brittany Loring, a young woman who had been at the Boston finish line, celebrating her 29th birthday.

"My daughter is also called Brittany," Loretta explains. "In fact if she hadn't gotten a stomach bug on the day of the marathon, my daughter would also have been at the finish line. My life could be very different right now," she tells us.

Another girl explains, "We're two sisters so we've taken the names of two brothers who were injured at the finish." Overwhelmed by the simplicity and yet the significance of these written gestures I can feel myself getting choked up just talking to them. We ask one of the policemen to take a photo of us all and then head off to grab our washing before the Laundromat closes.

*****

We have a look through our list of runners and realize we are fast approaching the 100th stage. Will Allender is running again in a few hours' time. His stage starts in the middle of nowhere at 3am and is number 98. When we left Will, the day before, he was feeling pretty wasted after running on and off over twelve hot hours. We knew he was concerned that one day's recovery wouldn't be enough to see him through the solo 15-miler which lay ahead of him. Leaving Cimarron, we send Will a text saying we'll be there to support him and then drive ahead to grab some sleep at his hand-off spot before he arrives. Despite the ungodly hour of his stage we want to be on hand to offer encouragement, although we can't guarantee that we'll be as perky as he'd seen us the day before.

Parking up in the darkness, we drift in and out of consciousness for a couple of hours. I am half woken by a car's bright headlights but instinctively close my eyes again. I haven't had nearly as much sleep as my body is craving. It takes Will's gentle tapping on the car window a few minutes later to jolt Kate and me both fully awake. On the horizon, we see a bobbing light. Will tells us it is Jim Blake's team of runners drawing near. It is very nearly Will's turn to run again. He says he'll be fine for the first 10-12 miles at least and insists we leave him to it, telling us to park up ahead and get some more sleep. Grateful for the opportunity we conk out for a couple of hours eleven miles up the road. By the time he reaches us, Will is looking pretty spent. Kate and I jump in for a few miles, handing Miles back to Will for the last few hundred yards.

Next, it's the turn of Curtis Chambellan. Curtis has been recruited by his daughter Amy, who has also brought her husband Aaron along to run a stage. Between them and Will, they've coordinated the collection from Albuquerque airport of another runner, Ty Thurlow, who is down to run over forty-five miles of the relay between now and sunset. Ty's a pretty key cog in today's machine.

Curtis hands-off to his daughter who then hands-off to her husband, as Will, Ty, Kate and I follow in convoy dishing out water, food, loud music and general encouragement. It's like one big happy family. But the heat is back and the asphalt is melting. We pass through tiny towns that straddle the quiet highway. Pretty much deserted, they look like ghost towns. In Roy, a huge white water tower dominates the town. It looks totally out of proportion to the number of people who must live here. In fact, it looks big enough to fit all the residents of Roy inside it for a nice big bath and still have room to fit the people living in the next two towns along as well. There

142

are two cafés both named after a mystery woman called Annette. Both are closed. We notice a shop with Christmas decorations still in its window suggesting that the last time it opened its doors to the public was at least six months ago. But judging by the dust, it could have been ten Christmases ago. When we first launched the relay, Kate and I tried to make contact with businesses in all these towns, thinking they could help us promote the relay to the locals and encourage some more sign-ups. I realize now why we got such very little response.

We pass the time by exploring some cultural differences. Kate and I learn the difference between dry heat and humidity. We've already experienced plenty of dry heat along the way but Amy promises it won't be long before we encounter the wetter, more stifling humidity of the central and eastern states. It sounded hideous. Somehow, I find myself explaining what an 'Essex Girl' is. It's the US equivalent to a 'Jersey Shore Girl' apparently. And Kate and Ty discuss the merits of the different judges on the UK talent TV show The Voice. The conversation is pretty highbrow.

When we reach Mosquero, it's Ty's turn to get ready. Ty, a handsome, dark-haired runner with skin that somehow contradicts the amount of time he spends on the open road in the sun, is the second of our ringers to be flown in from the east coast. He is a good friend of Gary Allen's but lacks the ego. Ty's best friend in the Philippines had heard about the relay and sprung Ty the flight to New Mexico to fill in some gaps. After finishing the Boston Marathon on April 15, Ty met up with his girlfriend, Jerusha, and got down on one knee to propose to the woman he wanted to share the rest of his life with. Jumping on the train hand in hand, her finger bearing the symbol of his eternal love for her, they sped back to their hotel to get ready for the post-race celebrations, but the celebrations are cut short by the bomb blasts.

Kate takes a photo of Ty next to one of the incredible murals that fill every spare inch of wall in the town of Mosquero. They really look awesome. It's just a pity there are no residents around to appreciate them. Kate posts the photo to Facebook with a quote from Ty:

"Running is different to other sports. No time outs. No referees."

Gary Allen immediately replies in a comment, "Ty Thurlow is so freakin' MaineStrong, it makes me hurt 2000 miles away!" I couldn't help it, but somehow this comment from the man with the ego grated with me. In just over 24 hours, we'd get to meet this Maine-iac in the flesh and I wasn't sure that I was looking forward to it.

Ty floats over the tarmac, as Kate and I scramble up a cliff in search of the perfect picture. From our perch, we look out over thousands of acres of ranch land and have a bird's eye view of Ty as he rounds a corner beneath us. We shout out to him and it echoes around the hillside. The rugged beauty of New Mexico is getting more and more epic with every footfall.

We go to meet Ron. He has obviously forgiven my early morning antics in front of the camera with him yesterday and invited Kate and me to join him for lunch with his girlfriend, Larraine and stepson, Scott. They are all staying in their RV near the start of Ron's stage. Scott has a condition which means he is extremely hyperactive and can be quite a handful! He can sense that they're about to be involved in something different and special and his levels of excitement rocket even higher than normal. Having the opportunity to share some family time with them gave me a new respect for Ron. When I'd met him a couple of days earlier, I'd found it hard to warm to his quietness and reserve. But inside the RV, I recognize that this is the way he has become used to acting around Scott in order to keep him calm. Scott finds it hard to sit still and marches around outside, shouting Ron's name and rehearsing his cheers ahead of Ron's run. It comes as no surprise to us that Scott is a talented athlete himself and competes in the Special Olympics. I think his energy levels could probably fuel a small city.

Ron's stage sits in the middle of Ty's four stages, giving Ty the chance to rest his legs for a couple of hours before he is back on. It is just before three in the afternoon, and the temperature is officially roast-a-chicken hot, even with a strong headwind. Having shared a stage with Will a few days before, Ron is determined to run all of the 15 ½ -mile stage himself. You can see it in his eyes. This man is not going to give up. Hill after hill, mile after mile, Ron pushes on with Larraine and Scott supporting him.

"This guy is one of the toughest men I have ever met," says Ty, who is a tough nut himself and has surely met a few tough cookies in his time. "Relentless should be his name."

Ron's pace begins to slow and it is painful to watch as he slows to a walk and then, summoning up all the strength he has, forces himself to get running again. We all want to jump in and help him but he has told us he does not want our help. He also does not want to hold the relay back, but since he started with an hour in hand, thanks to time made up by Ty on his first two stages, there is no good reason to stop him. Ron tells us that if we need him to relinquish Miles for the sake of the relay he will, but he is going to continue and finish his stage regardless of who is carrying the baton. I can see this is a matter of pride for him. He needs to finish this for the people who could not finish in Boston. Screaming with joy every time he sees Ron, Scott runs out and back from where Larraine is parked to cheer him along with such passion and enthusiasm. Each time Ron stops to have his water bottle refilled, Scott dances excitedly around him and even though he's feeling thoroughly worn out, Ron displays the patience and love of ten doting mothers.

The only person who is allowed to run with Ron is Scott. With one mile to go, Ron hands him the baton and they head off on the final stretch together. Scott is so excited he sprints forward ahead of Ron, but returns with the baton to finish by his side. Kate and I crowd together with Ty, Will and Larraine to witness this highly emotional moment. It is simply beautiful to behold. Later that week Will emails us to say that this was the most inspiring part of his One Run experience.

"What had been a fun and jovial and light-hearted adventure had just become as serious as a heart attack," he wrote.

It's Ty's turn again and having 24 miles in his legs from this morning, he is happy for us to jump in for a few miles as we head south to San Jon. A storm is chasing us; lightning crackles on the horizon, lighting up the sky and we can see rain heading in our direction. Will slips right back into his old routine of teasing me about all the downhill sections I appear to be getting. So I start keeping count of the uphills and shout the numbers out as I run past him. "Downhill Danny!" he shouts and I pretend to lose my temper. "Control your venom, Danny!" Will shouts back, reminding me of the baby rattler.

Eight miles from San Jon, Ty takes the baton back and Kate and I sit in the car, exhaustion etched across our faces. It is all beginning to get too much. The lack of food we can manage; the continuous driving is bearable, although our bodies have left human-shaped stains on the front seats. We have our own set of stinking sweat shadows. The heat is horrendous but that isn't the worst of it. The thing that is killing us is the lack of sleep. We have just gone about this the wrong way. We should have thought it through a bit. If we had penciled in six hours' sleep a night and stuck by it we might have been coping a lot better. Thinking we could handle life in the fast lane, on an average of two hours sleep per night was ridiculous. Our bodies are beginning to shut down. We just want to drive ahead and leave all these lovely folk to get on with it. Neither of us has a clue what day it is let alone what date.

Kate checks her phone. It's June 15. Both of us stop whining for a second.

It is two months since we were sitting in my barn, listening to the first reports of the Boston Marathon bombings. It is two months since three people lost their lives at the finish line. Two months since the lives of many, many more were changed forever. We knew many of the injured were still in hospital. Some were undergoing repeat operations on their limbs, in the hope they might be saved. Others already knew that this was not a possibility for them. As these thoughts are running through our heads, Ty is putting in a six-minute mile and giving everything he's got. He reaches our car and without saying a word, I take Miles from him. We continue the relay with no further thought given to the trivial hardships that we might be facing.

Chapter 15

Saying goodbye to Will in San Jon, at the end of Ty's final stage, is like saying goodbye to a brother. We've spent 160 miles with him over the last amazing few days. Sure, there have been some dark times in amongst the miles, but in many ways, it was just one long, sweaty party.

San Jon is a funny old place. Once an important stop on Route 66 and home to numerous gas stations and motels, it is now almost completely deserted. When the I-40 bypassed the village in 1981, the local economy went into freefall and most of the businesses shut down. Today, only one motel remains, the San Jon Motel. Check out their website and tell me it's not another Psycho sequel waiting to happen.

It's just before 10pm and Phil Blong, who we first met on his 'jog' up to the Palo Flechado Pass the day before (Holy Monkeys! was that really only yesterday?) is back. He is running the last 18 New Mexican miles, to the border of the neighboring juggernaut, Texas - The Lone Star State. Texas is given this nickname as a reminder of the state's struggle for independence from Mexico and its status as a former independent republic. It is a super-sized state; more than five times the size of England. In fact, it is so blinkin' big that if our relay route was to go a little further south and cross the state at its widest point, we could run continuously for more than nine days and still be in Texas. As it is, our route is taking us through the northern Panhandle part of Texas and we'll be in and out in a little more than 24 hours.

Kate and I are just about falling asleep on our feet and ask Phil if he's going to be alright on his own. It's a pretty lonely place out here and he hasn't brought any support with him but we have to get some sleep. We are so tired that the Stink Mobile is a car crash waiting to happen right now, with us at the helm. Phil says he'll be absolutely fine and we remind ourselves that he's in the US Air Force. We know he can take care of himself. Wishing Phil well and giving the San Jon Motel a wide berth, we wind up in the much more amusingly named Bonanza Motel, a little way down the road. We eat the ultimate comfort food of cereal and milk before crashing out in a room that smells like the lady behind the desk's personal smoking room, but we're too tired to complain about it.

Meanwhile, jaunting out of San Jon on the original Route 66, Phil leaves the bright lights behind him and is soon running alone on a dirt road in the pitch-black. Armed with only a headlamp, a blunt Swiss Army knife and a sizeable chunk of paranoia, he ventures on into the night, past pairs of unidentifiable glowing eyes. He presumes his route must have been mis-mapped due to the lack of civilization. He wonders whether there will be anyone waiting for him when (if) he makes it to the border. But mostly he thinks about Boston, of the victims and their families and of all the selfless runners out there, who have embraced the exact experience that he is savoring right now.

*****

We are woken early by a phone call from John Villalobos, one of the overnight runners. Kate takes the call.

"Where are you guys?" I hear John ask. "I have a present for you." Kate looks at me and pulls a confused face. "Where are we?" she mouths. We arrived so dog-tired last night that neither of us can remember. I shrug, pulling a similarly confused face. "Hold on a minute," Kate says, scampering outside in her pajamas in search of clues in the parking lot. There is nothing. She nips over to the motel reception and is hit by a waft of Indian cooking as she enters.

"Excuse me, can you tell me where we are?" She asks the first person she sees. Looking at Kate as if he's surely seen it all now, the motel owner tells her she's in Vega, Texas. "You still there John?" Kate says down the phone, "we're in Vega! We're at the Bonanza Motel in Vega!"

John says he is just down the road and will be there in ten minutes so Kate races back to our room to get changed. Ten minutes later the phone rings again.

"Are you sure you're in Vega?" John asks.

"Erm, pretty sure," Kate says, not sounding at all convinced. She nips outside again and eventually flags John down on the road outside the motel. John has brought us the most beautifully carved wooden plaque, in the shape of the state of Texas. It is engraved with the names of every runner that will be carrying Miles through The Lone Star State.

"Something for you to remember us all by," John says. We are so touched by the gesture we are speechless.

With the Tony Christie song looping round in our heads, we make our way towards Amarillo, stopping briefly ten miles out at the Cadillac Ranch to see the hand-off between Josh Backus and Shannon Puphal. Shannon has brought her whole family along for the ride, including daughter Avery, who insists on playing 'horses' with Kate, until Kate is broken. Shannon has Texan Cowboy hats to give us and magnets which say 'Don't Mess with Texas.' She also has a special vest for me with 'Epic Race Director" on the back. Cadillac Ranch is an outdoor art installation made up of ten Cadillacs half-buried, nose-first in the middle of a field. The cars stick out of the earth with their back seats and tailgates showing. The owner, the millionaire Stanley Marsh 3, encourages people to visit, armed with graffiti spray cans to make their mark on the cars. Kate and I are handed some leftover cans of paint by some visitors on their way out and, scrawling 'One Run

For Boston' as big as we can over the end car, we don't disappoint.

A couple of television crews turn up, thanks to the efforts of Lani Hall who is running her own stage later on. I am busting for a pee, so leave Kate in front of the cameras. There are no bathrooms around and too many kids to make peeing up against the fence an option. I remember what Shawn said back in Arizona about how peeing in public, especially with kids nearby, is perceived by the Police in some states. Not taking any chances, I run back to the car and relieve my bulging bladder into an empty water bottle.

It's Father's Day, and lots of families are out supporting their running dads today. Jason Garren's daughter, a talented artist, has decorated his pick-up with awesome cardboard signs wishing everyone a 'Happy Father's Day' and encouraging them to go online and donate to our cause. Santana Gonzales has brought his whole extended family with him and half his church, including the Pastor who is running with him for company.

"What an honor it is to run on Father's Day with my kids supporting me!" Santana tells us. Eighteen months ago, Santana was on the north side of 300lbs. He could swig his way through a 12-pack of Dr. Pepper in one day. He is half the size he used to be now, but twice the man. "Limits are what you set them at," he says, "We're all capable of doing more than we ever thought we could." Santana and his entourage are deeply religious. We see it in the signs of encouragement they hold up to will Santana on, and in the way they talk. Discussing some of the logistics of the relay with one of Santana's supporters, Tom Bonilla, Kate explains that we're still waiting on a permit from the Boston authorities which will allow us to finish at the Boston Marathon finish line. If we don't get the permit, we've been debating whether we should just go ahead and do it anyway.

Tom nods his head in agreement, "It is always better to ask for forgiveness, rather than permission," he says with a grin.

In the middle of the Texas Panhandle region, there is a town named, originally enough, Panhandle. The fact that it doesn't even have its own distinct name gives you an idea of how dull the place is. Flanked by giant grain stores and a freight line, not a lot has happened here since the town was scandalized in 1897 by the deeds of a local preacher, George E. Morrison. In scenes reminiscent of Snow White, Morrison killed his wife with a poisoned apple so he could marry his mistress Miss Annie Whittlesey of Topeka, Kansas. The one redeeming feature of Panhandle is that it has a Subway restaurant. Inside, we get chatting to a girl who correctly spots that we are not from round these parts –neither was she, originally. She was born in New Zealand but moved here as a teenager after her mum met a guy on the internet and he happened to live in Panhandle. "Moving here was quite a culture shock coming from Auckland, I can tell you," she says. On the one hand, it is pleasing to know that internet dating does work for some people. But as the girl tells us more of her story, we can't help feeling incredibly sorry for her. She had spent her teenage years waiting for adulthood, so she could return to her beloved New Zealand. But then she fell pregnant and now with two kids, she finds herself trapped in a dead end town with no prospects. We munch on our sandwiches, reflecting on how lucky we both are.

As we leave the restaurant, we notice a ticket underneath the windscreen wiper of the Stink Mobile. Thoughts of parking fines go through my head, but on further investigation, we see it is an envelope with a twenty dollar bill stuffed inside. A three word message accompanies the bill. It reads simply, "God bless y'all." Panhandle may be the arse-end of the world, but its residents sure do have big hearts.

We're coming up to Gary Allen's stages, and the anticipation of finally meeting the man we have heard so much about, mainly from him, is mounting. In White Deer, we meet a large group of boisterous runners, some of whom had been recruited only last night at a barbecue. "Look everyone, these two are from the Ukraine!" One woman introduces us, a little too excitedly. Miles is handed over to two friends who couldn't be more different. Mike Flores is small and softly spoken; he reminds us a bit of Ned Flanders from the Simpsons. Charlie Hennessy is a great deal taller, with long slim limbs and shorts that would have made my little red shorts look like long, baggy pants. Kate nicknames him 'turkey legs.' Charlie is a lot brasher than Mike, more typically American in my book, and he gives himself a good talking-up. But boy, oh boy, as we wait for the two pals to get going, we are introduced to a new kind of brashness. Gary Allen has arrived.

From the minute he gets out of the car, Gary talks non-stop about himself, his racing career, his journey to Texas from Maine and about the 33.5 miles he is due to run later tonight. I don't know whether they are just being polite, but the group who have just finished their run appear to be lapping it up. Perhaps they're just too tired to interrupt him. Kate and I say a quick hello, then take refuge in the Stink Mobile and head off to follow Ned and Turkey Legs. Kate tells me we must stop calling them by their new nicknames and to go back to using their proper names. She is right of course but I don't. Sometimes I can't help being a little naughty, and anyway I've forgotten what their real names are now.

We drive behind our boys, shielding them from the traffic. Kate is at the wheel but is finding it difficult to keep looking straight ahead as Turkey Legs' shorts start to reveal a little too much flesh. I have to tell her to slow down a couple of times, fearing she is going to drive into the back of them. It's not Thanksgiving yet, anyhow. After a blazing hot and sunny day, the air is cooling and we can see rainclouds and lightning up ahead. It looks like we are heading into a storm and we hope it's heading away from us, faster than we're travelling. Our hearts leap into our mouths as we approach a rail crossing and watch the two runners sprint across the tracks, just as the crossing arms start to lower and the alarm bell starts to ring, signaling the approach of a train. We wait behind the barrier and, to our relief, see them safely across to the other side.

Despite the cooler temperatures, when the men finish at Pampa, they are dripping in sweat. They take off their shirts and ring them out in front of us. It is like turning on a tap at full blast. Stuck waiting at the railway crossing, we missed their hand-off to Gary. By the sounds of it, he didn't hang about. Gary had been dropped off at the start of Ned's stage and offered to shuttle his car forward to meet him at the finish. But when they arrived at the hand-off, Gary sprinted off without telling them where he'd left the car key. Neither did he tell Ned what to do with the bag he'd left on the back seat full of energy gels. Taking the bag, we hang around until the key is found. Unbeknownst to Ned at the time, Gary has also run off with a pair of his reading glasses on top of his head. This guy is a nightmare.

We are a bit puzzled that Gary has left the bag containing all his gels. He isn't expecting us to support him through the night, is he? Our blood runs cold. The relay is running half an hour late which means Gary probably won't finish until nearly 4am. There is no way that Kate and I can continue driving until then. We are done in. A few days earlier we'd seen some chatter on Facebook in which Gary had been telling people what they needed to do to sort out his logistics. All he needed, he said, was a lift to the start of his stage. He was going to leave his hire car at the finish in advance, ready to drive back to Amarillo airport when he was done. Lani Hall had kindly stepped up to offer Gary his lift.

"Great, that'll give Danny and Kate a chance to sleep," he had written. We assume Gary must simply have left the bag on the back seat of Mike's car by mistake and so we set off to catch him up to work out where he wants us to drop it. We catch up with him a mile down the road. He is easy to spot in the distance. With lights all down his arms, and across his shoulders, he looks almost bionic, and a lot like Buzz Lightyear.

We pull over and I jump out to give him his bag, explaining that we are going to drive ahead to the finish of his three stages and get some sleep.

He looks me in the eye, "Well, I don't have any water on me."

I look at him, confused. "Erm, I thought you didn't need our help." Gary goes quiet for the first time that day, possibly his whole life.

"How about you just stop every five miles to give me a gel and water?"

Unaware of any other option that won't jeopardize the relay, I agree and stomp back to the car. Getting back in, I'm calling Gary every name under the sun as I slam the door.

As I rant, Mary texts Kate to ask how things are going. The timing isn't great and Kate texts back, "Just met our VIP. He is something else. Danny is already dropping the C-bomb."

Five miles later, we pull over, and it's clear we're catching the storm, or is it catching us? Standing silently in the rain that's beginning to fall, I hold a water and a gel out wordlessly for Gary. "Not now, I'll have it in a mile," he states. I stare back at him. Have I heard him right? I take a deep breath, mainly to stop me grabbing the baton and wrapping it round his head.

"Actually Gary, we were going to drive ahead 5 miles and get 25 minutes sleep," I tell him, "It's now, or in 5 miles." Picking up the slightest tinge of tension in my tired voice, Gary suggests we should drive ahead and leave a water bottle and a gel every five miles for him to pick up on his way. That way we can drive on to the finish of his stage and rest before he arrives.

As agreed, we pull up after another five miles. I search the car for full bottles of water to put on the roadside, wishing I hadn't thrown away the bottle of pee earlier.

We drive another five miles and put a second water bottle down. The sky really is bigger in Texas and the storm is apocalyptic. Wall-to-wall lightning fills the sky and appears much closer. We're entering the storm...

In my tired and angry state, I joke about what would happen if Gary got struck by a lightning bolt. "It would make a great news story and maybe the publicity would boost our fundraising effort…"

I love storms; they're hypnotic and beautiful – especially from your bedroom window. I've never seen anything like this before, though, and it suddenly feels like we're the lead characters in a disaster movie. Driving further into the storm, the lightning becomes more frequent and intense. With Kate at the wheel, I watch as a billion volts of electricity strike the ground within meters of our car. Fear takes me and I forget about Gary Allen, I just want to get out of the storm, fast.

These lightning bolts are getting far too close to comfort. The fact that there are no other cars on the highway tells us we probably shouldn't be here either. Before long the odometer tells us we've hit fifteen miles, and reminds us it's time for another water bottle for Gary. Lightning erupts around us again, hundreds of barbs smashing into the fields ahead of us. We turn to each other. Fighting to focus my tired eyes on the pale glow of Kate's skin, my shoulders sag. I know what's coming.

"We can't leave someone out in this alone, Danny, not even Gary Allen."

Driving back, the rain turns to hail. Pea-sized ice pellets hammer down on the windscreen so hard that I'm scared it will shatter. Lightning flashes illuminate the night sky and the landscape around us. We realize that there are no trees, shelters, houses or any kind of structures for miles and miles. We begin to really worry about Gary. Picking up the water and the gels that we left out for him, we hurry back along the road. With each turn in the road, we hope to see the unmistakable flashing of his body armor in the distance. Suddenly he's there, his technique looks strong and his posture is defiant. Just as we're approaching, a deafening clap of thunder joins forces with an almighty flash of lightning and the earth shudders. Turning in the road that looks more like a river, we pull alongside Gary.

"Do you want to jump in for a bit?" I ask, winding down the window which allows the rain to hit my face. It's raining harder than ever and a burnt smell hangs in the air. Lightning is coming at us from 360 degrees. Some bolts connect with the ground, others shoot horizontally from cloud to cloud. There even seem to be some lightning bolts spewing upwards from the ground like fireworks. We see Gary cringe every time the air crackles. Although he is 55 years old, at this moment Gary's face looks boyish and fearful.

"I'm going to keep running, thanks," Gary says, to our absolute amazement.

"Are you sure?" I ask, which at the time is subtext for, "Are you a complete mentalist?"

Gary explains that he has Boston in his thoughts and that he feels empowered.

"We can't leave you out alone in this," I say, handing him an energy gel. His face is full of gratitude,

"Thanks guys. That makes me feel safer." The edges of the road are flooding with water so Gary moves over to the middle and we slot in behind him, our headlights shining out his pathway.

Kate keeps an eye on her rear view mirror and honks her horn if a truck is coming, to let Gary know he needs to move over. Kate's eyes are drooping and I worry she might nod off and drive straight through Gary. But I'm obviously not so worried that I offer to take over and instead I fall asleep. Completely exhausted, I close my eyes and drift off, only to be woken every time Kate honks the horn. This starts to piss me off and when I realize she has begun honking not just to warn Gary of traffic approaching from behind, but in appreciation of Gary's play acting out in front, it pisses me off even more. Passing the middle of his stage, Gary has started to shoot down the miles each time we pass a sign-post advertising how many miles are left to Mobeetie. He draws an imaginary gun from an imaginary holster and shoots the sign before blowing the imaginary smoke away from the imaginary barrel and putting his imaginary friggin' gun back in the imaginary holster.

It is infuriating to watch. At least *I* think so. But Kate disagrees. Each time Gary blows away the smoke from the barrel of his gun, Kate returns her hand to the horn. I have a slight inkling she might be doing this just to wake me because she is jealous of me sleeping. I have to confess that when Kate fell asleep on our way to the motel the night before it had put me in a bad mood. So much so that I had 'accidentally' caught my foot on the brake a few times to jump the car and wake her up. Maybe she is just getting her own back? Each time Kate hits the horn and cheers, I wake with a start and snarl at Gary. I am angry at Kate too for enjoying this man's antics even though he is keeping us from another night's sleep. Eventually, I give up on sleep and get my camera out. I may as well capture the beauty of what could be our last hours before we're cooked by an accurate strike of lightning from the gods. The storm has been raging for over three hours, with no sign of a let up. But the onslaught only seems to be making Gary stronger. As another bolt of lightning fizzes past him, he holds his arms out wide and looks up to the heavens.

"Is that all you got? BRING IT!" He cries.

"Is he losing the plot?" Kate asks, concerned. This is turning into a scene written by our fellow countryman,

Shakespeare —the one where King Lear loses his marbles and ends up in the middle of the moor, ranting and raging against the elements.

Before I realize what is happening, a smile crosses my face. I wipe it off. This is not funny. But then it's back creeping from ear to ear. All of a sudden, there is something about watching Gary run through the most torrential rain, with bolts of lightning bouncing off everything around him, that makes me want to keep my eyes open. Worse than that, I can feel my heart opening as I watch Buzz Lightyear, running through this torrential rain, whilst lightning bolts bounce around him, with his imaginary gun, without any water.

At 25 miles in, the storm is abating. Gary beckons us to drive alongside him and tells us,

"I will run this mile for the thousands of runners who were stopped on marathon day." At 26.2 miles, the marathon distance, he shouts out, "Fuck you, Chechens!" He is referring to the two bombers. "We will not lie down and be beaten by you!" Only then does it hit me how emotional this run has been for Gary, how important it is to him to keep going, regardless of what the heavens may throw at him. I ask Kate to pull up beside him again and wind down the window. I extend my arm out the side of the car. Gary takes my hand in his and we grip each other firmly. We drive on for a few moments in silence, then hand-in-hand, I thank him for all he has done. He has put his life on the line tonight to honor those in Boston. There is no room for egos here. Both his and mine have been struck down by the storm and we hold each other's hands, knowing that all that is left now are two men thankful to have made it through the night unscathed.

Driving ahead to Mobeetie we meet Lani at the hand-off. Gary arrives a few minutes later. As I see him, I run to him and hold him close, thanking him again. He is soaked through and exhausted both physically and emotionally. Like a wet rag doll, he sags in my arms.

Chapter 16

We drag ourselves a few miles up the road and cross the border into Oklahoma. Slumped in our seats, we grab a few minutes' sleep before it is time to hit the road again. A couple of days before, I had an email from Monique Galmour, saying she was worried about safety along Route 6, the stretch of road that her stage was following this morning. She told me that Route 6 is known as 'Suicide Road', due to the high number of fatal accidents. We couldn't blame her for being concerned and promised we'd be there to watch her back. It was a no-brainer. So we rallied ourselves once more and drove on to meet up with her.

We arrive at the hand-off location to find that four other women will be running with Monique and they have each brought along a car full of supporters. It appears they have their own very large safety team sorted already. I don't know whether my eyes are deceiving me or if I am still asleep and dreaming. Miles looks up at us and shakes his plastic head. If he had eyes, I'm sure he would have rolled them.

"I thought you needed an escort?" I ask, dumbfounded.

"Oh no, we're sorted, thanks," Monique replies chirpily.

We have sacrificed our precious sleep only to be told we aren't needed. It's not often this happens, but words fail me. Life on the open road feels like it's giving us one hell of a beating.

With our energy levels at zero, we get back in the Stink Mobile and look at each other blankly. Is it best just to write off today? I wonder. Will it be OK if we just go and hide somewhere for the day? It won't matter if we are in the car, on a soft comfy mattress or a bed of nails; wherever we end up, we are going to sleep like a log on downers.

Suffering some kind of delirium, we decide to push on with Day 11. We go in search of Timmy and Joy Badillo. Of all the places we have been through so far, Oklahoma reminds us most of home. There are green fields full of black and brown cows alongside fields of golden wheat. Sure, it's a lot hotter than back home, but driving along in our air conditioned car, it really could be rural England on the one day a year that we call our British summer.

After a few wrong turns, we catch up with Joy who is supporting her husband Timmy. Joy has already run a stage early this morning. We ask her how it went, expecting her to give us a description of the hills or the heat. But instead, she says, "It changed me."

Joy had been a talented competitive runner at college but now, as a working mother of four, Saturday morning was her only time to run. Like so many busy mums, she says running had been her 'me' time. "No work, no kids, no phones, no anything, except those stupid dogs that like to chase me every time!" she says. But this was all going to change. "Because of One Run For Boston I'll be running for a different reason now. I'm not just going to run for my own selfish enjoyment," she says. "If my kids want to run with me, I will welcome it as a treat. When my co-worker wants help to get in shape, I will be pleased to go with her, even if it cuts into my running time. It's not about me anymore. It's about helping others. Every single time I run, I will tell myself, 'You're running for those who can't.' Before One Run For Boston I would never have thought like that."

We stay and cheer Timmy on a while, then drive off along the empty road. All of a sudden, there is a car on our tail, flashing its lights. I immediately clock it's not a police car – phew – but slow down anyway to let them pass.

Whoever they are, they must be in a hurry. I can't understand these drivers, who are obviously frustrated by having to share the road with other vehicles. I wonder what it must be like to get frustrated by something so ridiculous. This guy on my tail is persistent though. He is refusing to pass me and flashes again.

"What do you want me to do, punk?" I think out loud, waking Kate from her sleep. She looks round and suggests we just pull over to let them pass more easily. I swerve off the road onto the grassy verge and the car pulls up behind us. Kate and I look at each other, not knowing what to do. Kate locks the doors. We're now actually hoping that it *is* the cops because the alternatives of axe-wielding farmers and gun-toting rednecks that are circling through our heads are even less appealing.

"Let's just drive off and lose them," Kate suggests. I'm quite up for a car chase and am about to slam the gear stick into drive when I look in my rear view mirror and see a middle-aged woman getting out of the car carrying an array of boxes balanced precariously on top of each other. She looks innocent enough to me.

"Is that a pizza box she's carrying?" Kate asks, clocking her in the wing mirror.

"I dunno, but whatever it is she looks like she's about to drop everything," I say, unlocking the door and hopping out to help.

"You must be Danny?" She says. "I'm from Starvin' Marvin's, I've got a pizza delivery for you and Kate." How did this woman know our names and what on earth had we done to deserve pizza?

"It's from Bill, Frank and Harry." She tells us.

"Bill, Frank and Harry?" I say, confused.

Kate comes to my aid. "Bill, Frank and Harry! The guys from New Mexico?" We had spent only a few brief moments with Bill and yet it turns out that this miraculous pizza delivery to the middle of nowhere had been his idea. And Harry? Harry Barnes? I'd barely had a chance to speak to the fella. What a dude! Bill had been tracking the relay online and had tipped off the delivery driver with the location of where we were likely to be. The driver had been coasting this road for half an hour trying to find us. We take some photos next to the delivery van, then drive up the road to eat our feast in the graveyard of an isolated church. Let me make it clear it was a very picturesque graveyard, before you start thinking we're a bit weird. It was more like a public garden really. By the time we open up the box, the pizza is a little cold, but OMG it is so, so, so tasty! The pizza comes with a couple of boxes of salad and it is all gone in a matter of minutes! Delicious! We haven't eaten a proper meal in a while and my cheek bones and ribs have started to show. This pizza is exactly what my stomach needs. This random act of kindness is quickly followed by another.

Our phone rings. "Hello, this is Tom Love," the voice at the other end says. Tom and his wife Diana have been avidly following the relay since they signed up to run the group stage in Oklahoma City. They have tracked Miles through California, Arizona, New Mexico, Texas and now Oklahoma and have been surprised to see Kate's and my faces cropping up in nearly all the photos. When and where were we sleeping they wondered?

"Listen, where are you guys staying tonight?" Tom asks us down the phone. As usual, we don't have any plans, other than sleeping in the car again. We sense there might be an invitation in the offing, but feel a bit embarrassed to tell Tom the truth. We don't want to put him in an awkward situation, giving him no option but to invite us to stay with him.

"Erm, we haven't really made any plans…yet," Kate says vaguely.

"I'm going to give my daughter a call. I'll call you back." Tom says, hanging up. We're not entirely sure what Tom is trying to fix up for us but if it means we have a bed for a night then this is awesome news. Moments later,

Tom rings back and gives us the address of his stepdaughter's house. Alicia and her husband, Brandon, are both running in the morning. "They've already got quite a crowd staying with them but there's room for two more," Tom tells us. I am in love with Tom Love and I don't care who knows it. We're heading for our first proper night's sleep in days and I am ecstatic.

"I wonder what stages they're running tomorrow." Kate says, rifling through her notes.

"I don't know," I say, "but let's hope it's not til 10am at least so we can have a lie-in." Kate starts to giggle. "According to my notes," Kate says, sounding like a mock-professor, "Alicia will in fact be running at 3.40am." She looks at me and grins. My bubble is bursting.

"You're kidding me!" I say, snatching the papers out of Kate's hands. I scan through the list of stages and am gutted to discover the cruel reality.

*****

The Love family love running. They love to run together, crew for each other and cheer each other on at races. They are known as the 'Crazy Running Family'. Alicia was the first to get the running bug and ran her first full marathon in 2011. Her brother Nick, not to be left out, followed Alicia's lead in early 2011. Their proud mother, Diana, started going to their races to cheer them on and loved the running community so much she decided to trade her fast-walking for running. Her husband, Tom, jealous of his wife's shiny, new trainers, started running too. Alicia's husband Brandon hopped on board early in 2012 and the Crazy Running Family was complete.

We are welcomed over the threshold of Alicia and Brandon's home like new members of their family. With an early start, we know we ought to get some sleep but we stay up, chatting, laughing and joking late into the night. Eventually, as the clock creeps closer to midnight, we slope off for a shower. Alicia tells us she is getting up at

2am to make it to her hand-off in plenty of time. She doesn't want to be late! Yikes. It barely seems worth going to bed. But the good news for us is that Brandon is running the stage after Alicia and won't be leaving the house until 4am. We can have a 'lie in' until then.

*****

We head out of the house in the dark and follow Brandon and his friend Joe to the hand-off point. Soon enough, we see the familiar sight of headlamps bouncing along in the distance. Alicia's brother Nick and three other friends that were staying in the house last night have joined her for this stage. As they get closer, we can hear them chatting and occasionally we see the light from one of their headlamps turn to illuminate the face of another runner beside them. The sun is starting to rise and a beautiful sliver of orange and pink sits on top of the horizon, underneath a blanket of purple cloud. When the group reaches us, everyone is elated and barring Nick, they are happy to have finished the thirteen-mile stint. Nick is still full of energy and has no intention of stopping.

He looks at Brandon and Joe and says, "Are you ready to go boys?" They're ready.

"How fast do you want to go?" asks Joe. It's a question that is begging for a clever answer. Nick replies with a wry smile, "As fast as you wanna go!"

After just two years of running, Nick has gone from 5K and 10K races to half-marathons and marathons. He found the longer the race, the better he performed. Soon he was running 100 mile races and not just completing them but winning them. Competitors who had been running all their lives and had trained for two years, specifically for that one race, were being beaten by a man who had only been running for two years in total.

Nick qualified for the Boston Marathon in 2013. Diana and Tom could not imagine staying at home that weekend. Their son was running in the biggest race on the planet, they were not going to miss it. They flew out to Boston with Nick's wife Carrie and his 17-month-old son, Mason.

The family got a prime position next to the railing at mile 17, and when they spotted Nick, they yelled at the top of their lungs to make sure he heard them above everyone else's cheers. They jumped on the T and cheered him again at mile 22. Rushing to the T once more, they attempted to head to the finish line. But the trains were full and they couldn't get on the first two that stopped at the station. They knew that Nick would have finished running by now and begged their way onto the next train, pulling the "We have a baby!" card. Nick had been waiting a whole hour by the time the family was reunited. He was tired, cold and hungry so they scurried back towards their hotel on foot, avoiding the packed T system, and stopped at Panera Bread to get something hot to eat and drink. As they waited for their order, Tom and Nick started getting strange texts on their cell phones asking if they were alright. Some of the messages seemed quite panicky.

They didn't understand, until the people on the opposite table told them that they'd just seen images on their phones from the finish line and believed a bomb had gone off. It seemed unimaginable to Diana that the family had just left that area only 20 minutes earlier. Hearing the sirens and seeing the emergency crews pass by the café, they knew something terrible must have happened. In a state of shock, Diana tried to pray for those affected.

"What if we had not begged our way onto that train when we did?" She thought. "Where would our family be now?"

Five weeks later, a supercell tornado made its way towards Moore, a suburb of Oklahoma City. At work, Diana was far north of the affected area but knew her husband, daughter and son were all in the path of the storm. As she made her way to the storm shelter, Diana could hear one of her co-workers crying and knelt down next to her. She had just come off the phone with her mum who was at her house in Moore. Her mum was in the bathtub, crying because she could hear the tornado coming. Diana knelt down with the woman and they prayed and hoped that her mum would not be injured. The city of Moore took a direct hit. The tornado killed 23 people and injured hundreds more.

Diana's family was fine and so too was her co-worker's mum. But Diana felt numb. The emotions she felt were eerily similar to those she'd experienced after the Boston Marathon bombings, one month earlier. That evening, not knowing what to do, Diana took pillows, blankets and supplies to her local church to help those affected by the tornado. The next day she learned that an ex co-worker's nine-year-old son was missing in one of the schools destroyed in the tornado. Unfortunately, he was one of the seven children killed at the Plaza Towers elementary school in Moore.

*****

Nick was the first member of the Love family to find out about One Run For Boston. He had been looking for a way to support those affected by the Boston bombings and when he saw that the money raised by the relay runners in Oklahoma would be donated to the Tornado Relief Fund, he was in. It wasn't long before all the members of his Crazy Running Family had signed up to run in four different stages of the relay. But just one week before the relay was due to leave Santa Monica, another tornado had formed over Oklahoma City and this time it was heading straight for the homes of Diana and Tom, and their son Nick. The news reports were warning people to get below ground or travel south to avoid almost certain destruction. Diana knew that Nick and his family were already on their way to Arkansas for a trail race, so she and Tom collected up some treasured personal belongings, got in their car and headed south for safety. The traffic was crazy with everyone trying to do the same thing. Out of nowhere, a driver coming in the opposite direction decided to make a quick U-turn without checking the traffic both ways. He crashed into Diana and Tom's car, pushing them off the road into a culvert. Their car rolled over on the passenger side where Diana was sitting. Luckily, they were able to escape but their car flooded and their treasured personal belongings were ruined.

Kate and I had talked about the tornadoes with Alicia, Brandon and Joe the night before their stages. They told us that large swathes of housing had been flattened by the two tornadoes and that the clean-up process had barely begun. Alicia and Joe had driven out to scout legs 135 and 136 before the second tornado hit. They returned home with a good plan of where they would run. But after the second tornado hit the area a few days later, they decided they ought to do another drive through just to check the area was still passable.

"To put it into perspective," Joe says, "On our first scouting trip we paused by a lonely looking house being built and close to the final stages of completion. It had two stories and looked to have plenty of space. The outside was not yet complete, so no telling the plans for decoration. It looked nice." But by the time they went back for their second drive through, it was a very different story. "A big piece of the second story was missing and the entire house was ruined. A few miles down the road, we witnessed the same sad story. I recognized the roads we were travelling, but the area itself was not the same. Buildings were destroyed or simply gone. One building had been picked up and moved across the road. I barely recognized a place I have traveled through many times."

The route Joe had planned to run went through these ruined streets. His first thought was to take a detour and go around them. There was too much debris on the original route and he was worried it would slow him down and hamper the support team.

"But our thoughts quickly changed to the original purpose of the run," Alicia tells us. "We signed up to do this because we wanted to lend our strength and support to those who needed it. By running through these devastated areas, we hope that we will show the people who live there that our thoughts and prayers are with them." Joe nods his head. "I have to give full props to Alicia for that. She told me we have to stick to our original plan."

Even knowing all of this, we are not prepared for what we see on stage 136, as we drive through the suburb of El Reno. Roads that would have once been cramped with houses and people lie flat on the ground. We are travelling the exact same route the second tornado took. Normally super keen to take pictures of the environments I visit and the people I meet there, I feel I have to put my camera away. It feels intrusive to take pictures of the devastation. I can't even bring myself to take a photo of a hand-painted sign outside a half-ravaged house which says "Keep Out. We have bullets." In any other circumstances, I wouldn't have been able to resist. I don't want to be seen as a disaster tourist. Diana takes a picture of her son Nick, running down a street flanked by Brandon and Joe. On either side of the street, the remains of flattened houses are piled up beside the mailboxes. It is such a powerfully humbling photo. Captured on a mobile phone, the simple image represented hope in the midst of despair; something I had not thought was possible when I made the decision to put my own camera away. When Tom posts the photo on Facebook, it soon becomes symbolic of the spirit of the relay as a whole. Even ultra-marathoning legend, Scott Jurek, retweets it on Twitter. From Los Angeles to Boston, people were running so that others may be helped.

Having already run a 24-mile warm-up, stage 137 is the leg that Nick originally signed up for. He is joined by George Paylor from Texas, Joe on his bike and a Canadian County Sheriff's deputy. Meanwhile, Diana takes Alicia and Brandon reluctantly back to their house, so the pair can get ready for work. Alicia looks especially bummed that she could not take the day off work to spend time with her family and the running community. That girl loves running events! By the time Diana returns, the Yukon police have joined the convoy and the fire department have even got in on the act by pulling their fire truck out and flashing their lights and cheering.

After 34 miles, it is time for Nick to hand off to Dina 'Dinky' Hamman, on the shores of Lake Overholser. We say a fond farewell to Nick, not expecting to see him again. But ten miles later, at the start of the group stage in Oklahoma City, who should we see? Nick, of course. He can't stay away and has taken time off so he can run an additional five miles with his parents and the rest of the thirty-strong group.

At 11am, bang on time, we all set off together along the riverside path. It feels good to be running again ourselves. We cross the new Skydance pedestrian bridge, which we are told was inspired by the 'sky dance' of the scissor-tailed flycatcher, the symbol of Oklahoma, apparently. I'm not sure if they are making this up, I've never heard of a scissor-tailed flycatcher, but I nod along politely. We pass the Chesapeake Arena, home to the NBA's Oklahoma City Thunder, and the Devon tower. At 50 stories high, the Devon Energy Center is the 39th tallest building in the United States. (Just thought I'd throw that one in for all you fact fans out there.) These are all major landmarks for the city, but none is more significant than where we are heading, the Oklahoma City National Memorial.

On April 19 1995, Timothy McVeigh parked a rental truck in a drop-off zone underneath the Alfred P. Murrah Federal Building, in Oklahoma City. At 9:02am, the truck containing 4,800 pounds of explosives detonated, destroying 324 buildings within a 16-block radius. The bombing claimed 168 lives and more than 680 people were injured. In 2001, a memorial was built on the site of the former Alfred P. Murrah building and this is where we're heading now. Monumental twin bronze gates mark the entrance to the outdoor memorial. They face each other at either end of a block-long reflecting pool, formed by a thin layer of water flowing over polished black granite. The pool is surrounded by a field of 168 empty chairs, handcrafted from glass, bronze and stone, to symbolize each of the lives lost. The chairs represent the empty chairs at the dinner tables of the victims' families. An American Elm that survived the bombing thrives on the north side of the memorial. The inscription around the inside of the wall surrounding the Survivor Tree reads:

'The spirit of this city and this nation will not be defeated; our deeply rooted faith sustains us.'

But the first thing we see, as we run up the street, even before entering the memorial through the solid bronze gate, is the outside fence. It is covered in ribbons, flowers, flags, toys, messages and all manner of other tokens. It reminds me of the photos I have seen of the wrought-iron fence on Boylston Street, just beyond the Boston Marathon finish line. Since the bombings, the fence has become covered in ribbons and messages from people all over the country and across the world. Once inside the Memorial, we are struck by the tranquility of the space. After the frantic pace of life on the road these past twelve days, it is a perfect place to pause, to reflect and collect our thoughts. Brent Denton, who has travelled up from Dallas, Texas, to join us on this meaningful stage, sits quietly beside me.

"When I think about One Run For Boston, I can't help thinking of a quote from Christopher McDougall's 'Born to Run'," he tells me. The book, about a mysterious tribe of Mexican Indians, the Tarahumara, who live quietly in canyons and are reputed to be the best distance runners in the world, is one I've read and loved myself. "You know the bit where he says, 'Perhaps all of our troubles – all of the violence, obesity, illness, depression and greed we can't overcome – began when we stopped living as Running People," Brent says, staring ahead into the reflecting pool. "Deny your nature, and it will erupt in some other, uglier way."

I'm pretty sure that neither Brent nor I believed that running could seriously cure all the world's evils. But One Run For Boston had given us both cause to think that running was a pretty good place to start.

Chapter 17

We are given a ride back to the Stink Mobile in one of the runner's cars. Kate and I are both hot and sweaty and sit in the back seat trying not to leave a wet body print on the upholstery. We sit on our hands, figuring a couple of sweaty palm prints would be less embarrassing than leaving a print of our behinds. It's a relief to get out of the car and back into the trusty Stink Mobile.

It's just past midday and we are on the road to Tulsa when Kate has an idea that if we stop off at a hotel they might be persuaded to let us have a shower.

"They'll most probably still be servicing some of the rooms at this time of day," Kate says. "Perhaps they'll let us jump in and use one of the showers, before they clean up the bathroom ready for the next guests." It is good thinking and I'm happy to give it a go but on this occasion, I don't share Kate's optimism. She reckons that any hotel receptionist that smells us walking up to the front desk, let alone hears our story, will show some compassion and allow us a wash. "You do the talking," Kate says to me as we pass through the revolving doors into the reception area, before dashing off to take a phone call. Thanks. As I make my way to the desk, I'm hoping for an older woman, one who won't be able to suppress her motherly instinct to help us. But the only receptionist on duty is a balding, middle-aged man. This is more Kate's department, I think, looking over to where she is sitting, engrossed in the phone call. But I plough on regardless. The man listens intently to the favor I ask before saying "No."

Kate is not going to be happy with him or me. I wander over to take a seat beside her and listen in on the call. She is speaking to a reporter from The Boston Globe. From the way she appears to be bending over backwards to help him, The Boston Globe must be a pretty important paper. It feels a bit weird that we are sitting in the reception area of a hotel with the guy behind the desk, who has effectively just told us to bog off, watching us. I'm pretty certain he's going to come and ask us to leave in a minute. Kate's phone call is taking an eternity, but I know I can't interrupt. So I sit and wait, and sweat some more. When Kate gets off the phone and I break the bad news to her about the shower, I am surprised that she doesn't seem to care. She has much better news to share. Eric Moskowich, a Reporter at The Boston Globe is planning an article on One Run For Boston and he wants to fly out to Missouri to follow one of the runners.

"This is so awesome!" I shout, raising more than an eyebrow from the receptionist. "But let's get out of here. Fill me in as we drive." We scuttle back out of the revolving doors, giving the receptionist a cheery wave, and Kate starts recounting the whole conversation.

"There's a guy called Jeff Merritt who lives in or near Boston, I'm not sure which but I think he's running the last stage. Anyway, Jeff contacted The Globe and pitched the story to Eric and now Eric wants to write a feature! He's already started looking up some of the runners on Facebook. He wants to fly out and follow a few stages. But he's looking for someone to focus in on, to tell the story of One Run For Boston through their eyes. They mustn't be an elite runner, just a regular guy or girl. He wants to get under the skin of why people are running, why One Run For Boston is important." Kate talks so fast and excitedly that it's difficult to take it all in. "How many people read The Globe?" I ask her, trying to gauge what this sort of exposure could mean for the relay.

"I don't know but it's a biggy. It's *the* newspaper in Boston," Kate says. "Danny, this could be massive. This could be the breakthrough that really gives our fundraising a boost!"

*****

Joplin is a city in the south west of Missouri, not far from the border with Oklahoma. The relay route does not go through it, but comes pretty close, skirting south on Route 60. In the states of Oklahoma and Missouri, seventeen stages of the relay have the names of Joplin residents beside them. Put another away, over 5% of the 319 stages are to be completed by people who come from one small town in the Midwestern United States with a population of just 50,000, located 1500 miles from Boston. Why should this be so? It is no coincidence.

In 2011, Joplin was ravaged by a category five Tornado. The town lost 7000 homes and 161 lives. Everyone living in Joplin lost something that day. Some lost a loved one, others a job, a home, a sense of security.

"In those early hours, following the storm," Ken Schramm tells us, "we couldn't imagine how we would recover. The cleanup alone was unfathomable. Rebuilding seemed a distant dream. And, how do you heal emotional scars when everyone in town is hurting?" he says. "Then, they came. Volunteers from all over the world showed up to help with every task at hand. They used whatever skills they had to bring our community together. Those who couldn't travel to Joplin wrote letters of encouragement or sent donations. Our city was blessed with the kindness of strangers on a level I had never experienced."

After all, they've been through, the people of Joplin know what it means to have support in times of trouble and so the Boston bombing tragedy hit a nerve.

As another Joplin runner put it, "We know all too well that disaster can strike anywhere, at any time and we understand the suffering it entails. It is the silver lining in all of this. I think our hearts are bigger than they once were."

175

Through One Run For Boston, the residents of Joplin found a way to give back. On June 19 and 20th 2013, on the road between Claremont, Oklahoma and Republic, Missouri, they gave their time, energy and sweat, but most importantly their hearts, to support the people of Boston.

"It really is pretty simple," Ken says. "Pay it forward. Kindness always wins."

*****

We meet up with some Joplin runners in the town of Monett. Alison Nelson is waiting patiently with her family for her stage to begin.

"Where's Miles?" I ask.

"Oh, he's on his way," Allison tells us, "he's a couple of miles down the road with Shaun." That's funny. We'd been checking the tracker map on our phone and it had shown that Miles had already arrived in Monett. In fact, it was showing him right here in this very parking lot. Allison explains that on her way to Monett she had passed Ken Schramm who was running the stage before Shaun, two stages before her own. "Shaun was waiting with Ken's wife and told me Miles had had a rough night," Allison tells us. It seems some of the runners had been finding it more comfortable to run while holding Miles upside down. The weight seemed better balanced that way. Super speedy Nathan Sicher was one such runner. As he raced along, with Miles the wrong way up, the screw that was holding the plastic cover in place on what was meant to be the top of the baton, came undone. "Shaun told me that this 'thing' had fallen out of the inside of the baton," Allison says, holding up the GPS tracker! Realizing that the tracker was no longer inside the baton we see why Miles had appeared to be travelling ahead of schedule on the tracker map.

There are a couple of TV crews waiting to film the hand-off and we give a short interview, before returning to chat with Allison and her team. I can sense she is nervous

176

and put both my arms around her in a One Run embrace. She takes a few deep breaths and relaxes.

"Hey, do you guys know One Direction?" she asks, winking at us. Allison's beautiful blonde daughter, Michaela, is mad about the British boy band, but specifically the curly-haired heartthrob, Harry Styles.

"Oh sure," I say, loud enough for Michaela to hear. "We go out with One Direction all the time!" Michaela spins round and her jaw drops. "Harry and I party together all the time but sometimes we just chill around my house, chatting about his music and playing tunes on my ukulele."

Michaela looks up at me, impressed and jealous. "No way!" she says.

"On yeah." I'm getting into the swing of a good tale. "In fact they all wanted to come to Monett to cheer your mom on and to meet you, but they had to go on tour at the last minute." I might have overdone this last bit. Luckily, Allison steps in and asks if I could possibly get Harry to send Michaela a text message.

"No problem!" I say, making a mental note to send Allison a message later on from my English cell phone.

Michaela could not be more excited and she runs around the parking lot posing for my camera, dressed in her One Run For Boston T-shirt. Suddenly, we look up and see Shaun Steal running towards us with Miles. But something is wrong. He's holding Miles gingerly and the plastic covering is missing. Miles has taken a beating, no doubt about it. He's not looking good at all. I make a beeline to the car to get some first aid for Miles. At least the GPS tracker hasn't been lost. I look through our kit and find some duck tape to bind Miles back together. It may not look so pretty, but every scar will tell a story.

I hand Allison the new-look Miles, and she heads off down the street with her 14 year-old son and his best friend. Her husband-daughter support team jump in the car. But before they pull away Michaela jumps out of the car and runs back to Kate and me.

177

"Tell Harry I love him!" she says.

We say, "Sure thing!"

All in all, it's a pretty typical handover, barring the outrageous lies we've just told this trusting little girl about us rubbing shoulders with a band of teenage superstars.

*****

Running in itself can be a pretty solitary pastime. Especially if you have a family and only one parent can train at a time, while the other looks after the kids. You have to squeeze your runs in when you can, even if that is four in the morning and there is no-one else for company. But on the special days, the race days and the epic event days like One Run For Boston, running becomes a sport that brings everyone together. Not just runners, but non-running families and friends too; the supporters. I think back to the runners that Kate and I have done our best to support since starting out from Venice Beach. The runners we have helped through the heat and the hills, the altitude, the lightning storms and the dark, dark nights. The sad thing is that we know we can't be there to support every single runner on the route. We are doing our best, but it just isn't possible to be there for everyone. Yet Kate and I aren't the only support team on the road; far from it. Most of the runners have dedicated families and friends who come out to support them. These loyal supporters drive behind to shield their loved ones from the traffic. They fill up their cars with food and water to make sure their runners are well-fed and hydrated. They hand out high fives and hugs, wave placards and cheer at the top of their voices. They give up their time and very often their sleep, to ensure their nearest and dearest stay safe. And they do not expect anything in return.

Many of the runners who write to us after taking part in One Run For Boston speak of the love and appreciation they feel for those who support them when they run.

Our supporters put up with our incessant talk about running. Rabbiting on about our injuries, our nutrition, our mileage. They humor us, nodding and sympathizing at the right bits. On race day, they're the ones who drive us to the race, look after the children, carry our stuff and feed and water us when we need it. They study route maps finding out whether they can see us at mile 3 and mile 11 and still make it to the finish on time to welcome us home.

How often do they stand, sometimes in the rain and cold, frantically looking from one tired runner to the next, waiting for their opportunity to cheer with all their heart and soul? We acknowledge the noise with a slight lift of the head, if we have enough energy we hold out a hand for a high five. If we're doing terribly, we stop for an indulgent hug, and maybe a cry, to recharge us mentally and physically.

The most amazing thing is they don't just support us. They go wild for everyone. People who might not be the most outgoing in the office or at home are making a scene, dancing and singing in a way they wouldn't do normally. People come every year and perhaps they're addicted to this moment of freedom in their lives. The pride in watching such a united show of strength can't help but make you emotional as a supporter. When you're the runner who has hit the wall, every muscle in your body wants to stop. You slow down, then as you're about to change your stride length from run to walk, the supporters notice and like a sonic boom of noise they start to cheer you on. If you've got your name on your bib, they'll shout it! And if they don't know your name, they will latch onto any identifier and shout, "Go, short red shorts!" "Go, One Run For Boston!" "Go, pink tutu!" Others join in and it spreads ahead and behind you. You can't stop now. How could you? Every runner knows we couldn't do it without the support of friends, family and very often strangers.

These loved ones, the supporters, were the people the bombers targeted at the Boston Marathon finish line. They picked on people who were doing something absolutely and completely unselfish; helping others to achieve their dreams. Without the supporters, the Boston Marathon, especially at Boylston Street, would just be a line of very tired runners plodding on and stopping. It would be very grey indeed. The supporters bring the color to the day. They bring the noise. They are the atmosphere.

Every runner knows that without any support, we just couldn't do it, and One Run For Boston was no different.

Chapter 18

Stripped to their waists, two runners stand with their backs towards us, eyes searching the horizon. On Richard White's back, 'Boston' is written in large black letters. On Aaron Tucker's back, 'Strong' is written, just as boldly. Richard holds a white pole with a large American flag that flutters proudly above both their heads, framing the perfect picture. It is another image that sums up the beauty and the purpose of One Run For Boston. This peaceful scene is a world away from the previous baton hand-off outside the Bass Pro store in Springfield. Having followed Kevin Rorick through the previous stage, we had rocked up at Bass Pro ten minutes before him, to find a crowd of seventy or more runners, spectators, reporters and film crews. The store owner had set up a PA system outside and had been working the crowd up into a frenzy of anticipation as we arrived in the Stink Mobile.

"Stay tuned!" he announced, "History is about to be made!"

There was much ceremonial pageantry with speeches and a giant check presentation. We weren't prepared for any of this and Kate did a bunk down the road to check on Kevin, leaving me to entertain the crowd. When Kevin came into view across the parking lot, the atmosphere was electrifying. Everyone cheered, car horns honked and camera bulbs flashed. It was probably the closest we will ever get to a red carpet experience.

Now here we are in Strafford, no crowds, no cheers, and yet the same level of anticipation among those about to do their bit. Richard and Aaron are joined by three of Aaron's college friends. Zachary Kellner and Bryce

Heffington are running with them and another, who we know only as the Officer of Hydration, will cycle behind with the flag and water supplies. These guys are all competitive runners and we know they'll make short work of the next 13 miles. They do not disappoint. Averaging seven-minute miles for the duration, the guys soon reach Marshfield, where Darren Maute and his team of runners are waiting. They hand-off not just the baton but also the flag and as Darren's team disappear into the distance, the last thing we see is the stars and stripes, flapping in the breeze and disappearing over the horizon.

A couple of the boys' mums have escorted the group in their cars and they join Kate and me at the finish of the stage, to cheer their boys home, juggling cameras and handmade placards. Handing his sweat drenched headband to his mum, Aaron asks her, "Can I have a beer mom?" Aaron has just turned 21 and his mum replies, "Sure. You have your wallet and you have your ID. The store is over there." There's not much Aaron can say to that, even if he has just run 13 miles. So, he trots off across the road to get his beer. While he's away, a car pulls up and a man jumps out. He's wearing tatty clothes and his speech is very slightly slow and slurred, but his motive is clear.

"I saw you on the TV," he explains. "I want to make a donation." He's been driving around trying to track us down after seeing a news report on TV with footage filmed outside Bass Pro. He takes my hands and puts two screwed up dollar bills into my palm. It feels like the two dollars is a lot of money to this man. There are sacrifices he will have to make this week in order to afford it. It is an incredibly generous gesture and I thank him sincerely. Taking the notes from him, I explain how grateful we are that he has come to find us and assure him that his money will be put to good use by the One Fund Boston.

Fifteen miles away in Conway, the mother of a local firefighter has also been watching the TV. Realizing that the same trans-continental running relay is heading straight for her small community later that night, and will pass right by the fire station, she gives her son a call. The call is to play a crucial part in one of the most extraordinary nights of my life.

Dan Bohannon, or 'Danbo Hanan' as I believe he is called when he introduces himself to me, began running in the 1980s. "Back then if you were a runner in a small town and you weren't a high school kid or coach, people thought you were a bit weird," Danbo tells us. "I was neither a high school athlete nor a coach, just a middle of the pack runner, and so from the git-go, I was not normal. Whenever I ran, I got cat calls and people asked me if I needed a ride." But that didn't stop him. He ran to relieve stress, clear his head and to be alone. "I am not a social runner," Danbo admits. So when he signed up to run stage 173 through the rural Ozarks in Missouri, Danbo was expecting, looking forward to even, 9.5 miles of solitude. "Maybe I'd have an escort? Maybe not. Maybe another runner would sign up and join me? I was afraid that some fast person would sign up and take away my solitude," he confides. And yet, despite this introversion, Danbo had been a regular on the One Run For Boston Facebook group. He'd followed every picture and post, frequently offering up his favorite motto, "Excellent!" to praise and encourage other runners. When some members of the group grew frustrated at the delays that were occurring, due to the hot and challenging conditions, Danbo reminded them that this was meant to be fun. "Run, smile, drink water and don't die!" he posted lightening the mood, adding, "Blessed are the flexible, for they shall not get bent out of shape." If nothing else, Danbo thought, he would be an encourager while he waited for the relay to reach him.

Browsing through the Facebook scroll, searching for a runner who would epitomize the very essence of the relay, The Boston Globe reporter, Eric Moskowitz, became intrigued by Dan Bohannon – this unassuming, middle of the pack runner who had held off from signing up to run at first. He had been anxious that he may not be up to it; concerned that this event was not for amateurs like him. Eric noted that Danbo was down to run a late-night stage through the heart of rural America, along a narrow stretch of Route 66 that his grandfather had helped to pave. In Dan Bohannon, Eric Moskowitz had found his story.

We meet Dan waiting with Eric by the side of the road, just as the sun is setting.

"Danbo!" I say, giving him a hug and a slap on the back, "Are you all set?"

He nods and says "I think so!" in his typically upbeat yet self-deprecating way. "But I have something to give you and Kate first before we get going," he says, rummaging in the back of his car. "I promised Kate I'd bring you both one of my homemade blackberry cobblers." Dan lifted out a polystyrene box, wrapped in tea towels. Inside, the cobbler sits, still nice and hot. It smells delicious and I can't wait to tuck in.

"I said we'd eat it all together at the end of Dan's stage to celebrate!" Kate says. Damn Kate and her sharing, caring ways, I think to myself, putting the cobbler out of temptation on the backseat of the car. At that moment, a Conway Fire Department truck pulls up and an officer gets out.

"My mom saw you guys on the news," he says, then looks at Dan and asks, "Do you want an escort?" Dan looks at us. We look back at him, grinning.

"That would be excellent," Dan says, "Thank you."

When Darren and his team arrive, they lash the flag they picked up at the start of their stage to the back of the fire truck.

"Be safe out there," Darren says to Dan.

"I will, I'll be paying attention," Dan assures him. Then the fire truck drives off, lights flashing, and Dan falls in behind, holding Miles firmly in his hand.

Eric sits with The Globe's photographer on the tailgate of the truck, looking back at Dan and scribbling furiously into his notebook. He records everything, as Dan gives a commentary of the road he knows so well, pointing out features and landmarks as they pass by. We enter Conway, population 788, and see the fire station lit up in a blaze of fluorescent lights. A fire engine is parked outside, with an American flag hanging from its ladder that is stretched out high above the road. A grandstand of twenty people has gathered in deckchairs, opposite the fire station, and they cheer as Dan runs by. He smiles broadly and holds Miles up to acknowledge them. A man and a woman wearing running kit jump out from the crowd and ask if they can join Dan for the last five miles.

"We go to church with your parents," the woman explains, "and they were telling us all about this." Another reporter is standing in the crowd, writing in her notebook. She is just 14, and has been woken up by her family so that she may get her scoop. Nights like this don't come around too often here.

Up ahead, we see Dan waving to a couple of elderly women who are standing on the road outside their house. It is Dan's mum and his aunt. They are joined by Dan's dad, who has stayed up after 9pm for the first time in years so that he may see his son run by. We stay and chat with them for a while and they tell us about all the different travelers that they have met while living on this road. It's not the first time that they have entertained people who have been making a coast-to-coast journey either.

"One time there was a group of church folk who came from all over the world," Dan's mum explains to us. "They were walking right the way across the country. One of them, a Russian woman, was very overweight and suffering, so I invited them all in for pop and cookies. I couldn't understand most of them but they were very friendly. When my husband came home he didn't know what to make of it, all these strangers in our house!"

185

Dan's stage finishes in a deserted parking lot, just before midnight. Aside from a gas station, which is closed this time of night, the only other building nearby is a tired-looking store that proclaims itself to be 'The World's Biggest Gift Shop.' The location seems a bit of a letdown after all the excitement we've encountered en route. That is until the fire engine and the ladder truck show up, shortly before Dan's arrival. The whole fire station crew has turned out and they illuminate the entire parking lot with two enormous spot lights. We're joined by Dan's wife, Regina, Dan's parents and three runners who are waiting to take their turn on the next stage. As we wait, Dan's dad beckons me over with one hand behind his back. I bound over to him smiling, and he produces a small, yellow rubber duck from behind his back.

"I like to give all the children a little gift," he tells me, placing the duck into the hands of a 34 year-old *man*. I am so utterly touched. I often think of myself as a seven-year-old trapped in an aging body. This is something my therapist says is true of everyone, it's just with me, my childlike instinct is a little stronger.

Flanked by the runners he picked up in Conway, Dan enters the parking lot and we all go wild. There are high fives and hugs and back slaps galore. We cheer the next group of runners on their way and then I remember the cobbler! Taking the delicious blackberry pie out of its box, we offer it around with a bag full of plastic spoons. In return, the firemen offer us a ride up into the sky inside the bucket of their ladder truck. I'm torn between the ladder truck and the pie and solve the problem by taking the pie up with me. Dizzy with excitement, it feels like we are at a fairground. As we look down at the ground and marvel at how small everyone looks, I turn to Dan and ask him,

"What do you normally do on a Thursday night?"

He says, "I watch films that Regina doesn't like while she's at her mom's house."

I cannot see how Thursdays can ever be the same again for Danbo.

We don't want the evening to end, but know we must be on our way. Like an exhausted child, Kate falls asleep in the car before we even leave the parking lot. Her head droops until she is almost bent over double, nudging the gear stick with her nose. We are both completely wiped out. I make a decision to find a motel for the night. We are in desperate need of a proper night's sleep. I drive along, keeping my eyes open for neon signs by the side of the road. Each time I have to wait at a red light my eyes close automatically and I fall asleep. Somehow, my body has programmed a 30-second alarm and every time I nap, I wake myself before the light turns green. If I oversleep by a few seconds and the light changes before I wake, the car behind is always kind enough to toot their horn to send me on my way again. There are no motels to be seen and we soon reach Lebanon, the next hand-off location. I don't think either of us has the energy to meet any more runners tonight and I intend to drive straight through. But there they are, waiting at an intersection, Jeff Beatty and his team. They've spotted the Stink Mobile and are cheering and waving in our direction. I give Kate a prod and tell her to wake up. She shudders awake, scrunching her face up as she opens her eyes.

"Where are we?" she asks, disorientated. But I'm already out the car. And now we're here, it feels rude not to wait and watch the next hand-off. So we hang out, chatting with the runners for another hour and watch as Miles changes hands again. We ask one of the runner's wives if they know of any motels nearby.

"I think I know of one nice motel," she says.

Kate looks at me, as if for backup, and interrupts the woman saying, "Oh, we're not looking for nice," she tells the woman, "cheap and nasty will do us."

The woman looks at us a little strangely and says, "Oh, OK, follow me. I'll take you to have a look at a couple."

187

So, we follow her to some of the most skanky motels that I have ever seen in my life. The first one has no vacancies and there is no answer at the next one. Judging by what they look like from the outside, we've probably had a lucky escape. "I'm sorry, I don't know of any more," the woman says, apologetically.

"No worries!" I say, trying my best to sound perky. "There's bound to be some other options up the road." We thank her for taking the time to help us out and head back to the car.

"What do we do now?" Kate asks me, deflated. We had both been looking forward to a comfortable bed for the night. I look at her and realize she is as done-in as I feel. I know exactly what to do. I fire the car up and drive a quarter of a mile up the road to the nearest layby. We pull in, recline our seats, lock the doors and immediately fall asleep.

*****

"We can't miss Pete Leyva and John Kohler," Kate says, as soon as she wakes up. Exactly two weeks in, and the relay is infiltrating our dreams as well as dominating our days.

"Oh yeah, why's that?" I ask curiously.

"I'm not entirely sure, but their names are stuck in my head," Kate says. We've got some driving to do to catch them up, so we stop for some fuel and a coffee to help us on our way. We pull up beside the pump and as I open my door, I am suddenly hit with a wall of warm, sticky air. This must be the humidity that everyone's been talking about. It is like being inside a greenhouse. I can't wait to get inside the gas station with its lovely cool, dry air conditioning. I grab a couple of coffees and go to the counter. The woman at the till is drinking from a five-liter barrel.

"What is that?!" I cannot stop myself from asking.

"This?" The woman looks at me, astounded that I would not know. "This is my soda for today." My God, this is grotesque. The thought of this woman slurping down five liters of soda in one day, turns my stomach. How does she manage to hold down a job? She must need to nip to the bathroom every five minutes. Thinking about this woman's obvious soda addiction makes me consider the coffee I am about to buy. I had been drinking more and more of the stuff since I arrived in America, which is funny because I never drink coffee back home. But over here, coffee tastes altogether different with the array of scrummy flavorings and creamers. Kate and I are drinking countless cups every day. I think about it for a while. The coffee I am drinking over here isn't just sweetened; it is basically just caffeinated syrup. I am no better than this poor woman with her soda habit. I have become addicted to sugar.

Sugar is hard to avoid in America. For many Americans, sugar is present in everything they eat, from their first bite of food in the morning to their very last mouthful at night. It's in all their snacks, all their drinks and all their meals. They have become, often unwittingly, non-stop sugar consumers. Sugar is used to sweeten soft drinks, fast food, pies, pizzas, canned vegetables and even Biltong – the ultimate, innocent, high-protein snack that I have always believed contains nothing but meat. How wrong I am. In America, sugar is in pretty much everything. We have a lot of in England too, but nothing on this scale!

Many tests have been conducted comparing the effects of sugar with that of cocaine or heroin. A book, 'Deep Nutrition' by Catherine Shanahan says, "If a child were given a dose of heroin, the chemical would trigger a flurry of neural activity in the pleasure centers of his brain. Sugar results in the very same response." Both sugar and heroin occur naturally on our planet and both are harvested by humans to abuse our bodies.

Even as an adult, I have been told by my girlfriends that I'm not allowed to drink fizzy drinks when I'm around them as it makes me hyperactive and 'annoying.' I question the latter but agree with the former. It makes me talk uncontrollably and want to move and have fun. Whether Catherine Shanahan is speaking the truth or not I don't know, but I'm a complete sugar addict. I can eat two packets of hobnobs (my favorite English biscuit, or cookie as the Americans would say) in a day. I will often open the first packet as I take them from the shelf in the store and devour half of them before I even get to the checkout. I'll then finish the packet off on the way home in the car. The second packet, I'll rip open the moment I'm through the front door. I'll have my dinner, and then polish them off with a nice cup of tea. One of the things I love about running, is that it allows me to indulge my hobnob habit without gaining weight. I don't like to think about what the hobnobs are doing to my insides, meanwhile. As long as I can't see what the junk in my trunk is doing to me, I haven't been concerned about it up until now. Since being in America, my sugar cravings have grown even more intense. It seems each time I feed the monster, the monster wants more. No wonder there are so many obese people in America. They all have their own little sugar monsters inside them.

That said, most of the people we are meeting on our journey all look to be in mint condition. Some even look jaw-droppingly fantastic (*cough* Holly Miller). In a very strange way, this was disappointing to me. You see, certain aspects of my True American Experience just weren't living up to my grand expectations. I had not encountered as many American stereotypes as I had hoped and in particular, I hadn't had the pleasure of meeting any truly massive people. Until, that is, we went to an all-you-can-eat diner. The doorways are apparently built a little wider in these types of restaurant, to allow the people who visit most often to fit through the door. I guess it makes good business sense. When we walked through the doors of this particular diner, with no problems I might add, we were presented with two options: $7.50 for unlimited soup and bread or $10 for as much as you can eat of anything on offer. The menu included: soups, stews, fish, cold meats, roast meats, potatoes done every which way you can imagine, pasta, rice, bread, pastries, ice cream and desserts. You name it, you could pretty much have it. At the last minute, perhaps a little intimidated by her surroundings, Kate backed out of the $10 deal and opted instead for the $7.50 soup option. The woman behind the counter looked at Kate as if she has just walked through the door naked. She could not have been more shocked or surprised. It's probably safe to say that no one in the whole history of this diner had ever come in and asked for the $7.50 option. I put the woman right back in her comfort zone by saying, "I'm all in for the $10 plate, please."

She looked relieved. I could see she was thinking. "Just wait till I get home and tell my family about the day I've had!"

Kate got busy with the soup while I did a couple of laps around the giant buffet tables filling my plate with a little of this and a little of that until I could not fit any more on it. Feeling a little self-conscious at my over laden platter, I scuttled back to join Kate at our table and started digging in. I polished off every last mouthful and have to say I was absolutely stuffed. I struggled to manage even the smallest of desserts. Kate was ready to go, but I insisted we stayed a little longer. We were here now and we may as well see what happened. We watched in stunned silence as, again and again, the same people returned to the buffet and piled their clean plates up to the ceiling with food.

"How do they do it?" Kate asked, "Where does it all go?" Without exception, these people were big, really big. So it was fair to say they all had fairly large internal storage tanks.

But I knew what Kate was thinking, "Boy, the bathrooms here must take a hammering."

*****

We drive away from the gas station, leaving the woman behind the counter in peace to guzzle on her giant soda. It's a beautiful route to Newburg, where local policeman Pete Leyva is due to hand off to John Kohler. It is very, very green with steep, wooded slopes on either side of the road and stone bridges crossing trickling streams. Overnight, one of the runners had reported seeing skunks, raccoons and possums on the road. We spot a bit of roadkill, including the odd armadillo, but not a lot else. We roll into Newburg, a tiny town on the old Route 66. As soon as I see John, I recognize him as the incredible guy in the Facebook group who was inspired by the actions of Will Allender, Gary Allen and Ty Thurlow and paid for Steve Bender to fly out to New Mexico. John's wife, young son and baby daughter are with him and as we chat, we learn that they are the reason why John took up running in the first place. When he and his wife made the decision to start a family, John had realized that his lifestyle had to change.

"I was a smoker with high cholesterol and my physical activity consisted of walking a few blocks a day between offices at work," he says. His diet, needless to say, was no better. "I started running because I wanted to be around to watch my kids grow up." Within a few weeks, a friend told John that he was entering a local marathon and encouraged John to join him on his training runs. "My wife unintentionally told the rest of my family that I was also running the marathon! But I thought 'why not?' and my first ever road race was a marathon. After that I was hooked and Boston became my goal."

John set himself a two-and-a-half-year goal to qualify for Boston and be part of the greatest athletic tradition in the United States. On April 15, 2013, John achieved his dream, sprinting across the finish line on Boylston Street. He joined his family at the Forum restaurant where they heard the first bomb go off.

"I thought it was some sort of celebratory cannon," John says, "but the second bomb went off and the windows shattered; the building shook and the only thing I remember hearing was my wife telling me to get our son."

With his wife cradling their three-month-old daughter, John grabbed his son and together they ran toward the exit. "I'll never know why," John tells us, "but as we were running toward the fire exit in the back of the restaurant, I quickly stopped, set my son down and told him I loved him. It was a strange feeling, not knowing whether the safest place was outside or inside the building. In the back of my mind, I was fearful for what we would possibly encounter outside." John picked his son back up and the restaurant staff calmly escorted them out the back. They passed people carrying injured restaurant patrons outside, and John shielded his son's eyes for fear of him remembering the scene that no parent ever wants their child to witness.

At home two days later, John felt a mix of feelings pouring out of him. Sadness for those injured and killed; guilt, that his family had to cope with the emotions of the event; disappointment, that the race would never be the same, (guilt, for feeling this way after what happened), and anger at those who changed that.

"I just kept asking myself all these questions. Why do we continue to do this to ourselves? When is humanity going to realize that working together is easier, and less painful, than working against one another? Why can't we realize that our differences are why we've made it to this point, and that if we were all the same it would lead to our extinction (literally)? Is there any hope?"

About a month later, John saw a tweet about One Run For Boston. Curious, he went to the website to see what it was all about. Debating whether or not to sign up, he thought it may have been some sort of hoax but his wife encouraged him, saying he would regret it if he didn't. "When I joined the Facebook group a few days later, that is what really transformed the experience for me," John says. "It was amazing how everyone rallied together to get the stages filled, to ensure the relay would be completed. I've never been part of an experience where you meet a group of people online and feel so connected. We all came from different walks of life, but felt as one, as we raised money and awareness while trying to get the baton across the U.S."

One of the first pictures John remembers seeing after the marathon, was of Carlos Arredondo, the man in the cowboy hat who had famously rushed to the aid of Jeff Baumann in the aftermath of the bombs. In the picture, Carlos was standing holding an American flag. John started thinking about how great it would be to get a flag to travel from his hometown in Kansas, all the way across the country somehow, to the Forum restaurant as a gesture of solidarity and gratitude. One Run For Boston turned out to be that opportunity.

While we wait for Miles to arrive, I play Peek-a-Boo with John's son who is wearing the T-shirt he wore to support his dad in Boston. On the back is a quote from TS Eliot, "Only those who risk going too far can possibly find out how far one can go." It certainly sums up the relay. Across the road, a local woman walks back and forth, wearing a sign round her neck which simply reads, "Thank you." A group of children from the nearby summer school are starting to line the street and we get them to practice a Mexican wave. They cheer loudly and wave flags, as Pete Leyva arrives. I look over at John and see he is fighting back tears. The two men embrace as Miles is transferred between them and soon John is off, with Miles in one hand and a small American flag in the other. His family follow and the local kids return to their classroom, the woman with the sign walks back to her home and the sleepy town of Newburg returns to normal.

Finishing in Rolla, eleven miles later, is "one of the single greatest memories of my life," John tells us afterwards. He hands Kate the small flag he has been carrying and says,

"Please do your best to help it reach the Forum restaurant for me." We both recognize the significance of this gesture and are concerned about how we can best fulfill this great responsibility. We decide to tape the flag to the aerial on top of the Stink Mobile and drive off listening to it tap, tap, tapping on the roof above us.

As we drive, I think about something that John said to me as we left him.

"There is this saying that I keep seeing recently," he told me. "The phrase is, 'Be the change you want to see in the world.'" I had nodded vaguely as my fuddled brain tried to work out what John meant. He could see I wasn't 100% with him. "If I want to change the world, I cannot be a spectator," he explained. "I must be a participant. One Run For Boston has taught me that."

*****

The heat, combined with the humidity, is making life difficult for all of the runners today. It is a rough day for running. You can see steam rising off the road. In the early afternoon, we pass a small group of runners who are looking as rough as the road in the challenging conditions. Kate jumps out and offers them some water which they knock back in an instant. Our hearts immediately go out to them. They have a police patrol car following behind them, but we realize they must be running without any other support. They have already got through the water they were carrying with them and there are five more miles to go.

"Do any of you want to jump in the car with us for a minute?" I ask, willing them to say "Yes." This is no moment for martyrs. "You can take it in turns to have a little rest then all finish the last half-mile together," I suggest. But there are no takers and I'm not sure what to do. We drive ahead another mile and Kate gets some more water ready while I dart back to have a word with one of the policemen in the escort car. As he winds down his window to speak to me, I see that one of the runners is sitting in the back seat, looking dreadful.

"An ambulance is on its way," the policeman tells me. She is clearly suffering from severe heatstroke and dehydration and a wave of different emotions washes over me. I feel guilty but also a little angry. Why on earth didn't she jump in with us a mile back? I feel relieved that an ambulance is on its way but most of all I feel concerned. This runner does not look well. I hope she is OK and that this hideous experience won't put her off running for life.

Chapter 19

With few exceptions, every runner we meet comments on the extraordinary community that the One Run For Boston Facebook group has forged. They are absolutely right of course, but we cannot take the credit. There is one person in the Facebook group who has been ever present from the beginning. From the outset she instinctively became chief 'meeter and greeter,' providing a warm welcome to every runner who joined and offering friendly words of encouragement and support at every opportunity. Mary Hoatlin turned a random group of a thousand runners into a tight-knit running family. In my eyes, she had become the mother of One Run For Boston. I run this thought past Kate on the way to Mary's house in St. Louis and wonder if she'll take offence, thinking her own position has been usurped. But Kate is the first to admit she's not the maternal type and agrees this title is much more suited to Mary.

Mary had also become a crutch for Kate and me throughout our journey. Helping us keep everyone informed, answering lots of silly questions (from the group and us!) and plenty more clever ones, while nipping any bickering in the bud and making sure everyone plays nicely. Well, nearly everyone. Mary was also at the center of a well-orchestrated and highly effective twitter bomb campaign that had seen One Run For Boston retweets from a number of celebrities, including her heartthrob Kevin Spacey. She'll have to fight Kate for Kevin if the three ever find themselves in the same room. We knew if we needed help with anything, anything at all, Mary was ready to leap into action to help us further. And now that we had arrived at her house, she was going to feed us and tuck us into bed for the night. She'd also promised Kate a cup of English tea. Could this woman be any more saintly?

Entering her gorgeous, air-conditioned home, we find Mary busy on two computers. One screen has the Facebook page loaded up and the other displays the online tracker map so Mary can follow Miles's every move as he is carried across her beloved country. It's no surprise to us really. This two-screened approach explains how Mary has been able to keep so on top of things. Kate and I have questioned many, many times how Mary is managing to keep her job and marriage going while devoting so much time online to One Run For Boston. With Mary's help and dedication, we are now 2,000 miles into the relay and are beginning to allow ourselves the slightest expectation that Miles may actually make it to Boston.

Mary is the first to admit she's not an elite runner. "Running doesn't come easy to me, but I always feel better after I do it," she tells us. She's been running on and off since 1996 but went into 'semi-retirement' after doing two marathons back to back in two weeks. The experience drained her so much that she didn't run for over six years after that. But after her mum died, Mary got back at it and hasn't looked back. She is splitting her stage with her husband Patrick and a few other friends to be certain that they keep on pace.

Patrick describes himself as Mary's 'worse half.' In fact, he is an absolute diamond geezer and is cooking up a storm in the kitchen, preparing a delicious dinner packed with all the fresh vegetables that Kate and I are craving. We're not allowed to lift a finger to help. He hands us both a beer and we stay and chat while he chops.

"I have never fancied myself as a runner," he says. "As a matter of fact, I have been known to be a fierce opponent of running. I played soccer for most of my life and chose to play in goal just to avoid having to do so much running." It was Mary who encouraged Patrick to start running. "I baulked a bit at first, but eventually worked my way out there," he admits. "The first day of my new-found running career was quite humbling. I was able to run the length of a city block before bending at the waist and heaving uncontrollably. In my defense, it was a very fast 48 yards!"

Both Patrick and Mary work as Clinical Social Workers in a local jail. It makes for a lively conversation round the dinner table, packed with amusing anecdotes. But in amongst the stories, Mary makes a serious point. "In prison, Patrick and I spend a lot of time seeing the worst in people and it has been hard for me to keep my work experiences in perspective," she tells us. "But One Run has helped give me a better outlook on people. This experience has been just what my soul needed." Patrick and Mary's professional lives could not be more different from our own and Kate and I are intrigued. We ask about gang culture in America and we get on to the subject of what various tattoos mean. Kate tells Mary about the guy we met at Venice Beach just after we arrived in Los Angeles.

"Danny had his photo taken with this bodybuilder down at Muscle Beach," she tells Mary.

"Oh yeah, I saw the photo on Facebook," Mary says, nodding. Of course she did. If it was on Facebook, Mary had seen it.

"He had these tears tattooed underneath his eyes," Kate says, "Have you seen that before?" Mary and Patrick both nod. "That can signify a number of things," Mary says. "Sometimes it means the person is mourning the loss of a family member, or that a close friend of a gang member has died and they're seeking revenge," she explains. Kate and I mull this over for a few seconds. It seemed pretty hardcore to get any kind of tattoo on your face.

"Of course, it can also mean they've killed someone," Patrick says between mouthfuls. Kate and I stop eating and look at each other. Holy Schmoly!

Cheri Becker, a friend of Mary's who is running with her in the morning, arrives with presents for everyone. But she also brings news that the mighty Mississippi, the river that famously rolls along past the city of St. Louis separating the state of Missouri from Illinois, is on flood alert. This is a little irritating given that tomorrow's group stage in St. Louis is due to follow the riverside trail for four of its four and a half miles. It's possible to reroute it, but if the protective flood wall is closed, it means we'll have to relocate the start too. This could be a major headache. Cheri gives the police a call and confirms the worst. Bollocks. It's getting on for 10pm and even with a two-hour delay due to the heat and humidity today, the group stage is due to start in less than ten hours. We make a new plan and do our best to let the fifty or so runners know about the change via email and Facebook. Mary starts trying to contact the TV stations who have promised to send crews along, including Kate's pal John Pertzborn or 'Pertz' as we have all taken to calling him. Patrick has wisely left us to it and sloped off to bed and I decide to do the same.

"What time are we leaving in the morning?" I ask Mary as I head up the stairs.

"I'll come and wake you at 1am," she answers. Err…what?! 1am? OK right. We're getting up at 1am because you're running at 3am?

"Sure! Brill! Great!" I say, trying to sound enthusiastic while my insides fall apart.

*****

In another deserted parking lot, in another town in the middle of another night, we meet another group of awesome people. One of them is Bernard Mann, or 'Skip' as he is better known. Skip was always a good athlete but

200

in high school, he got into some trouble and was banned from taking part in sports. By the time he went to College, the only 'sports' Skip took part in were drinking, smoking and 'otherwise unhealthy events,' as he puts it. He quit college after a year and joined the Navy where he continued to smoke and drink heavily. He married, started a family, left the Navy and eventually joined the army, hoping to become a Combat Medic. This is where he started running in order to pass the fitness test. Skip developed his own interval training plan which involved running a mile, smoking a cigarette, running another mile and smoking another cigarette.

"Might have been the best cigarettes I ever smoked," Skip tells us. He hung on to his bad habits but started really getting into running. He ran weekly races and though he never won anything, he says, "It was giving me something that I seemed to need. Partying and good times and otherwise unhealthy events continued, but at a lesser rate and my self esteem began to change. I started to think that I might actually be intelligent and a good guy." He went back to college and did a course in nursing. Getting a job in a children's hospital Skip quit smoking and felt he'd finally found a purpose. But caring for the sickest babies in the Nursery, he had held too many dying babies and it was starting to get to him. He began drinking to escape, rather than just to party. "After one night shift in particular a bunch of us went to a drinking breakfast and this turned into lunch and I was totally drunk and tried to drive home so I could pick up the kids from school, as was my responsibility," Skip says. "Thankfully, I got stopped by the police and that was the best ticket that I ever got. It made me man up to the drinking monster that was trying to own me. It was time to be honest with myself and to change my life."

Running became Skip's new addiction and he entered the US Air Force Reserve as a Commissioned Officer. "2nd Lieutenant Mann sounded great, and I was not going to

201

trash this opportunity to be a good and respected Flight Nurse and Officer," he explains. As soon as he qualified, Skip was off to Germany for Desert Storm and for the next 16 years, he was a top notch officer. He retired in 2005 a decorated Veteran. His last drink was 23 years ago.

During this time, Skip got a mailer from Team in Training, a fundraising program of The Leukemia & Lymphoma Society. It simply said, 'Run a marathon and help save lives.'

"The Team in Training program changed my life and gave me so much positive energy," Skip says. It's where he met Mary Hoatlin, Cheri Becker and Jim Berding who are all standing in the deserted parking lot with him now, ready to run stage 189 of the relay.

Through conversation, photos and many, many jokes (some too rude for these pages and we have Skip to blame for that!) we make the most of the short time we have and get to know each other; in some cases a little too well. Tracy Wall is among the gaggle of spirited runners who hand-off to Mary and her team. She comes bearing gifts for Kate and me that she hopes will make life in the Stink Mobile more tolerable. She has brought wet wipes and hand gels, air fresheners and deodorants. But also fake mustaches and glow-in-the-dark fairy wands. Opening the contents of the bag, it feels like all our Christmases have come at once.

Manchester Street is normally one of the busiest roads in St. Louis but not at 2.30am. The sidewalks shine under a full moon as Mary and Cheri head off to run the first few miles of the stage. A few miles down the road, they are joined by Skip, Patrick and Jim and an escort from the Po-Po. As I may have told you before, Kate is about as streetwise as a fairground goldfish. She has never heard the Police referred to as Po-Po before and finds it hilarious. She films the procession on her phone giggling at the Po-Po. The smile is soon wiped off her face when the second full moon of the night appears in front of her. As we pass the group, with Kate leaning out of the window filming, Skip whips down his shorts to show off his butt. They don't call Missouri the *Show-Me State* for nothing!

We come across several spectators along the way, despite the early morning hour, although, as Patrick observes, it's not clear if they are actually spectating, or simply waiting for a bus. Whoever they are, they cheer anyway. At one point, Kate jumps out to persuade a group of overnight construction workers to replace their tools with flags and come over to the runners' side of the street to cheer them on. They duly oblige. After all, as Skip points out afterwards, "Who could deny Kate?"

The group finishes with a two and a half mile climb which they totally own. They hand-off to Andy Koziatek, the runner who had joined Mary in the Fox studio for that very first TV interview with John Pertzborn two months ago. He's planning to run at a six and a half minute mile pace. No wonder he is running on his own! It is music to our ears, as the relay is running behind, as ever.

Before he leaves, Skip likens the relay to his experience of marching as a soldier. "There is the creation of energy via synergy when you march," he explains. "As the precision movement of the group becomes sharper, a bond of harmony develops and individually you do not want to get out of sync, for fear of letting the group down. You have a responsibility to the group. You are not doing this for yourself but for something greater than you. There is power with each foot hitting the ground. Sometimes folks break out in chant or song because it truly can be joyful," he tells us, remembering his military days. He is right of course. As we speak, One Run For Boston is marching into morning, getting ever closer to Boston.

*****

The group stage in St. Louis is our first chance to meet John Pertzborn in person. The Fox Anchorman, who had at first questioned whether the relay was a hoax, before

Kate convinced him otherwise, had been promoting the relay with all his heart and is even running this stage himself. There are other news crews too, but they don't have their sneakers on. The flood risk has meant that we"ve had to shift the start of the stage down the road to the steps of the iconic St. Louis arch. It couldn't have been a more perfect location. Sometimes the universe aligns and things just happen for a reason, don't they?

A nice group is assembling, which is good because it means that our messages alerting everyone to the change of plan have got through. As we all gather waiting for Miles to arrive, we take turns to pose for photos under the arch with our giant stars and stripes flag. We meet Danny Howell and his wife. Danny is running to support Boston and in memory of his friend who died in Afghanistan. We spot the familiar faces of Dan Bohannon and Pete Leyva who have travelled up from the Ozarks to run another stage. We congratulate a couple who are newly engaged and 'ooh' and 'aah' at the sparkling diamond. And then, at the top of the steps underneath the arch, we see them. It's like a reverse Rocky moment, as the group of four run down the steps towards us, holding Miles aloft. I can feel myself welling up as I hear John Pertzborn behind me reporting live to camera,

"This is it, St. Louis!" he is saying excitedly into the microphone, "the relay has arrived at the Gateway Arch and now we are going to see the baton safely over the Mississippi river and into Illinois." I have to stifle the urge to jump in front of the camera and paraphrase that classic Anchorman sign-off, "Stay classy, St. Louis!" But Mary has told us that, if we play our cards right, Pertz might take us home with him so we can have a little siesta later on. I keep my feet firmly rooted to the ground and whoop and cheer the approaching runners instead.

Miles is passed into the hands of Linda and Eric Larson and with the TV cameras tracking their every move, they lead a torrent of royal blue T-shirts toward McKinley

Bridge. As we turn the first corner, a woman jumps out of her car, makes a kissy gesture in the air and bolts away from the vehicle to join our group.

"Are you here for the relay?" I hear Kate ask.

"Yes! Yes I am!" The woman blurts out breathlessly.

"Awesome stuff!" Kate says, slipping in beside our new recruit. "Don't worry, you haven't missed much." I have to laugh. I'm not sure I've heard Kate lie before.

I run along with a bag full of water bottles making sure Miles collects as many fingerprints as possible whilst Kate brings up the rear to ensure no-one is left behind. I run alongside Linda Larson while, 500m behind us, quite coincidentally, Kate runs next to Linda's husband, Eric. Over the next four miles we both listen, separately, to the same story told from two different perspectives.

At 5.30am on April 15, 2013, Linda left the hotel in Cambridge and made her way to Hopkinton for the start of her first ever Boston Marathon. Twelve years previously, she had been a slightly overweight, beer-drinking, middle-aged woman about to be blessed with her first grandchild. To have even got this far, was a big deal for Linda. At 10am, Eric left the same hotel with some friends and headed to the 26-mile marker to claim a good vantage point from which to see his wife finish her race. At 10.40am, Linda crossed the start line and was off and running.

"This being my first Boston Marathon," she tells me, "My goal was to have a good time, enjoy and take in all that the Boston spectators have to offer, and that is a lot!" The entire course, she explains to me, is filled with spectators. "They come in all ages and sizes, some dressed in costume, others holding signs, handing out fresh oranges, grapes, candy, popsicles, beer, high fives and kisses. Just when I felt like I couldn't go any further, their cheers would pick me up and 'lift' me to the next mile."

At mile 26, Eric watched as elite runners Kara Goucher and Shalane Flanagan crossed the finish.

"They easily glided by me like gazelles!" he tells Kate. "Linda qualified with a time of 4:07 so, when it came time, I started watching closely for her. The anticipation was incredible and my adrenaline was in overdrive with the anticipation of seeing my bride fulfill her dream. This is when I heard the first explosion," he explains. "I told the lady next to me, 'that can't be good!' but she just told me that transformers blow up all the time. When I smelled gunpowder, she replied, 'it's just sewers.' At about that time, there was a second explosion about 285 yards away and it was close enough that I felt, saw and tasted it. It took me a couple of minutes to digest what had just happened, but the first words out of my mouth were 'Fucking terrorists!'"

Chapter 20

With their ears ringing, and with no idea where to go, people ran. They ran in all directions. They ran for their lives. They didn't know if there would be another bomb. As pieces of shrapnel tore into the bodies of those around them, some wondered if a gunman was on the loose. Only one thought occupied the minds of most people and that was: Get me out of here.

Boston was in need of a superhero. But no caped crusader came. There was no masked defender of the city. No signal shone on the clouds, summoning assistance. It wasn't needed.

While buildings vibrated and debris filled the air, the superheroes who came were the runners, the other spectators, and the passers-by; regular people, with no known superpowers other than their selflessness and compassion. As people ran from the scene, these heroes fought the tide of bodies and, suppressing their natural instinct to flee, tried to help their fellow man.

At the site of the first bomb blast, Carlos Arredondo appeared in a cream cowboy hat. Carlos was born in Costa Rica and had spent his early years working as a Rodeo Clown, dodging aggressive bulls and occasionally leaping the odd fence or two, to save his life when the bulls got a bit too angry. On April 15, 2013, Carlos was back leaping fences again, only this time they were the barriers beside the Boston Marathon course and it was other people's lives he was saving. Landing in the road, Carlos began tearing down the barriers to allow the medical teams to access the injured. As the dust cleared and visibility was partially restored, he couldn't believe what he saw. Stepping over the bodies of the dead, Carlos saw people who'd had their limbs torn from their bodies and others with shrapnel wounds that gushed blood like running taps.

Arriving in America in 1980, and being granted amnesty by President Reagan in 1985, Carlos had begun training with the Red Cross, where he learnt skills that were desperately needed now. He moved from victim to victim doing what he could to help comfort them and stem the flow of blood. Then he saw Jeff Bauman.

Jeff Bauman, 27, had been waiting for his girlfriend to cross the finish line when the first bomb exploded, removing both his legs below the knee. Looking down at Jeff's graying face, Carlos pictured his two sons. His eldest, Lance Corporal Alexander Arredondo, had become a Marine and gone to Iraq. Carlos was proud of his boy but, like any parent would be, concerned for his safety. One day, Carlos was outside working in his garden when three Marines arrived in a truck. They had come to tell him that Alexander had been killed in battle. Overcome with emotion, Carlos told the Marines to leave but they insisted on staying with him. So Carlos snuck out the back door, went to his shed and picked up two canisters of gasoline that he used to power his lawn mower. He carried them over to the Marine's truck and splashed one canister around inside the cabin, leaving the other outside on the ground. Taking a seat inside the truck, Carlos struck a match and dropped it to the floor.

The cabin went up in flames that started to lick, and then devour, Carlos' skin. When the flames found the full tank of petrol there was an almighty explosion which shot Carlos out of the door and onto the ground. The Marines came running and Carlos' life was spared. But he suffered third degree burns on his arms, legs and face; and his heart was broken.

The news of his son's death impelled Carlos to become an anti-war campaigner and he forbade his youngest son, Brian, to sign up to the army. A week before Christmas 2011, Brian was found dead. The feelings of anger and guilt that he had felt since his brother's death had grown stronger each day until Brian had taken his own life.

Carlos was left devastated. He would often wonder why his life had been spared from the flames inside the Marines' truck. At 2.49pm on April 15th, the question was answered. Standing over the body of Jeff Bauman, Carlos had a reason to live. He tore the sleeve off his jersey and tied it round one of Jeff's legs. He got another helper to take off his belt to make a more effective tourniquet for the second leg. When the medics arrived they lifted Jeff into a wheelchair and ran him to one of the waiting ambulances. Carlos ran alongside, squeezing shut an artery that protruded from Jeff's leg.

Outside the Forum restaurant, America's former soccer goalkeeper, Matt Reis, was standing with his parents-in-law, Karen and John Odom, his brother-in-law and his family. They were all waiting for Matt's beautiful wife, Nicole, to finish the marathon.

The Odoms had travelled to Boston from California to watch their daughter run her first marathon. They had chosen to wait for her near the finish, so they could look on proudly and share her moment of joy as she crossed the line. The second blast knocked John to the ground and within seconds, the left leg of his pants was soaked with blood. Immediately Matt realized that the leg needed a tourniquet applied above the wound so he pulled his belt from around his waist and began tightening it around John's upper thigh.

When Matt and his family had left home that morning, he hadn't been wearing a belt. But as they headed out onto the street, they realized they'd forgotten the banners that the neighbors had made for them, painted with messages of support for Nicole. Matt ran back to the house to grab them and while there he decided to pop upstairs and get a belt for his trousers too. How very different things might have been, if he had not gone back home for the banners that morning!

John was taken to hospital by ambulance with his wife Karen. On arrival, he was placed in the care of Dr. Jeffrey Kalish. Kalish had been at the finish line too, supporting his wife who was running. After making sure she was safe, he had gone straight to the hospital. John suffered cardiac arrest twice on the operating table, and twice Dr. Kalish was able to save him. He broke five of John's ribs giving CPR and when asked about John's chances of survival, he was cautious.

"What do we do tomorrow?" John's wife asked Kalish when he left the operating theater.

"If I see you tomorrow, it's been a good night," he replied. "I have to tell you this. I don't know of anyone who has lost as much blood as John and survived."

Chapter 21

Standing beneath the 'Welcome to Illinois' sign on the far side of McKinley Bridge, I look back over the Mississippi River to St. Louis, cheering as the last few runners cross. A group of us attempt to spell out the letters of Illinois with our bodies but somehow only get as far as 'ILL.' "You look *ill*, Danny!" some clever person says, making everyone laugh. I don't doubt it. It feels like jet lag combined with being sat on by an elephant. It's not quite 8.30am, we have the whole day ahead of us, and that thought alone is making me feel quite sick.

As we've been hoping, Pertz scoops us up and takes us home to his house. This guy is on the TV every morning, he's clearly quite a local celebrity, and yet he doesn't bat an eyelid at opening his home to two scruffy, sleep-deprived Brits. We follow him in the Stink Mobile, feeling a bit apprehensive as it seems weird going to visit someone you've not met before, knowing that they know all you want to do is shower, sleep, eat and leave. Pertz doesn't seem to care though. In fact, I think he is quite enjoying himself. His wife is out of town for the weekend and he is at a loose end. Kate and I seem to be filling a hole in his Saturday morning, but not for long though, as we're about to pass out in his spare room.

If you stumbled upon Pertz's house in the middle of a country estate in England, you might think it was a genuine part of history. But the fact that the grand driveway, leading to his house, is lined with other similarly impressive-looking mansions, somewhat gives the game away. Nonetheless, Kate and I can't believe where we've come to when we pull up outside the Pertz residence. It is the kind of place that makes you remember to take your shoes off at the door. Pertz could not be more hospitable. He shows us a spare bedroom with a couple of beds and a shower room where we can get scrubbed up. He nips off for a couple of minutes, as we bring our bags in, and returns with a stack of fluffy, white towels. Honestly, if his viewers only knew what this guy was like at home, his ratings would soar even higher.

Leaving Kate to take a shower, I go online and post a few photos to Facebook from the night before. I include a couple of pictures in which I've discreetly planted Danbo's dad's duck and wonder if anyone will spot it. If they do, I tell them they can have a copy of my last book about my cycle ride to India. Kate is taking an age in the shower and whilst I'm online someone spots the duck and asks if I've heard of Boston Strong Ducks. I click on the link but Kate distracts me. She creeps back in the room with a look of horror on her face.

"I have totally wrecked Pertz's bathroom!" she whispers loudly, pulling one of the Wallace and Gromit faces she does so well.

"You've done what?" I say. "How?"

She drags me along to the bathroom to take a look. She hasn't quite wrecked it but she's had a pretty good go. The rail that is supposed to be holding the shower curtain is lying on the floor and there is a lot of water everywhere.

"What on earth did you do?" I ask, picking up the rail and curtain and working out how to get it back on the wall.

"I'm not really sure," she says. "One minute I was standing there enjoying the nice hot water and the next thing I know I'm toppling over and I had to grab hold of the rail to stop me falling out of the shower. I guess I must have fallen asleep in there."

I manage to repair the damage and just hope that maybe the rail was a bit loose anyway. I have a shower, avoiding all contact with the curtain and rail, and clean my teeth in front of the mirror. It's not a pretty sight. I realize how sitting in the car for such long periods of time has rounded my posture. My normally strong back and chest have curved to fit the shape of the car seat and my muscles have deteriorated, leaving sharp, angular bones protruding from my shoulders and ribs. I look years older than normal. I haven't been eating enough and am literally living on hugs. I read a journal once that said humans need twelve hugs a day to thrive. I believe it and I try to stick to it in my own life. Since the relay began, Kate and I had been giving and receiving hundreds of sweaty hugs a day. Without the hugs, I know we simply wouldn't have survived this far.

After our nap, unaware of Kate's earlier efforts to trash his bathroom, Pertz pulls out all the stops to serve us up a super tasty lunch before we hit the road once more. There is even some English tea in a proper china pot. This guy has class, no doubt about it. We collect our shoes at the front door, climb back in Stink and head off down the drive, waving madly at Pertz until long after he has disappeared back inside his house. Then it starts to rain; big fat, heavy rain.

*****

It buckets down on the windscreen, forcing me to slow down so the wipers can catch up. It is even wetter than the Texan storm we'd driven through following Gary a few nights before, only minus the thunder and lightning …almost. Right on cue, we hear a rumble of thunder followed by an all-too-familiar flash of white. This cannot be fun to run in. We catch up with a runner sporting a yellow polythene poncho.

"You OK?" I shout above the sound of raindrops landing like bullets on the roof of the car. "Do you need any water?!" I ask, puckishly. He looks at me without saying a word, but I get a slight hint of a grin. Kate tells me I am lucky not to get two fingers.

"How are you feeling?" I ask Kate as we plough through the puddles in search of the next hand-off location.

"Pretty rubbish," she says, "You?"

"Yeah, not great. I was hoping that nap at Pertz's place would have perked me up. But I think it's done the opposite. I feel dreadful."

"Maybe Pertz put something dodgy in our tea?" Kate jokes. I don't even have the energy to muster a laugh. "What are you thinking?" Kate asks me.

"I think we need to get a good night's sleep. What time is it now?"

"About 3 o'clock."

"What say we call it a day," I suggest. "I can probably manage another hour before it's game over for me. Let's just drive on now and find a hotel." I'm testing the water. Even though I know she's completely done in too, I'm pretty certain there's no way Kate is going to go for this idea. At best I'm hoping she'll agree we ought to stop a little earlier than normal and get a proper night's sleep tonight. But as soon as the words are out of my mouth I see Kate's face flood with relief.

"Cracking idea," she says, "let's do it." I've barely driven a mile before Kate's head is lolling by her chest and she is fast asleep.

I decide it's time to treat ourselves. We're going to splash a little cash on somewhere to stay. I pull off the interstate at Terre Haute and park up outside the Holiday Inn. We sleepwalk in to the lobby, check-in and go to find our room, already dreaming of fluffy pillows and the twelve hour sleep we plan to have. Our room is on the first floor, but in order to get to it we must navigate our way through the gigantic leisure complex which takes up most of the ground floor. We walk round and round the kid-infested swimming pool searching for a way out. The noise is deafening and disorientating. Playful shrieks and screams bounce off the walls and ricochet around the five-storey high, glass atrium. I'm beginning to think that there may not be a way out, when we spot a wooden staircase behind a large display of tropical plants. We clamber up the stairs and end up on a walkway that circles the entire atrium, overlooking the pool. The back wall of the walkway is made up of floor-to-ceiling windows and numbered doors. Stopping beside another flight of stairs leading up to a second identical walkway, I realize that every room in the hotel faces out onto the whirlpool of screaming children below. Finding our room, we shut ourselves inside. The door does little to deaden the noise from downstairs and I collapse on the bed with my ears ringing. Any hopes I might have had of peacefully snoozing the afternoon away are disappearing fast. I collapse face down on my bed and pull a pillow over my head, holding it tight against my ears to block out the noise. Shutting my eyes I wonder how the hell I'm going to sleep through this. Ten seconds later, I am sleeping like a baby.

I wake up fourteen hours later, completely befuddled. I've no idea where I am or what I'm supposed to be doing. Assuming I'm on holiday, I roll over, shutting my eyes again. But as my lids close I catch sight of another body in the room. It's pitch black, but I can just about make out the outline of someone looking at their phone. Think Dan, think. Who can it be? Did I get lucky last night? If I did, I can't remember any of it, let alone her name. This could be awkward. Maybe if I go back to sleep she'll just leave, saving us both any embarrassment. But what if she's really hot? What a wasted opportunity that would be. I decide to chance it and sit up.

"Morning..?" I say, more as an inquiry than a greeting.

"Oh good you're awake," says a familiar voice. "Listen, we had better get going. We've got a birthday party to get to."

"A birthday party? What time is it?" I ask, confused.

"Nine o'clock," the voice replies.

"AM or PM?"

"Jesus, Danny!" Without warning the lamp goes on. "Are you OK?"

I'm not sure. "I think you just blinded me!" I yelp, blinking frantically. Eventually, the room comes into view and I see Kate staring at me, dressed in her One Run For Boston T-shirt and ready to get going. I'm disappointed to find that she's not some girl I pulled last night. But at the same time it's quite a relief. It means there's no awkward morning-after chitter-chatter required.

"Whose birthday is it?" I ask.

"I'm not entirely sure," Kate says. "I think it's someone called Cheryl. She's running the stage into Terre Haute this morning. Marta Mason's organizing it all. It's going to be an English tea party themed birthday celebration! They said there'd be cake." Kate didn't need to say another word. I was up and out the door in less time than it takes to boil a kettle.

Marta and her team have chosen to host the tea party on the grass outside the courthouse in Terra Haute. They've brought a table along and furnished it with a lace cloth, vases of flowers and plates full of scones and cakes. I take a swig of tea out of a dainty china cup and immediately realize that it is not only black, it is ice cold. I glance over at Kate as she lifts her cup to her mouth. I know that she'll be expecting the tea to be hot, if not milky, and her face is a picture as she takes a gulp of the cold black liquid. In pride of place on the table is a framed photo of the Duchess of Cambridge, and Marta's friends bombard us with questions about the recent royal wedding and the royal baby that they say is due soon. Neither Kate nor I are clued up on such matters and I sense we're a disappointment in this department. I try to make up for this by telling a story about one of my best buddies who is a bit posh like Kate and went to university with the royal couple at St. Andrews in Scotland. She once danced with Will and her boobs fell out of her dress as he swung her round. Come to think of it, she was probably swinging him round. OK, so maybe she's not all that posh. Without a doubt, the Royal Family is far more popular in the US than back home in the UK. Barring a minority of patriotic older women, including my Grandma, we Brits don't really follow the Royal Family with too much passion. In my eyes they're just another family who live in a big house down the road.

The finale to the birthday party is a giant bunny cake. At least it was shaped like a bunny before it hopped from the front seat into the foot well of the car on the way over. It now looks more like road kill, but that doesn't stop me diving in for seconds and thirds. The green grass icing is particularly delicious. Fired up on sugar and E-numbers, we hug the women good bye and sing Cheryl another chorus of 'Happy Birthday' before bundling back into Stink.

*****

Cheryl's stage had brought Miles across the border from Illinois into Indiana, our eighth state. We were certainly rattling through them now. In less than twenty-four hours we should be in Ohio and then there will be just six more days before we are due in Boston.

This realization prompts me to think about all the runners we have met so far and the ones that are coming up shortly. Excluding the group stage in Indianapolis, thirteen of the next fifteen stages across Indiana are going to be run by men. This is contrary to what has been the case in the rest of the relay and I point out this fact to Kate.

"You and your girls Danny," Kate said, "When are we going to find you a girlfriend?" Poor Kate has had to put up with my daily musings on the runners I liked the look of, but barring the occasional bit of banter in response to the odd topless male, and some chat concerning Kevin

Spacey, she has remained fairly tight-lipped and professional in this department.

Kate is of course a happily married woman, but to pass the time I'm keen to find out if any of the runners we've met so far have ticked Kate's boxes. It's clear she's not in the mood to play along with my little game.

"Go on," I say, refusing to give up. "There must be someone who's made your heart flutter. I promise I won't tell Steve."

"You only want me to play along to help you feel less of a pervert," she retorts. She certainly has a way with words.

"Don't be so silly," I answer back. "It's only a game." I can see the next runner up ahead and have an idea. "What's this fella's name?" I ask Kate, pointing to the pile of crumpled papers on her lap.

"It should be Greg Pottorff," she says. I wait a few seconds.

"OK, so have a look out of your window and tell me on a scale of one to ten, how fit is Greg?" Kate looks at me disgusted. "Let me out," she says, "I'm going to see if he needs some water." I pull in and leave Kate to get the water out of the back while I take a peek at Greg in the rear view mirror as he approaches the car. He looks younger than us, a rugged-looking pretty boy. I'd give him eight out of ten if anyone asked for my opinion.

I watch in the mirror as Kate hands Greg the water. He takes a sip, then pours the bottle over his head, drenching his T-shirt so that it clings tightly to his chest. We're halfway up a long hill and Greg looks a little knackered, but I can hear him and Kate laughing, so I assume he must be good to carry on. He's taking his time though and I'm about to go and see what's happening when Greg runs past me modeling his newly wet T-shirt. Kate's face appears at my window grinning, a magical glint in her eyes, and she mouths the word "Nine," at me before pursuing Greg up the road with more water.

After stopping every half-mile to check Greg wanted for nothing, Kate ajumps in and we cruise ahead to meet Mickey Reigeluth, the brother-in-law of Amy Horton, whom we'd met back in Arizona with her husband, Shawn. Standing by the roadside in front of one of Indiana's many, many cornfields, Mickey asks us about our road trip and, in particular, what our favorite meal has been along the way. Barring a couple of delicious home-cooked meals and the pizza that Bill and co. had delivered to us in the middle of rural Oklahoma, we struggle to come up with any other memorable feasts. We explain how we had tried to buy fresh vegetables from a couple of supermarkets, but the veg. had soon rotted in our inadequate polystyrene cooler, forcing us to abandon that idea pretty quickly.

"I guess we've pretty much been living off whatever we can find at gas stations," I admit.

"Yeah, we've eaten a lot of burritos and Danny's drunk his weight in root beer," Kate adds. I can see Mickey's mind working away and I wonder what he's thinking, but Miles arrives before I can ask and within seconds they're both gone.

All this talk of food reminds us that we had better get a proper meal in, before the group stage in Indianapolis tonight. On the outskirts of the city, our burrito radar kicks in and we find a Mexican restaurant offering free Wifi. Perfect. I log in to Facebook and find we've been tagged in hundreds photos, messages and posts. Working through as many of the notifications as possible, I look to see how many I have still to answer. The number is now higher than it was before we started. We realize answering all the messages is an impossible task. How Mary manages to keep on top of everything, I simply do not know.

Giving up on responding to emails I do some research on these Boston Strong Ducks that are all over Facebook. Little yellow rubber ducks with a stars and stripe flag and a message stamped across them 'Boston Strong.' As I delve deeper I find the woman behind the ducks called Lori

Tosches. Like us she'd wanted to do something for the people of Boston. She was sick of the media focusing on the bombers, and our tendency as a human race to hate rather than love. She started a Facebook group to share the positive stories that emerged from the aftermath of the Boston bombings. She focused on the stories of people like Carlos, who had gone to the aid of those struck by the blasts, and the inspirational survivors.

Many of the amputees were making such huge steps physically and metaphorically towards their recovery. Lori tried to keep the group free of any talk about the bombing suspects. I was trying to do the same with our own Facebook group and page. I wanted everyone to focus on the positivity.

Inspired by a gift of 500 rubber ducks that brought emotional healing to the children after the Sandy Hook Massacre, Lori decided she would use the same tool to try and help Boston heal. She made a tag for the ducks that read:

"I am a Boston Strong Duck. Please perform a Random Act of Kindness and pass me on. Please take a photo with me, and post it on www.facebook.com/bostonstrongducks"

The ducks were Lori's way of encouraging people to be good to each other. She started by putting the ducks on the start line in Hopkinton and then gave them away to people. Before she knew it, pictures were coming in from all over the state of Massachusetts and soon from states all over America. People would take a picture of themselves with the duck, then do a good dead for a friend, neighbor or stranger and left the duck as a calling card, encouraging them to do the same.

I think that this is brilliant and drop her a message. No sooner do I hit send I have a response from Lori giving me more information.

"I would reach out to some of the injured when I found contact information and ask their permission to

220

post updates. I got to know many on a very personal level. I have always maintained a certain level of trust. I have been given a special gift. They shared things with me that were not shared in the media. There have been many nights that I have chatted online with several of the injured. Nights can be very hard for them and having someone just checking on them at 3:00am helped. It also gave me a personal connection to these perfect strangers who became dear friends. I would send them ducks.

"They all would get such a kick out of the photos and were so truly grateful to have their information shared. It was one of those chats that brought me to one of the severely injured, Jarrod Clowery."

Jarrod was the man who'd jumped the fence to help the victims before the second blast went off right underneath him. Lori continued, "He could not sleep and we chatted online for well over an hour. He was scared, in pain and feeling lost. We were both laughing by the end of the chat. He asked me to come see him in the hospital. The next day I went and even used a secret code to visit. Even though we were strangers he greeted me with a warm hug.

He told me to 'Please, keep doing what you are doing. You helped me so much and I want you to know that. I want you to know what you are doing is good. It is helping. Don't Stop.' It felt so amazing."

On the way home from that hospital visit Lori felt numb. It was all so crazy. With every duck request came a story. People felt connected. People were seeing the good.

There were so many requests for ducks. Lori didn't say no to anyone. During a Disney vacation that her family had been planning for ages, her daughter offered to help write 'Boston Strong' on all the ducks to help her fulfill all the orders. Without them it wouldn't have been possible.

Unknown to me, Lori was in fact already talking with Jamie and had helped us get some great exposure in the media. She had also been speaking with a few people she had been supporting, to see if they wanted to meet us at the finish in Boston. I am excited to think that Lori could be the person to help us reach out to some of the people the relay was all about and involve them in the finish of One Run For Boston.

Back in the Mexican, Kate's mind is also on the finish as she takes a call from Jamie. He is worried that with over 600 runners signed up to run the final stages in Boston, we still haven't got the necessary permits from the authorities.

"Tell him I think we should just go ahead without the permits," I say to Kate, loud enough for Jamie to hear. "I can't see how the police can stop us. They can try and arrest us, but where would they put us all? I doubt they've got enough cells to accommodate all 600 of us."

Kate relays this to Jamie, but it is clear from the conversation that he does not share my point of view. All this ticking boxes, dotting I's and crossing T's is not my thing, as I've explained, and I leave Kate to it and turn my attention back to Facebook.

Some way below the pictures of Kate and me standing with John Pertz, is a photo of a girl, proudly wearing her official T-shirt with the signature red shorts that have become a key part of the One Run For Boston uniform. She is looking into the camera but suddenly it feels like she is looking at me. There is something about this picture, this girl; I can feel myself getting pulled into the frame. My heart skips a beat and time stands still for a moment. Suddenly realizing I've been holding my breath, I gasp for air and Kate looks over from her phone call to make sure I'm OK. I give her the thumbs up, and then turn back to my lap top. This girl is still there, looking at me. She's pretty for sure, but there's more to her than that. I can feel her energy and I swear it feels like I can see into her soul. There's a look in her eyes, something about the way she stands, something about those shorts. I kick myself for coming for food when I should have been meeting the runners. I should have been meeting her... I glance up to the name above the post. I should have been meeting Joan Meagher.

*****

Distracting me, the owner of the restaurant comes over to introduce herself as Sally, and tells us that our meal is on the house. She has seen the relay on the TV news and gives us free meal vouchers to pass on to our runners. Heading outside for a cigarette, she runs back in seconds later. Running over to our table she breathlessly shouts, "I can see them!" she takes a deep intake of air, "They're running this way!"

Running outside with my camera, I sit on the curbside snapping pictures of the runners as they go by. It's getting dark and I'm not sure I've caught anything more than the fluorescent blur of their vests so I look back over the photos to check. In the first photo the runners are nothing more than small shadows in the distance. In the second photo they are closer, yet blurred. But the third picture is a peach; three runners perfectly synchronized mid-stride. Suddenly I realize I recognize one of the faces. I take a closer look, zooming in on the runner on the far side of the road. Is it? It is! It's the girl from Facebook, Joan Meagher.

Chapter 22

I pick up some water bottles from the car and sprint after them. It's not easy to run with three bottles and a camera round your neck, but I manage to catch them up and jump in front to give them the water. Joan throws her arms around me and hugs me tightly. I'm left dumb. I can't speak. But a smile has spread across my face like the Cheshire Cat. Hugging Garvin and Kristin, Joan's fellow runners, I feel the *Dannyness* that has been missing for the last few days returning.

I hate to do it, but for the sake of the relay I must tell them to get going. Visibly energized and inspired by their mid-run hugs the group disappears down the road at a rate of knots, twice as fast as before, and in the distance I catch Kristin saying, "Do you think we could slow down a little?"

Collecting Kate and my laptop from the restaurant we race ahead to the next hand-off. We arrive in time to see Joan, Garvin and Kristin holding each other in a three-way hug that seems to last forever. Tears are falling from Joan's eyes. My heart is melting. Joan turns to hug Kate and then me. I feel like I have been plugged in to a power socket. I may never know what has passed between our two souls, but at this moment I know that I don't want this embrace to end – ever. My energy levels have been restored and I have never felt better.

There is one more stage to go before the Indianapolis group stage which Joan and Garvin are also running. So we make our way in convoy to the group assembly point, which would have been at the Indiana Tower had it actually existed. When Kate first plotted the route she had noticed the tower marked on Google maps and assumed it would be a well-known local landmark that would make a good meeting point for the group stage. As soon as the stages went live on the website, we started getting emails from people asking what and where the Indiana Tower was. Kate couldn't understand it. How could anyone living in Indianapolis not know? The 750ft high obelisk must surely dominate the skyline. But a quick internet search soon revealed that the Indiana Tower had never actually been built. The building had been put forward as part of the plan to give Indianapolis a facelift. But the design, which many locals thought looked like a corncob, failed to get support and the plan was ultimately scrapped. Google Maps had obviously got a bit ahead of themselves.

Kate had also intended for the route to follow the riverside trail beside the zoo, until someone kindly pointed out that the trail actually went through the zoo and was closed at night when the group stage would be happening. Luckily for us, a local runner, Ed Cooning, had stepped in to rework the route and take charge of the stage. He had done an awesome job. By the time we arrive, holding glow-in-the-dark fairy wands for no reason other than that we are starting to lose our minds, over sixty runners are already waiting with Ed at the hand-off location. The local media are out in force, with TV cameras at the ready and newspaper reporters poised with notebooks in hand. There is quite a hubbub as the runners introduce themselves to each other, chat excitedly and take photos. But as Kate and I approach the group, everyone falls silent as they turn to look at us. It actually makes me feel quite uncomfortable. Irrationally, I wonder if I have food on my face – always possible - or maybe I've forgotten to put on my shorts, another distinct possibility since my memory is shocking. I've driven to cycle races without my bike before. I've run to work only to arrive and find I had forgotten to pack my shirt and trousers. I am just starting to panic when the silence is broken by someone shouting, "It's Danny and

Kate!" and the crowd starts to cheer and clap. We feel, and no doubt look, a little ridiculous wondering through the parking lot at midnight clutching our luminous fairy wands, but no one seems to care.

I hear another voice behind me say, "isn't that Joan from Boston?" and I watch as every single runner in the crowd walks up to hug, high five and kiss her. I can't help but do the same while wondering why everyone here knows who Joan from Boston is and I don't.

Miles is running two hours late and, as we wait for him to arrive, Joan asks me if she can say a few words to the group.

"Go ahead!" I say, relieved. I can sense the crowd is waiting for someone to say something and I would rather it be Joan than me. Joan asks if I can get everyone's attention. Now, that I can do! A piercing whistle and a loud shout later and all eyes are on me. I step aside for Joan to talk.

"I just want to thank you all for being here, for taking time out of your lives to come together for such an amazing cause." I cannot take my eyes off Joan as she talks straight from the heart, barely able to hang on to her emotions. "What you are doing, what this relay is doing, is helping me and so many others back home in Boston start to heal. Your support is overwhelming and so very much appreciated. Thank you."

As soon as Joan has finished speaking, someone spots a headlamp across the parking lot. Miles is almost upon us. Instinctively we form two lines, creating our very own scream tunnel. Holding Miles in one hand, and high-fiving with the other, Talha Khan runs down the middle of the tunnel and we cheer him like we would an Olympic champion.

Escorted by Ed's team of marshals, the group wends its way out onto a canal path that is so pristine it is hard to believe we are in the middle of a city and not a well kept theme park. Compared to London's ancient canal paths, this place feels positively futuristic. I find myself in the middle of the pack, moving Miles forward, quicker than normal, in an effort to catch up with those red shorts up in front. Eventually I make it to the front, leaving Miles to fend for himself while I run and chat with Joan. There is so much I want to ask her. Why on earth has she flown a thousand miles to run in Indianapolis when the relay will finish in her home town of Boston? And why has One Run For Boston had such an emotional effect on her?

"It's almost impossible to explain just how important One Run For Boston has been for me, how it has forever changed me," she tells me. "My story begins long before Marathon Monday."

Joan ran a lot in high school but stopped running altogether not long after she joined the Army. When she moved back to Boston in 2009, she started running again and soon confided in her mum that she wanted to qualify for Boston.

"My mom got a twinkle in her eye," Joan remembers, "She said that she would come and watch me run if I ever ran Boston." Little did Joan know that when she would finally get the chance to run Boston, her mum would not be alive to watch her. In December 2009, Joan took a call from her Dad. Joan's mother had been diagnosed with small cell lung cancer. "Now, working in an industry surrounded by scientists and doctors, I knew this was bad news," Joan tells me. "Small cell lung cancer is a guaranteed death sentence. It was not a matter of if, but when she would die."

One of Joan's siblings was out of town and the other two had issues which had led them away from their mum. Joan knew she was all her parents had and told them she'd do whatever was needed to help them get through the difficult weeks and months ahead. She went to the hospital with her mum for every scan and supported her through three cycles of aggressive chemotherapy. When she learned that the cancer had spread to a number of other organs,

Joan put her own life on hold to be with her mum. "I stopped running, stopped spending time with my friends and rearranged my work schedule so I could work from home to be with her," Joan explains. She skipped her first marathon which made her mum mad because she knew how hard Joan had trained and didn't want to be the reason she gave up the race. So Joan made a promise to her. "I told her, 'I'll make you a deal. I'll miss the Disney marathon this year because of you, and I'll run Boston next year because of you.'"

After Joan's mum decided to stop the chemo, she was moved to a hospice and Joan spent every single moment with her there. "The days were hectic and stressful because my mom's family is huge – she has 22 siblings and just about all of them have kids – so managing the crowd of visitors was a challenge," Joan says, staring straight ahead. "But the nights were brutal. Everyone would go home and I would stay with mom. Sleeping was impossible, because the act of dying is not really peaceful, no matter what the hospice nurses wanted me to think, and mom fought death the entire way. The nurses explained to me that mom was experiencing terminal delirium. I witnessed many things during those overnights that I wish I had never seen and those images are forever burned into my memory."

We're running pace for pace. Surrounded by runners on every side, I can only see Joan. Shortly after midnight on April 5th 2013, Joan's mum passed away. With her four children reunited around her, she took her last, shallow breath and was gone. Joan was inconsolable. "Four months of being strong, four months of holding it all in and four nights alone with mom watching her die, it all came crashing to the surface," she says. Over the next few days, as the family made arrangements with the funeral home, Joan was still unable to sleep or eat. "I was completely exhausted and running on fumes. My dad pulled me aside and told me how worried he was about me. He knew that if something didn't change I was going to crash and burn." Joan's dad reminded her that in just a few days she was due to be volunteering at the Boston Marathon with her friends. Since moving back to Boston, Joan hadn't missed a Marathon Monday. "Dad knew how much I enjoyed being at the marathon. He knew it was just what I needed to help pull me out of the deep despair that I was in. He insisted that I go, promising me that I would feel better if I went."   And next year she wouldn't be volunteering; she had a promise to uphold to her mum.

On race day, Joan travelled to Newton with a carload of friends. "My friends were so uplifting and I started to feel a little less sad, but thoughts of mom kept popping into my head and I couldn't stop the flow of tears that seemed to steadily pour out of my eyes." When they got to Newton they made their way to mile 17 and the Power Gel stop they would be manning for the day. "I got pumped to see the wheelchair athletes fly by and before long the elite women led by two Americans, Kara Goucher and Shalane Flanagan! I couldn't help but smile and somewhere along the line, I stopped crying."

But it was when the regular Janes and Joes started coming by that Joan really got lost in the moment. "These ordinary people were doing something extraordinary. I could feel my heart swell and a permanent smile on my face as I got swept up in the excitement of it all and started to feel alive again." Joan spent the next few hours cheering and shouting out names on runners' bibs while tossing packets of Power Gel to those stuck in the middle of the mob, unable to make their way over to her. She felt the sweat of runners' hands as they grabbed gels from her hands and saw the excitement on their faces and thought, "This is why I am here. This is the reason I volunteered – all these awesome courageous people. Through their smiles, their pain, their exhaustion, excitement, sweat and tears, they were making me feel connected again."

With the last of the runners safely through, Joan and her friends cleaned up all the empty packets of gel, took down the signs and removed the barriers. As they piled into the car to go home, Joan's phone rang. It was her ex-fiancé.

"Tell me you're not at the finish line," he said. Joan couldn't hear what he said next because the girls in the car were talking so loudly, still pumped from their marathon experience. Totally out of character, she *shushed* her friends and asked her ex to repeat what he said. This time she heard him loud and clear, "Two bombs have gone off at the finish line."

What was supposed to be a day of healing, a day of inspiration, turned into a day of unspeakable horrors.

"I can't begin to describe the terror I was feeling, that we were all feeling. So many of our friends were running whose families would have been waiting for them at the finish. I will never, never forget that awful feeling in my stomach when I heard someone I knew, a friend of mine, was directly impacted by this unimaginable act of terrorism."

Her friend and running buddy had been running the marathon. Her friend's partner and three year old son had been at the finish line, waiting for her. The blast went off right beside them. Both were rushed to hospital with injuries and unfortunately her husband lost his leg that day.

In the days that followed the marathon bombings, Joan closed herself off from everyone. "I didn't want to talk, I stopped 'living' and just started going through the motions. I became a shell of myself, overwhelmed with emotion and pain – unbearable sadness over the loss of my mom, fear for my friend's family and sympathy beyond words for all of the other victims. I tried to get on with life, tried not to think about everything but I couldn't get it out of my mind. Horrible, horrific images from the bombings scrolled through my head, combined with the awful memories of the final week of mom's life. I felt so incredibly alone and lost hope that I would ever feel normal again."

Running, which had been a source of comfort for Joan became something she struggled with and dreaded. "It was too much time alone with my own thoughts and I couldn't erase the images that kept flickering through my mind." Joan slows her pace a little and for the first time since I'd caught up with her she turns her head to look at me. Her eyes lock with mine for a moment and I am suddenly aware that I have spent the last four miles running with my head turned 90 degrees, unable to take my eyes off her. Joan has captivated me with her honesty and openness. My soul is in thrall to hers. We have reached the canal end and follow the path around the basin to run back in the opposite direction on the other side. I deliberately slow my pace, afraid that we will reach the hand-off before Joan has finished her story. Silently, I will her to continue. She holds my gaze and tells me, "Then suddenly, in an instant my life was completely changed. One Run For Boston began." From the moment it started, Joan had followed the progress of each and every runner, unable to tear herself away. "Before I realized what was happening, I was completely drawn in to this crazy, ridiculous relay. One Run For Boston and everything it stood for began to replace so much sadness with happiness, fear with triumph, despair with hope. So many horrible images and memories etched in my mind were being replaced with funny, inspiring stories and photos from the relay."

As Miles made his way from city to city, state to state, Joan was moved by the displays of enthusiastic support from runners all over the country and felt inspired to jump in. "For the first time in my life, I didn't think about what I was doing. No over-analyzing, no second thoughts. On an absolute whim I opened the One Run For Boston registration page and looked at where the relay was headed next." Joan clicked on Indiana and sent a message to Garvin Adamson, lead runner for stage 215, introducing herself and asking if he would like some company on his stage. Of course Garvin had said he would love some company and they decided to sign up for the group stage together too. Three days later, in the very early hours of a muggy Indiana morning, Joan is leading the group on the final mile of stage 217 and I feel privileged to be running with her.

At the hand-off, Joan kisses Miles goodbye, promising they'll meet again in Boston. Side-by-side, we stand and cheer every last runner home. I grab Joan and ask Kate if she'll take a photo of us together. Taking the camera, she assumes I want a group photo and starts gesturing for others to join us. I manage to stop her in time saying, "No, no. Just me and Joan."

It's gone one in the morning, but more than half the group stays to chat and take photos. No one wants the night to end, least of all me. Something very special is happening and my head is clearer than it's been for days. I see how everyone here, not just Joan, is taking strength from what's been created. Together we are raising a lot of money to help those impacted by the bombings, yes. But, more incredibly, One Run For Boston has become a powerful movement of positivity that has brought strangers together and formed bonds that will be hard to break. I'm enjoying a rare moment of clarity as I recognize that the risks we have taken and the enormous pressure we have put ourselves under to get this far have all been worth it.

It's just as well, because it's not over yet and there are six more days to go before we get Miles to Boston.

Chapter 23

Eventually we drag ourselves away from the group and head back to Stink. Crossing the deserted car park, Kate suddenly remembers that Talha Khan, the runner before the group stage, had offered us a place to stay tonight. It's almost two in the morning and we've dallied so long chatting that there's no sight of Talha, he must have gone home. As we get nearer to Stink, I reach in my pocket for the keys and press the button. The doors unlock and as the lights flash we see a figure waiting by our car.

"Do you guys still want to come back with me?" the voice says. It's Talha. We cannot believe he has waited all this time for us. Kate and I look at each other in happy amazement. "Yes, please!" we shout in unison, before starting to apologize. But Talha could not be more understanding and we are soon back at his place, tucking into watermelon from the fridge while setting several alarm clocks to wake us up in three hours' time.

*****

We get up at 5.30am to support Texan fly-in Sean Maguire on stage 222. Searching for something that might help get us through the day, we have a little rifle through the bag of goodies given to us by Tracy Wall in Missouri. There are a number of cleaning and washing products that we discard, then I pull out a stash of random stick-on mustaches! I am a great fan of mustaches. Until recently, I sported a pretty nifty handlebar mustache, like a circus strongman without the muscles. I would take great pleasure in waxing either end to an even curl each morning. My mustache attracted many strange looks but also had its fair number of admirers and became a bit of an obsession amongst some of my friends who couldn't resist the urge to buy me mustache-themed merchandise at every opportunity. Thanks to my mustache, I am now the owner of a mustachioed jumper, iphone cover and socks. But far and away my favorite novelty gift is the Powertache card game. Think Top Trumps but with mustaches instead of cars or football players. Playing that game was a revelation. The gents whose facial hair features on those cards have taken mustache-growing to an entirely new level. They have made it into an art form. Immediately inspired, I began wondering where my mustache would take me next. I was heading down the path of a Salvador Dali or Fu Man Chu, when one fateful night I rashly ended it all.

Waking up at 3am, with half a soggy mustache halfway down my throat, I got out of bed and shaved it all off. It's a decision I've been regretting ever since. So when faced with a packet of six ready-to-wear mustaches I know only too well the power it contains and Kate doesn't need much persuading. I select a neat little Hercule Poirot while Kate goes all out with a bushy Texan number, in honor of Sean's home state. We pop on the cowboy hats that we'd picked up in Amarillo to complete the look.

Feeling pretty pleased with ourselves, we rock up outside a whitewashed US Post Office building in the middle of nowhere and introduce ourselves to Sean. I am thrilled to see that he is himself sporting a most excellent homegrown mustache of his own. Until, that is, it occurs to me that being an authentic facial hair wearing gent, Sean might wrongly assume that with our stick-ons we are making fun of him. Luckily, he barely bats an eyelid. Sean tells us that he flew into Indianapolis late last night, picked up a rental car and has been following the relay since about 3am. He is surviving on 5-Hour Energy Shots and knocks out twelve quick miles to get us to Dublin.

By the time we've waved the next runner on her way and said goodbye to Sean, Kate and I are so hungry our mustaches are drooping. Needing some grub, and fast, we ask a passerby to direct us to the best breakfast joint in town. A few minutes later, we're sitting amongst a noisy bunch of regulars in a busy little café poring over the menu. Immediately, the old guy next to us strikes up a conversation and, perhaps worried he will scare us off, the waitress hurries over to shush him and take our order.

"What can I get you today?" she asks, pen and paper at the ready. I fancy eggs on toast and ask her to run me through the many different styles of egg on offer. I already know exactly what I'm going to have but never tire of hearing all the quirky names that Americans have for their eggs, especially fried ones. "Over easy, over medium, over hard, sunny side up…" the words drip from her tongue like a runny yolk. After she seems to run out, I order what I wanted initially, scrambled.

"And for you?" the waitress asks Kate who still has her nose buried in the menu.

"Oooh, I don't know. What would you have?" Kate asks her. My mouth practically drops to the floor as I hear this. This is definitely not a Kate thing to say.

"I'm over easy every time," the waitress says. The man beside us barely manages to stifle a snigger.

"Sounds great, I'll have mine over easy too please," says Kate, giving me a grin, eyes twinkling. As soon as the waitress turns her back to take our order through to the kitchen, the man beside us starts chatting again. If you met him in an English bar, you'd know him as the local drunk, the sort of guy who'll talk to anyone about anything, but usually himself, for hours on end. But this guy appears to be totally sober and it is fun sitting back listening to his life story. Our breakfasts come and go and he eventually turns the conversation to us, pointing at our T-shirts and asking what two Brits could possibly be doing in the middle of rural Indiana. We fill him in and when we've finished ask for the check.

"I'm getting this," our new friend tells the waitress, holding out a twenty dollar bill.

"Oh, it's already taken care of," she replies smiling. She looks at our baffled faces and explains, "Your eggs are on the house."

We thank them both and leave the café, once more marveling at the kindness of strangers. Turning the corner we hear a shout from behind and look back to see the man from the café rushing towards us.

"Hold on!" he calls.

I look at Kate and whisper, "Hang about, you've got an admirer!" She gives me one of those glares. The guy is out of breath and unsteady on his feet so we jog back towards him. Catching his breath, he pulls his hand from his pocket and hands Kate a twenty dollar bill. "I couldn't pay for your breakfast so I'd like to make a donation to your charity instead," he gasps. We thank him enthusiastically but he raises his hand to silence us. "It's nothing, really," he says, and turns to stagger back to the café.

*****

In Centreville, Indiana, we meet Jason Williams, his wife and their three impossibly polite kids. They seem to have things sussed and so, once the customary hand-off photos have been taken, we drive off and leave them to it, hoping to catch a cheeky nap up ahead. But as we look at the map, working out where Jason is due to finish up, we spot the state line between Indiana and Ohio and know we cannot miss Miles being carried over into state number nine.

"Aren't you supposed to be sleeping?" Jason shouts as he approaches the border.

"Yeah, we scrapped that," I shout back. "Welcome to Ohio!"

I had assumed that as we got closer and closer to Boston and the likelihood of finishing became more probable, Kate and I would find it easier to take a step back and detach ourselves from the relay. But I was wrong. Although we're both asleep on our feet, it still feels like our baby and we can't shake off the parental instinct to watch over and protect. It is always hard to leave Miles, even though we have nothing left to give.

Stumbling blindly on throughout the hot afternoon, we meet and greet on autopilot. I remember being taught that 'wicked pissah' means 'really awesome' if you live in Massachusetts, and that it didn't sound right tripping off Kate's tongue.

"I feel as though my lights are on but no-one's home," I tell Kate as we drive away.

She looks at my sagging eyes and puffy skin and laughs, "I'm not even sure your lights are on right now. Perhaps you need to replace a few of your bulbs?"

"I just have a good dimmer switch," I say, defending myself from the mock abuse.

"Come on, let's go," Kate says, "Columbus is calling me."

It is early evening when we arrive in Columbus, Ohio's state capital. We drive past Genoa Park, where the group stage is due to start at 6am tomorrow, and spot children playing in the fountains as we cross the Scioto river. The roads are quiet and the whole city feels as though it's sleeping. We check in to a hotel and Kate decides to take a walk.

"If I'm not back in an hour, phone 911," she says, heading out the door. I assume she's just joking but wonder if I should have gone with her. Plugging in my laptop I reassure myself that Kate is an adult who can look after herself. I'm relieved when she returns an hour later. She'd been down to the river to scope out tomorrow's group run.

"Oh yeah, what's it like?"

Kate wrinkles her nose. "Well, I don't think it's the smartest part of town. I did bump into one or two dodgy characters along one section."

237

"What do you mean by 'dodgy'?" I ask, trying to hide my concern.

"Oh, you know, just a bit shady. I think they'd had a bit to drink but they were friendly enough."

"Really?"

"Yeah, they didn't say too much. Just, 'Hello, how are you doing?' That sort of thing."

"And what did you say?"

"I said hello back and said that I was very well, thanks. It seemed rude not to."

O to the M to the G, I can't believe that this is the same girl who, only three weeks ago, refused to go two meters from the car without locking it, for fear some 'shady character' might steal our stuff. Kate had come as far metaphorically as we had physically on this trip.

*****

Early next morning, we join a motley crew of 26 runners on the banks of the Scioto. The leader of the gang is a kilted man sporting an enviable Mohican hair do. Stuart and his sidekick, Amanda, have volunteered to chaperone the group by bicycle to, "keep everyone safe." I don't really read too much in to this comment at the time; I'm too busy imagining what Kate might look like with a Mohican. Back in California, she told me she would get a Mohican if we ever made it to Boston. It's probably about time I reminded her of that.

The run starts pretty calmly and we manage to stick together in one pack chanting O-H-I-O as we go, passing Miles back and forth. But the pace soon starts to quicken and I realize that Miles has taken off. Planted in the hand of Nik Cannell, Miles appears to be making a break and the rest of the group are struggling to keep up.

I am used to seeing the effect Miles has on those who hold him. He gives people an energy boost and makes them feel super human. Nik shows no sign of slowing and I'm worried there are others who may miss their chance to carry Miles. Deciding to give chase, I eventually catch up with Nik.

"We should maybe try and keep together a bit more and give everyone their moment with Miles," I say, trying not to knock the wind out of his sails.

"I was just trying to get Miles to the next hand-off as fast as possible to make up some of the lost time." He's right of course. We're an hour behind again and we could really do with speeding things up. But as much as I want Nik to go on, I know I can't let him. Not just yet, not until everyone has had their own moment with Miles.

"Bear with me," I tell him, "I'm just going to run Miles back a bit, just to be sure everyone's had their turn." I sprint back to find the pack and pass Kate who is helping Stuart up off the tarmac. It looks like he's come off his bike and there is blood oozing from his knees and elbows. "Are you guys OK?" I shout as I pass.

"Yeah, don't worry about us!" Kate yells back, "I'll fill you in later." It seems a bit strange that Stuart has come off his bike on a straight bit of path when he can't have been going more than five miles per hour. Maybe his kilt got caught in a wheel? I guess that must be an occupational hazard for kilt-wearing cyclists the world over. Getting on with my mission, when I'm sure that everyone has had their turn with Miles, I sprint back to the front of the group and hand him to the faster runners, urging them to go on ahead.

By the time I reach the hand-off location, Miles is already safely on his way to his next destination. Tucking into some home baked cookies that have magically appeared, we stand cheering every last runner home. Posing for photos sitting down, I'm shown a full frontal of what an American wears under his kilt. Slightly lower down, the sight of Stuart's grazed knees remind me that I have yet to find out what happened earlier down by the river.

"So, did your skirt get stuck in your spokes?" I joke. Kate butts in before Stuart can say anything.

"No, those are the wounds of a total hero!"

I'm intrigued. "So what happened?"

"One of the locals got a little up close and personal with Kate and so I had to step in," Stuart explains, a little mysteriously. It turns out that one of the 'shady' yet 'friendly' locals that Kate encountered on her walk last night had jumped out of the bushes, bounded up to Kate and tried to push her over. Forgetting that his feet were clipped in to his bike pedals, Stuart had leapt to Kate's rescue but, still attached to his bike, he had come a cropper. The man still got the message though. He took one look at Stuart writhing on the floor, blood pouring from his knees, and decided he was not prepared for a tussle and that was the last they saw of him.

Making plans for us to join a small group of runners for a post-run breakfast, Kate is calling the next runner along to let them know the relay is heading their way. I glance over and see a look of panic on Kate's face that I know means, "We've mucked up." She is cradling the phone in between her shoulder and neck, as she uses her free hands to frantically rummage in her bag for the battered scraps of paper containing all the stage information. "Don't panic Victoria, I'll give Todd a call and warn him that you're not going to be at the hand-off when he gets there. No, don't pass out. Just put your foot down and get there as soon as you can." The relay is already an hour behind and it sounds like it will soon be running even later.

"What's happened?" I ask as soon as she's off the phone.

"I just rang the next runner, Victoria Dugger, to say Miles is about half an hour away and she started to freak out. She's still some way off in the car. She says that she'd added on the hour delay to her start time and worked out

Miles wouldn't be getting to her for another hour and a half."

This is bad news indeed. "How far away is she?" I ask.

"She's not too far off, she was planning to get to the hand-off a bit early anyway, but it sounds like Todd may arrive with Miles before she gets there. I guess he'll just have to wait until she shows up." Kate stares at her papers, trying to work out how Victoria could have got the timing of her stage so wrong. "Oh... hang on a minute," she says eventually, a smile creeping back across her face. "I think I see what's happened here." It turns out that Victoria is right. Her stage isn't scheduled to start for another hour and a half. When Kate was planning the route, she had accidentally added an extra hour to stage 236, the stage before Victoria's. It means we now have a spare sixty minutes we didn't know we had.

"But this means..." I ponder, "We are no longer behind. In fact we are bang on time!" If Todd has to wait a few minutes for Victoria to arrive at the hand-off, it's really not that bad; we are basically back on track!

Kate tries to convince me that she built the extra hour into the schedule deliberately. "You may call it an error, Danny, but I say it's a stroke of genius! Just call me Einstein from now on!" And somehow the name stuck.

*****

I like sleep, I love sleep even. With all my running and adventures, I need 8 hours a night to function. I was becoming quite the opposite of Einstein. My brain was shutting down. The days were blurring into one as I dragged my sorry self through the day. I remember Chocolate Pretzels being given to us, and Kate and I getting the chocolate all over the seats and someone asking me "What *is* this? Mount Fucking Ohio?" The laughter that followed sounded like a record player had slowed it down so that it seemed like a hallucinogenic dream tinged with evil. Shaking myself, I see Meghan Crosby smiling at me, passing a water back to my hands, as if to say "You need this more than me." She was right, I am wilting; in contrast, she's switched to Beast Mode.

A familiar face is waiting to accept the baton at the next hand-off, but my brain can't compute who it is. Eventually I realize it's Nik, the blond-haired, blue-eyed guy from this morning's group run who took a telling-off from me when he ran off with Miles. He has flown all the way from Hawaii to be part of the relay and will fly straight back after he's done. Now that is commitment to the cause. There's a news crew waiting on the bridge to film the hand-off and we hang around to talk to them while Nik continues on his way. He has entrusted his car to Kate who will drive ahead to meet him at the finish, while I give the last runners a lift back to their car in the Stink Mobile. By the time I catch up with Nik again it has started to rain and he is starting to flag. Kate is doing her best to keep him motivated but the pain is evident on Nik's face. He only has a few miles left to go and assures me he's cool to carry on. There's not much I can do, so I tell Kate I'm driving ahead to check out the next hand-off and pull in for some comfort food. I spy a McDonalds and with a burning of rubber and screaming of tires I turn in before I even realize I'm doing it.

My relief at sinking my teeth into sugar and fat junk food is mirrored by Nik's relief when he reaches the hand-off. If he's heard about Kate's driving, it could of course be that he's just relieved to see his car is still in one piece. But I suspect it's more than that. His legs are sore and he's had to dig deep to get Miles here. He hands-off to a fresh-legged trio in a motel parking lot as thunder rumbles in the distance. The skies are dark and ominous. It looks as if there's more rain to come. Kate and I make a plan to stick with the relay for the next stage then head on to the state border with West Virginia to park up for the night. The urge to sing John Denver's song, is irresistible and we motor off half singing, half humming as we struggle to remember the words.

"Country Roads, take me home
To the place I belong
West Virginia, mountain momma
Take me home, country roads."

Halfway to the next hand-off, Kate decides to have a look through the day's photos and scrabbles around for my camera but she can't find it. Pulling over in a layby, searching for the camera, my stomach clenches as I realize my beloved camera, along with every single photo I have taken since arriving in Los Angeles, is missing. There's no camera.

"When did you last have it?" Kate asks. "Back at the last hand-off when Nik finished you were clicking away." I can't imagine I could have left it there. We were in a motel parking lot, there was nowhere I could have put it down. Unless…Oh god. It occurs to me that I may have put the camera on the roof of the car again and driven off. This had happened a few times before with the camera and the phone but luckily we or a clued-up runner had managed to spot it before it was too late.

"Shit!! We'd better head back there." We race back to the motel slowing down half a mile out to scour the road for camera debris. There is nothing. My heart is in my mouth as I pull in to the parking lot. Still nothing. A woman runs over, waving at us, and I wind down my window. "Did you guys leave your camera here?" she asks.

"I think so, have you got it?" My hopes soar.

"No, I don't," and just as quickly my hopes are smashed to smithereens. But then she continues, "The blond-haired runner has taken it. He drove off to find you." I could kiss her. But there's no time for that. I call Nik and we eventually catch up with him in a gas station down the road. I thank him profusely and wonder what I can do to show my gratitude. But he has to get going; he has a flight to catch.

The events of the last half-hour alone have exhausted me further. Taking my life in my hands, I tell Kate she'll have to drive. I simply can't go on.

Kate is keen to get back behind the wheel again and since she managed to drive Nik's car without crashing it, I have a little more faith in her driving skills. She maneuvers out of the gas station with ease, winding around a number of obstacles.

"This is great, Kate," I tell her before she turns the wrong way on to the highway and stops in front of an oncoming juggernaut…

My life flashes before my eyes as the huge truck bears down on us in the fast lane. Kate freezes as I instinctively adopt the brace position. Seconds away from collision, the truck manages to switch lanes hooting its horn and Kate gets us back on to the right side of the road. Pumped with adrenaline, we find ourselves laughing hysterically, after I've stopped screaming.

By the time we get to Steubenville it's almost midnight and the storm we saw in the distance has gathered a head of steam. Again our runners are going to be running against the elements tonight. Neither of us fancies sleeping in the car. We're afraid the metallic bodywork of the Stink Mobile might act as a lightning conductor and we could be frazzled to a crisp. Lying in our beds, in a dilapidated hotel, we hear the rain lashing down outside, hammering on our windows, and the wind rocks the building as if ushering us towards sleep. Even though the curtains are closed, we see the room flash alight with every lightning bolt. A thunder clap erupts overhead, shaking the whole room.

"Shit! That sounds close," Kate sits up and turns the light on. I ask if she's OK and she replies, "Not really, this is pretty frightening. It feels like the storm is about to blast through the walls." I know what she means. "Do you think the runners are getting this right now? How far did we drive on in front?" Kate asks. I have to think about it. We must be at least sixty miles ahead. Depending on which way the storm is heading, it's possible the runners won't run into it. "What should we do?" Kate asks, but I'm not sure of the answer. We consider driving back, like we'd done for Gary in Texas, but knowing that each of tonight's runners has their own support vehicle we decide it isn't necessary. But Kate is worried that the runners may try and take a leaf out of Gary's book and just keep on running regardless. "I'm going to text them all," she says as another clap of thunder rattles my rib cage, "let them know not to take any risks tonight and only run if it's safe to do so."

Chapter 24

We wake to a clear, bright sky but the Facebook feed is full of stories and photos from last night's runners showing a very different picture. As we feared, the storm had hit them full on. But it seemed all the runners ignored Kate's pleas. We flick through photo after photo of determined runners, soaked to the bone, battling through flooded roads that resemble fast flowing rivers. It looks apocalyptic, biblical even. I half expect to see Noah and his ark floating around in the background of some of the pictures where the runners have water over the knees. We check the GPS tracker map and to our utter amazement we see the little dot blipping along, not more than an hour behind schedule. Ohio has truly rocked it.

We head straight for Pittsburgh for this afternoon's group stage. Unlike the last group stages in Columbus and Indianapolis, no local runners have stepped up to take charge of the stage and so the responsibility is very much on our shoulders. We just have to hope that when we turn up there's at least one person in the group who knows the route. Kate may have been the one who mapped it out online, but neither she nor I have a clue where we're going to be running. As we drive, Kate takes a call and I can tell immediately from her serious tone of voice that it's someone important. I'm right, it's the Pittsburgh Police.

"OMG!" she cries, hanging up the phone. "I thought they had a problem with what we're doing at first. The officer sounded all heavy and said he'd just found out about the relay. I swear I thought he was going to tell us we were breaking the law and he was going to stop the run," she gabbles excitedly. "But he just wanted to see if they could help us out with a parking spot for the Stink Mobile near the start of the group stage. Apparently his girlfriend is going to be running with us and she was worried we'd have nowhere to park! But that's not the best bit. Danny, you should have heard him, it was so funny. He told me we have to head to this hotel and look out for a Chevrolet with blacked-out windows. It'll have a plain-clothed cop inside who is going to sort out everything!" It all seems like a scene from CSI to me and I absolutely love it! If it turns out to be half as cool as I'm imagining, this will definitely score high on to my list of authentic American experiences.

Driving along the 376 Penn Lincoln Highway, you cannot see the city of Pittsburgh as you approach. There's a great big mountain in the way and you have to drive through a tunnel which goes straight through the middle of it. One moment you're driving along a narrow tunnel with various lights flashing and blinking at you before it opens out to a wide expanse of cityscape. It's like finding a hidden city in a Sci-Fi film. By the time the tunnel spits you out the other side, you're on a bridge over the Monongahela River with the Pittsburgh skyline right in front of your nose. You can even peer over into the Heinz Stadium, home to the Pittsburgh Steelers, as you drive across the bridge. It's a great way to arrive. We head for the Wyndham Grand hotel, as we've been instructed by the police officer.

"I'd be really disappointed if this is all a hoax," Kate says, as we both keep an eye out for the blacked-out Chevy. But sure enough there it is. We pull in behind it and before I've had a chance to turn off the engine, a super-sized guy in dark shades is standing at my window. "Welcome to Pittsburgh, I'm going to park you right over there," he says, pointing over at the hotel which is as grand as its name would suggest. We move to the other side of the road and are mobbed by smartly dressed valets waving their arms and shouting, "You can't park here!" They look unaccustomed to having Stink Mobiles drive by, let alone park up, outside, their hotel. I wind down the window to explain, but hear the deep voice of the Police officer who has once more appeared unnoticed beside my door.

"I'm from the Pittsburgh PD," he tells the valets. "I need you to do a little favor for my friends here. They're going to be leaving their vehicle with you for a couple of hours." The valets look a little taken aback but nod their heads. "Leave your key with these guys and they'll take care of your car," the officer tells us. I jump out and hand the key to the nearest valet. It is not his lucky day. I feel more than a little guilty as I see him gingerly sit down on the sweaty driver's seat and hesitate a second before putting his hands on the grubby steering wheel. For his sake, I hope that the garage isn't too far away. He drives off with the windows down.

We thank the officer and head on over to the fountain where the group stage is soon to start. It's all been a bit surreal. As we walk, I can't help but think about how the police and other services have come out in force throughout our journey to help support One Run For Boston.

There have been police officers, sheriffs, firemen and ambulance drivers present on many of the stages. Some have responded to a request from a runner, others have simply shown up to volunteer an escort. Quite often they have arrived unexpectedly and, without ceremony, just slotted in behind the runner, lights flashing, to shield them from other vehicles. In some cases, runners have approached intersections to find that all the lights are red and the traffic has been deliberately held to allow them to cross the road unhindered. But at hand-offs the escorts frequently disappear without fuss, before we, or the runners have a chance to thank them.

I think of police officers and other first responders, both on and off-duty, who helped in the aftermath of the bombings in Boston. They had set to work helping others without a thought for their own safety. They took control of a crazy situation and saved many, many lives that day. I think about how, within minutes of the bombs going off, a line of ambulances had arrived to take the injured to hospital, how police officers made tourniquets out of anything they could get their hands on and how, in the days that followed, one of their own had lost his life at the hands of one of the bombing suspects.

At first, the police had no clue as to who the suspects may be. The Mayor of Boston, Thomas Menino, checked himself out of hospital where he'd been recovering from a fractured leg to address the city. "We will get through this," he told his people, but could add little more. The police had no leads. One man changed all that.

Thirty hours after the bombings, Jeff Bauman regained consciousness in hospital. He tried to speak but couldn't. Asking for a pen and paper, he wrote down seven words, "Saw the guy. Looked straight at me." Bauman was able to provide the FBI with a detailed description of the man who had placed a backpack at his feet just two and a half minutes before it exploded at the Boston Marathon finish line.

The bomb blast shattered both of Bauman's legs and, in the hours that followed, he had quickly become the face of the tragedy after a photograph was published of him being carried away from the wreckage by a man in a cowboy hat, Carlos Arredondo. Bauman's information allowed the police to reconstruct photo fits of the bomber's face and sparked one of the biggest manhunts in the country's history. But shortly afterwards, before anyone could get to them, the bombers shot and killed MIT Police Officer, Sean Collier, as they tried to steal his gun. Less than an hour later, police caught up with the suspects in Watertown, less than eight miles from the marathon finish line. There followed a shootout, in which Tamerlan Tsarnaev was killed. His brother Dzhokhar managed to escape, but was caught the next evening as he hid under a boat in a backyard .

Boston police soon announced the arrest via Twitter: "CAPTURED!!! The hunt is over. The search is done. The terror is over. And justice has won. Suspect in custody."

As the news spread, people poured out onto Boston's empty streets to celebrate. The residents of Watertown turned out to cheer the Police as they left the scene of the capture. And the nation breathed a collective sigh of relief.

*****

There are 25 runners standing by the fountain waiting for Miles to arrive at the start of the Pittsburgh group stage. We quickly identify Danielle, the runner responsible for getting us our VIP parking space. As we stand chatting to her, Miles arrives and the runners look around, searching for someone to hand him to. Instinctively, Danielle stretches out her hand to take him and soon we are on our way. It is brutally hot, and as the sweat soaks every inch of my shirt, Danielle, running alongside me, says, "Wow, I've got swamp ass!" Neither Kate nor I have a clue what she means by this so we get Danielle to enlighten us. "Swamp ass is when it's so hot that your butt and undercarriage area get all..." She pauses looking for the correct word, "Swampy." It is a perfect explanation and I take great pleasure in confirming that my ass is definitely a little swampy right now. Kate admits that she is also suffering with a touch of the swamp ass and when the group stage is over, we cure ourselves of the affliction by jumping in the Point State Park fountain fully clothed. It's not quite the shower we've been longing for, but it is better than nothing. We turn up at the Wyndham Grand Hotel to pick up the Stink Mobile dripping from head to toe. The valet looks at us as if he's seen it all now. Handing us the keys, he looks on in disbelief as we haul our soaking bodies into the car without changing and drive off.

Our steaming carcasses soon make the inside of the car feel like a rainforest, only without the trees, and by the time we reach the next hand-off in Turtle Creek my skin is so shriveled it's like I've been sat in the bath all day. I strip down to my Stars and Stripes shorts and stand outside the car, airing myself. A car whizzes past and an angry-sounding man screams out of the window, "Put some clothes on!" Never one to miss an opportunity, Kate takes a photo of me and posts it to Facebook with the caption, 'Down and Out in Turtle Creek.' It sparks a conversation about my lack of a suntan.

"Danny Bent has travelled all the way across this country but where is his tan? I met him on leg 24, three weeks ago and there has been no change in color. None at all!" posts Todd Glieden.

"It's because he hasn't had his clothes off enough. Keep the clothes off and work on the tan!" replies Joan Meagher. OMG! Joan is flirting with me! Awesome! I decide there and then I need to smarten up a bit and, spotting a barber's enroute to the next hand-off, I tell Kate we're stopping for a haircut.

"Great idea!" says Kate, "My hair could do with a trim." And a nice little innocuous trim is exactly what she gets. Meanwhile, the woman tries to refashion my hair into some kind of bowl cut. I'm guessing that must be the gents' cut of choice in these parts. If it wasn't for the fact that I'm losing a little of my hair on top, I might have ended up like a ginger Jim Carrey in *Dumb and Dumber*.

"Maybe you could take the sides a little shorter?" I ask, hoping I don't piss her off. I've learnt through experience that it's never a good idea to annoy a woman with scissors in her hand. Kate is sitting on a chair behind me and I catch sight of her in the mirror sniggering. Oh God, if I look this bad from the front, I can only imagine how bad I must look from Kate's rear view perspective. Once outside, Kate reveals I look like the Sloth from *The Goonies*. Even I know that is not a good look. I've got just four days until I see Joan again in Boston. Four days to grow my hair back. I am going to have to start wearing a cap. I drown my sorrows in a S'mores flavor DQ Blizzard, courtesy of runner number 255, Scott Farley, and live to fight another day.

Chapter 25

Stage 265, Canoe Creek Lake to Alexandria, is a gem of a stage. It is seventeen miles long, mostly off-road and flat, along an old canal path and an abandoned railway line. According to the Rails to Trails website, bald eagles and ospreys have been spotted along the trail and many beautiful and rare plant species grow beside it. The trail passes the historic remains of lock keepers' houses, mill streams and abandoned stone quarries, as it winds its way through the trees. Craig Murphy definitely knew what he was doing when he signed up to run this particular stage. But it was not to be.

A few days before he was due to run, Craig received the devastating news that his father had passed away. The funeral was set to take place at exactly the same time as Craig's stage, so he emailed to let us know that he would not be able to run. Craig was deeply apologetic that he would not be able to fulfill his obligation to the relay but we reassured him that it really wasn't a problem and that we'd find another runner, no sweat.

"You know, we could always run that stage ourselves," Kate had suggested. "We could run it in honor of Craig's dad." Although I had never met Craig and I had never met his father, it didn't seem to matter. It was something that just felt right, and something I very much wanted to do.

By the time the relay reaches Canoe Creek, it is an hour and a half behind schedule. I work out we can maybe make up half an hour between us over seventeen miles, but Kate says we can shave off over an hour.

"I'm not being funny Kate, but unless you've had some serious steroids for breakfast there's no way that's going to happen," I tell her.

"You're right. But there is another way," she reveals. "If we ditch the trail and take the road we'll cut out five miles, that's nearly an hour of catch-up in itself and if we rotate every couple of miles, we'll easily chop some more minutes off between us."

"But what about the bald eagles and the ospreys?"

"We'll just have to make do with spotting road kill instead."

A lunch date has been arranged for us in Alexandria by Mickey Reigeluth. We'd met Mickey in Indiana, shortly before the group stage in Indianapolis and I thought at the time that he seemed weirdly over-interested in what we were eating along the way. It all became clear when, three days later, he called us up to say he'd arranged for an Italian restaurant in Alexandria to feed us after we'd run our stage for Craig. Taking inspiration from our pizza delivery in Oklahoma, Mickey had planned for the Italian restaurant owner to drive out and meet us. The only problem is that when we arrive in Alexandria, it is lashing down with rain and we agree that it is going to take the edge off our treat if we eat our fancy Italian meal cooped up in the Stink Mobile. So we ditch that idea and rather than let the restaurant come to us, we go to them. Mickey has gone to town and ordered us the full Italian works. It is super gorgeous and there is plenty of it, so we persuade a runner called Joel to share our feast with us.

Leaving Alexandria, we enter Amish country. The Amish people are traditionalist Christians who by modern standards live simple lives. Their culture bans them from using electricity, telephones or automobiles. As we drive across the state they are easily recognized by the horse-drawn buggies they use to get around in and the men's impressive beards. Amish men traditionally shave until they marry and then they let their beards grow. But you won't find an Amish man with a mustache. The Amish people came to settle in America to escape persecution in Europe. At the time mustaches were common among their persecutors and so Amish men shave their upper lips to set them apart. It's not a look I would choose for myself but every man has their own facial fuzz favorites.

With no electricity, there are no modern distractions such as televisions or computers, and possessions are very low on the priority list. These aspects of the Amish way of life appeal to me, but the fact that everything in their lives is so regimented definitely does not. Children are not allowed to be cheeky or mischievous and woe betides any who step out of line; Amish parents are big fans of corporal punishment. School ends at 8th grade, which most kids would think was awesome if it wasn't for the fact that the boys are expected to start work in manual jobs straightaway and the girls have little choice but to follow in their mothers' footsteps by getting married and popping out babies.

As night falls, there is barely any sign of life from any dwelling that we pass. Only the faint glow of candlelight is visible in the windows. We consider turning in for the night, but decide to carry on, as we so often do, for 'just one more' hand-off. The rain has stopped and there's a freshness in the air that we haven't felt in a while. We park up in a gateway and keep our eyes peeled for Joe Church who has signed up to run this stage on his own. Five months ago, Joe lost his beloved wife Eileen to cancer. We only knew this because yesterday Joe had posted to Facebook that it was going to be a tough day for him - the relay was passing through Eileen's home town of Turtle Creek.

Turning off the headlights, we notice the field beside us is alive with green and yellow sparks. I've never seen anything like it but know they must be fireflies. These creatures are magical and mesmerizing. Soon, a couple of white lights appear out of the darkness. They are too big to be fireflies. We hear voices in the distance and eventually the familiar pat of feet on tarmac. We recognize Joe straight away, but don't know who the other guy is. After shouting a few words of encouragement we drive on, stopping a couple more times as much to play with the fireflies as to support Joe and his pal.

We catch up with the support crew at the hand-off and learn that the man running with Joe is Craig Murphy whose stage we had run earlier. Returning home from his dad's funeral that afternoon, Craig had messaged Joe to ask if it was OK for him to join Joe's stage that night. It seems as though the universe has been at work to bring together these two runners who had both lost someone special recently. For us to be able to meet them both is pretty special too. Joe's friend, Linda, joins them to run the last few hundred meters and, once Miles is safely handed-off, Craig's wife suggests we say a little prayer of thanks. We stand together in a circle in the dark, holding hands. As a non-believer, it feels a little odd at first, but the words are so beautiful and the positive energy between us so strong and palpable, I can't help but feel soothed. We hug and say goodbye as the fireflies dance around us.

Chapter 26

Driving by the mini mart in Snyders, Pennsylvania, we do a double-take.

"Did you just see what I just saw?" Kate asks me.

"You mean the license plate?" I say, flinging the car round to take another look. The blue and yellow plate with BOSTRNG is too much of a coincidence. Since the bombings, the two-word motto 'Boston Strong' had been everywhere in Boston. As The Boston Globe observed, 'Boston Strong' quickly became, "handy shorthand for defiance, solidarity, and caring. In its ubiquity, 'Boston Strong' presents a united front in the face of threat." The phrase had found its way onto T-shirts, hats, wristbands, Facebook banners, buses, and now license plates. I pull into the parking lot and roll up alongside the BOSTRNG car.

The earlier floods have paved the way for another heat wave and the car occupies the only slice of shade around. We wander over and see a woman sitting in the car, beside a panting black pug dog. The woman introduces herself as Jennifer Wargo's mum, and her out of breath canine friend is Suzy B. Jennifer is running the stage that starts in Snyders and she is waiting round the corner for Miles to arrive.

"Jennifer asked me to go into the store and stock up on some water," Mrs. Wargo tells us, "But I can't leave Suzy B. on her own in the car." She asks if we'll nip in and buy the water for her and hands Kate a ten dollar bill. As Kate dashes into the store, I ask Mrs. Wargo what her plans are.

"Are you going to follow behind Jennifer or drive ahead and stop every couple of miles?"

"Oh, I don't think there's really anywhere to pull in along that road, so I was just going to see Jen off from here and drive on to wait for her at the finish. She's handing off outside the Pleasant Trees Senior Center." I envisage Jen running on her own with ten dollars' worth of water strapped to her back for the entire nine-mile stretch and tell Mrs. Wargo that we will help her support her daughter. I reassure her that Kate and I have become highly practiced in illegal roadside maneuvers over the past few weeks and that she will be fine if she follows us.

So, with Suzy B. at her side, Mrs. Wargo slips in behind the Stink Mobile and trails our every move as we career along the 895 to Ashfield, on a mission to keep her daughter hydrated. The BOSTRNG plate is ever present in our rear view mirror as we pull in and out of the shoulder, U-turn across the road and park up every mile or so in a series of ditches, verges, private drives and other unsuitable stopping places. Mrs. Wargo seems exhilarated and Suzy B. is panting harder than ever. It's probably a good job they haven't followed Stink the whole way from Los Angeles. Suzy B. might well have had a heart attack.

Somewhere in Kate's decaying paperwork, hidden amongst the endless lists of runners, is a name that is immediately recognizable to just about any American who has ever laced up a pair of running shoes. After coming under pressure from the One Run For Boston Twitterati, Bart Yasso signed up to join a small group of runners on stage 287, near his home town of Bethlehem, Pennsylvania. Dubbed the 'Mayor of Running', Bart Yasso is one of the best-known figures in the sport. As the Chief Running Officer at Runner's World, his job is to turn up at races across the nation to encourage, motivate and inspire. A sub 2:40 marathoner in his time, he now relishes the opportunity to run further back in the pack with the lopers and the stragglers. On his website, Bart says, "I have run on all seven continents, but it's not the details of the races I recall, it's the people I meet."

Neither Kate nor I had heard of Bart Yasso until One Run For Boston. We had struggled to understand everyone's excitement at first, and are wondering if our experience of meeting the man could ever really live up to all the hype. Introducing ourselves to Bart as he hangs out with the stage 287 team, in Walnutport, it takes no time at all for it to be confirmed that this man is an absolute legend. Despite his high profile celebrity status, Bart is as down-to-earth as they get.

When the TV cameras turn up to interview him, he tells them, "It's Steffi you should be talking to, not me." Steffi Park Eger, had been the first to sign up to run this stage, long before Bart had thrown his hat into the ring. "This is Steffi's stage," Bart reminds them. Bart signs the banner and stands for photo after photo until everyone has their keepsake picture of him on their cameras. He is relaxed and casual and doesn't stop to question me when I ask if he might pose for a photo inside the Stink Mobile, with one leg out of the window and a yellow duck on his knee.

When Miles arrives, we watch as the group set off down the road with Steffi out in front and Bart falling in somewhere behind. The runners have their own support crews but we decide to follow behind for the first few hilly miles, anyway. Half an hour in, a car whizzes by in the opposite direction and does a quick U-turn. As the car catches us up and creeps by to ride side by side with the runners, we spot a pair of red shorts hanging out the passenger window. The mad man inside the car is shouting, "I got shorts, who needs red shorts?" which is greeted with uncontrollable laughter from the runners in front of us. Scott Allender has arrived.

Scott Allender is the older, quirkier, brother of Will. The day before One Run For Boston began in Santa Monica, Will had emailed his brother a weblink with the message, "You should join one of the runners out in eastern PA! Gonna be fun!" Scott had been off work so didn't pick the message up straight away. But a week later, just after he'd read his email, he picked up a copy of USA Today and saw a picture of his younger brother, who had always been a non-runner, running through New Mexico, carrying a baton in an epic cross-country relay.

"Just days before that," Scott starts to explain to us, "my older brother, Pat, had won three gold medals at the Pan Am Masters Swimming Championships. And where am I, when I learn of both these things?" He asks us, not expecting an answer. "On the couch! So right away I know that I have to get off the couch!"

Scott had signed up on the spot to join another runner on stage 286 in New Jersey. A day later, Will introduced his brother to the Facebook group, "My triathlete brother, Scott Allender, has thrown his hat in the ring for stage #286 in NJ. Dr. Allender has been tirelessly doing benefit athletic events for cancer research since I can remember. Really happy to have him on board. Cheers bro!"

Spotting this at the time, I promptly replied, "Scott, you have a lot to live up to. Will is one of the most epically awesome people I've ever met – please don't disappoint! ☺"

"I'll bring it!" Scott had replied and 'bring it' he does, in the shape of a liter of locally distilled gin and a whole side of home-smoked salmon. So, on a curbside in Pennsylvania, not far from the border with New Jersey, we find ourselves knocking back the local hooch with Allender No. 2, while we wait for Steffi, Bart and the rest of their gang to arrive. I'm a little concerned to see just how much of the gin is disappearing down Scott's throat given he's due to be running in a few hours. But that anxiety pales into insignificance when we wave him goodbye and watch as he crosses the road with a rather dramatic limp.

As soon as Scott is out of earshot, Kate whispers, "Shit, have you seen the way he walks? Do you think he'll be OK to run tonight?!" I'm thinking the same thing. It's especially worrying since a last minute drop-out means that Scott is going to be running a stage on his own with no-one else to share the strain. We wonder why Scott hasn't mentioned the limp to us and stew about what we should do. Jamie has just arrived in New York City from the UK and we've arranged to meet him there tonight. We've got beds booked in a hotel and everything, courtesy of a very generous runner from Arizona who has fixed them up for us. It would be a major bummer if we had to stay and run Scott's stage for him instead.

"Maybe he was born with a limp? It doesn't have to mean he can't run," Kate says optimistically. I know I should call Scott to ask him straight out if he's actually going to be able to run tonight. But something is stopping me. I feel a bit embarrassed to ask, especially if the limp is something he was born with and doesn't like to mention. I decide to call Will.

"Hiya Will, we've just met your bro!" I say, cheerily down the phone.

"Oh yeah? How is the old man?"

"Oh he's fine, I think. He's certainly ...." I tail off as I try to find a polite way to say that on first meeting Scott appears to be as mad as a box of frogs. "He's certainly very different to you!"

"He's quite a guy, isn't he?"

I cut to the chase. "Listen Will, does your brother normally walk with a limp?"

There's a pause at the other end of the line but I have no option but to plough on.

"Kate and I are just a tad concerned that he may not be in the best shape for running his stage tonight. He was limping quite badly when we met him earlier. Is that normal for him?"

"Let me see. He has always had a slightly unusual gait, I guess."

That is certainly one way of putting it.

"But he's OK to run?"

"Yeah, should be. Did he say he wasn't?"

"No, no. He didn't say anything to us. Which is why I didn't like to ask him."

"I think he'll be fine."

"OK, that's great. Thanks Will."

I hang up and reassure Kate that all is well. "It's just the way he is."

We drive on to New York City, blissfully unaware that Scott's limp is a badly sprained ankle that he picked up two days ago, which will later torment him through most of his stage.

Working away behind the scenes while Kate and I lap up the limelight, Jamie is the One Run For Boston equivalent to the Wizard of Oz and it feels like a lifetime since we waved him goodbye. We are looking forward to the reunion. As we drive towards the Empire State, I think about the hundreds of goodbyes we've bid to all the runners that we've met along the way. It seems fanciful to think that there will ever be an opportunity to reunite with more than a few of these awesome people in the future. With the end in sight, every goodbye is leading us one step closer to Boston and it hits me that this will all be over before we know it. In just a couple more days we, like everyone else, will go back to our normal lives. But what Kate and I don't realize is that a new paradigm of normal is forming within the One Run For Boston community. As the relay reaches its conclusion, people aren't simply returning to their old lives, old habits, old friends. They are staying in contact with the people they've met and new friendships are being forged across the country. Even though it's days and in some cases weeks since they ran their stage, runners are continuing the conversations and are making arrangements to meet up with each other for runs, meals, coffees and fun. But that isn't all. After someone happened to post on Facebook, "So, who's going to Boston?" we've been hearing story after story of cancelled vacations, skipped family engagements and hastily arranged sick notes for work. Regardless of how many hundreds or thousands of miles away they live, everyone wants to be in Boston to follow Miles as he takes the right on Hereford and left on Boylston.

But Miles still has a long way to go and if he has as many problems as Kate and I are currently experiencing trying to navigate our way into New York City, it's quite possible Miles may yet not make it to Boston. We can see the Empire State building lit up in colorful rainbow lights and know that's where we need to head for, but none of the roads on our spaghetti-like map seem to tally with what's under our tires and we loop round and round, racking up toll after toll after toll.

After three wasted hours, and countless wrong turns we find our hotel and take Stink down into the garage below. Not for the first time, we are chased by an angry-looking valet as we try to find a parking space. It turns out we should have left the car outside and got the valet to park Stink for us. This valet parking malarkey is not something we've come across in the UK. I suspect it's because neither of us have ever stayed at a posh enough hotel. We park up and unload our bags from the car as the valet looks on, scowling. He may not have had the opportunity to earn himself a tip by parking Stink for us, but if only the valet knew what we had just saved him from, he would no doubt be tipping us.

We quickly drop off our bags in our room, fill the mini bar with Scott's smoked salmon that he'd left with us, and set off in search of Jamie and his girlfriend, Sophie. We've agreed to meet them in Times Square but it's Friday night and the whole area is crazy busy, with tens of thousands of people buzzing back and forth. I begin to think we should have been a bit more specific about our rendezvous location, but as we wait for the green man's permission to cross the street, I spot the unmistakable pale features and well-trodden face of our third amigo. Jamie has been keeping the same ridiculous hours as we have, albeit from the comfort of his home, rather than an SUV on the open road, and looks no better for it than Kate or I. Over dinner, in a food hall the size of an aircraft hanger we catch up on the news and slip back into the same easy banter as if we'd never been apart. It's approaching midnight and it's tempting to make a night of it and hit some bars, but we all know we've another big day ahead of us tomorrow and can't afford to let things slide now. Since Jamie is staying in a different hotel to ours, we make a plan for the morning before we go our separate ways. Kate and I will meet the runners at the 9/11 Memorial before heading up to Central Park for the group stage. Jamie and Sophie will head straight to Central Park and wait with the runners there. The streets are still heaving as Kate and I make our way back to our hotel.

We call in at a 24/7 to pick up a big rack of water bottles in case we don't have time in the morning. It's a struggle to carry them, so I balance them on my head with my left arm to stop them from falling and scoot off down the road. I assume that the unusual way I'm carrying the water is the reason why I'm attracting so much attention. But Kate knows better.

"It's gay pride weekend, Danny. I think you could get lucky tonight if you were up for it." I look down at what I'm wearing and realize that still dressed in my skimpy running shorts and tight tank top with a 24 pack of bottled water on my head, I look as gay and proud as anyone else on the streets of New York tonight.

Chapter 27

When United Airlines Flights 11 and 175 crashed into the twin towers of the World Trade Centre on September 11th 2001, I was backpacking in Australia. I remember turning on the TV in the youth hostel and seeing pictures of blazing buildings and wreckage. I thought it was just another Die Hard movie and turned it off. I spent most of the next 12 hours on an overnight bus and didn't find out until the next day that the scenes I had watched on TV were not from a movie, they were breaking news from New York City.

Waking up in the Big Apple, Kate and I leave the hotel at 6am, and take a cab south through Manhattan to the 9/11 Memorial. At this time of the morning, the Memorial is usually closed to the public but we have been given special permission to be there for the hand-off between stages 291 and 292. Arriving early, we wait outside a side entrance and I realize I have butterflies in my stomach. Kate and I are quiet. Our minds are just too full for words. The silence is broken by the sound of a voice from behind, tentatively calling out to us.

"Danny? Kate?" We swivel round to see a face that has come to be familiar to us, although we have only ever seen it on Facebook.

"Ian!" we shout out in unison, before leaping to give him a hug. At last it was time to meet Ian Alden Russell, the runner from Rhode Island who had popped up out of nowhere on Facebook before the website had even been launched, to offer his support. Since then, Ian had helped us in so many different ways. He'd spread the word, of course, but he had also attended meetings on our behalf and liaised with various organizations to help make this all possible. We owe him a huge debt of gratitude but we hope our hugs will do for now. Since he'd signed up early on, Ian was able to pick one of the most special stages of the entire relay, the one which would start at the 9/11 Memorial in New York City. He has decided to run it on his own and I wonder if there is a significant reason for this. I don't have time to ask, as the three of us are joined by Boston-based *USA Today* Reporter, Melanie Eversley. It was Melanie's article that had put us on page 3 of the newspaper with the photos from New Mexico. She has been following the relay ever since and has persuaded her boss to let her travel to New York to write a follow-up article. If you were to meet her, you might never know that Melanie, or Mel as we call her, is a heavyweight reporter for one of the country's top daily newspapers. She comes across as light hearted, mischievous and fun. I like her straight away.

As the four of us stand chatting outside the 9/11 Memorial, Miles is making his way across the Hudson River from New Jersey. The lead runner for this stage, Lorrie Krebs, has arranged for a local Captain called Jim to take her little group across the river by boat. We can hear them almost as soon as they land at Pier 25. "When I say Jersey, you say proud! Jersey!"

"Proud!"

"Jersey!"

"Proud!"

"When I say Boston, you say strong! Boston!"

"Strong!"

"Boston!"

"Strong!"

The group turns the corner from West Street onto Liberty and makes a beeline for us. One of the runners carries a hand-made 'Welcome to New York' sign, one has a City of Boston flag and another wears red socks up to her knees. I try to gulp back the emotion and just about succeed, until we step inside the Memorial. We pass the two enormous reflecting pools that occupy the footprint of each of the twin towers and we gather together by the Survivor Tree. The charred trunk of a Callery pear tree was pulled from the smouldering rubble of the World Trade Centre site after the 2001 attacks. It was nursed back to life and, like the survivor elm tree in the Oklahoma City Memorial; it has become a living reminder of resilience, survival and rebirth. I look across at Lorrie and Ian as they stand by the tree, clinging on to Miles, in a tight embrace. Suddenly, the emotions I am feeling become too much for me to hold in. I have to turn and walk away, tears flowing from my eyes. The tree mirrors the human survival spirit, the spirit that possesses each of us at times. A spirit I hope we have brought into One Run For Boston. Again what has been achieved by One Run For Boston in the last few weeks is hitting home. The realization of what the relay has meant to everyone involved, as well as what it has represented and symbolized to the outside world, engulfs me. I am joined by the other runners who can do nothing but sob as we hold each other.

Shortly after 9/11 my parents had stepped onto a plane, destination New York. They had signed up to the New York Marathon nine months previously and were not going to let terrorists stop them from doing what they loved. I was so nervous for them the day their plane left UK air space. Now, standing by the survivor tree twelve years later, I think of my parents as I realize our runners are doing the exact same thing; refusing to let terrorists stop them doing what they love.

My parents' experience was the first time I heard about the warmth of American people. The reception they were given for visiting at this time of unknowing and fear was something that would stay with them forever and something that touched my soul, as they recounted the number of people who expressed love and affection towards them. It was a reception I didn't think I would experience in my lifetime. But this was what I had lived for the past three weeks. Strangers hugging you close, whispering their thanks in your ear. Thanking us for coming such a long way to do something so important for their country and community. I think back to Mum and Dad at home and know they are proud, which starts my tears again.

Ian's keen to set off and leaves with Miles.

"We'd better be going," I say to Kate. Mel is planning to follow the next few stages with us and expertly hails us a taxi outside on the street. She sits in the front, scribbling into her notebook as we chat, all the way to Central Park. The traffic is terrible and I'm convinced that Ian will make it to the hand-off before us even though he's on foot. Leaping out of the cab halfway up Fifth Avenue, we race into the park, past Strawberry Fields and on towards the Bethesda Fountain. At the top of the steps, overlooking the fountain, we spot Jamie, we are taken aback to see he is sporting a kilt. I've no idea why he's wearing it but it suits him. He is standing with a group of thirty runners and among them is Ian, who, as I suspected, has beaten us to it. The plan had been to take Miles on a lap of Central Park before sending him off on the next stage to Bronx Zoo. But with the relay running two hours behind, we ditch that idea and Miles heads north with a small group led by Vince Varallo and Martha Muñoz while we lead a fun run round the park with anyone who wants to join us.

As we leave Mel, she confirms to us how she wants to refer to us in her story. "Danny, you are clearly the fun-loving Imp, of One Run For Boston," I think of my favorite of all Shakespearean characters, Puck, another fun-loving Imp, from A Midsummer Night's Dream and smile. My favorite line of his is, "And those things do best please me, that do befall preposterously." – I'm flattered to be compared to my hero.

She looks at Kate and says, "I think you are the reasonable balance to Danny's whimsy"

We laugh and say in unison, "That's about right!"

Having been on the road, just Kate and I, for three weeks, it is taking a bit of getting used to having Jamie and Sophie sitting in the back seat of the Stink Mobile. There's barely room for them amid all the memorabilia that we've accumulated across 3000 miles and twelve different US states.

"Eurgh! What are these doing here?" Jamie asks, fishing out a damp pair of my underpants from the pocket in the side door.

"Oh, I see you've found my dirty washing pile," I say, cheerily, grinning at him in the rear view mirror. Sophie keeps quiet. Her entire body is rigid, no doubt in an effort to minimize the parts of her that are in contact with the Stink Mobile's grimy surfaces.

"You've been eating well then?" Jamie says, referring to the empty chocolate wrappers, coffee cups and soda bottles that are strewn around the floor by their feet.

"You might find some leftover popcorn from Ohio if you're lucky," Kate tells him. "It's delicious, a mix of salty and sweet."

"I think I've already found it," Jamie replies. "Most of it is stuck to the bottom of my shoe."

"Just so you know, Jamie, you and Sophie might need to duck the odd missile in the back from time to time," I warn him.

"What?"

"Kate's developed a habit of chucking her empty coffee cups over her shoulder when she's done."

Kate starts giggling. "I'll try and restrain myself while you're in the back though," she says.

"Thanks. I'd appreciate that," says Jamie, dryly.

With four people instead of two, everything takes a lot longer, from packing up the car to stopping for a coffee. I can feel myself getting impatient with the time it's taking

269

us to get out of New York and the traffic jams aren't helping. I need to get us to Greenwich for Molly Barrett's stage, but the others don't seem to understand my urgency. I've been emailing back and forth with Molly pretty much since the relay began. She is incredibly cheerful and has recently asked if I would like to run with her on stage 297. I am super keen to do it and have told her I'll be there. Unbeknownst to me, as we battle our way out of New York, Molly and her friends are involved in an important discussion. Molly, or Marathon Molly, as she is more widely known, is wearing a yellow tutu. She's wearing it in honor of her mother, who has recently passed away, who loved watching her race in this silly attire because it meant she wasn't taking running too seriously. In her left hand is a spare red tutu. She and her friends are debating whether they'll be able to persuade this guy from England to wear the red tutu for the run.

Her friends decide there is no way this will happen saying things like, "What man would wear a tutu, let alone with people he doesn't know?" But Molly thinks there may be a chance and of course she is right. With minutes to spare we arrive at Molly's hand-off and she presents me with the red tutu. I grab it with delight and slip it on over my shorts.

Even at a young age I loved dressing in my mum's old clothes that she would cast off into the dressing-up box for my sisters to play with. It was probably one of the reasons why, when I was 16, Mum told me that she and my dad would love me no matter who or what I was.

"I'm not gay, mum!" I told her, catching onto what she was getting at. I was always just a bit different. I used to think I was abnormal, an alien in this world. Through my teenage years I strived to fit in but failed miserably. Only my sporting achievements kept me from being bullied on a daily basis I'm sure. It took years for me to realize that I am just me, nothing more, nothing less. But by just being me, I am the best *me* I can be. It is the people who feel they must change to be someone other than themselves we should feel most sorry for.

Jamie is clearly suffering withdrawal symptoms from being away from his computer and since Kate has yet to drink her body weight in coffee today, even though it's the middle of the afternoon, she is easily persuaded to drive on to find a Starbucks for coffee and WiFi. Thinking back, I wonder whether Jamie and Sophie were just embarrassed to be around a man wearing a bright red tutu. Either way, they leave me to it. Molly, her friends and I have an absolute ball. Their support team has made up placards which they hold up as we run past.

'Run now, beer later' one says, while another reads, 'You're the shit!' whatever that means. But it's the one that has a telephone number with the invitation to 'Call me, maybe?' that has me in stitches. I make a mental note to get someone to take a photo of me with Kate and Jamie each holding a sign later.

We get a few friendly toots and waves from passing traffic but none of us can quite believe it when an ambulance pulls over and the driver jumps out to take a photo of us.

"One Run For Boston!" Molly shouts, "Look us up!" By the time we finish the stage the photo is all over the web.

A police officer shouts, "Why are you running?"

Molly holds up Miles and proudly shouts, "BOSTON!"

"Why the tutus?"

"My Momma," Molly calls as we run past and the police officer turns on the siren as if to say, "We're with you."

At the end of the run, I leap a random poppy somehow existing amongst the crack in the sidewalk. Molly looks back at it with a small look of shock on her face. She sees the question in my eyes and says, "It's my Mom's favorite flower."

Molly's stage has brought us into Connecticut, the penultimate state, and from here on in it feels as if there is a party kicking off at every single hand-off. The groups of runners are getting bigger, the support crews even wilder and fancy dress continues to be a theme. I'm pretty certain that the Canadian we meet in Westport, who has adapted the itinerary of his family's RV vacation to South Carolina in order to be part of the relay, had no idea what he was getting himself into when he signed up to run. He is pretty much outnumbered 10:1 by women and looks to be enjoying himself. He says afterwards that it was well worth the 800 mile drive. I don't dare ask if his wife and kids agree.

The female contingent is known as the 'Dirty Dozen'. A group of twelve like-minded, adventure-seeking ladies whom I'd been joking with on the internet since the day they signed up. These girls love to party, love to flirt, love to love and aren't afraid to show it. The ladies want a Danny sandwich hug, in which I am very happy to be the filling to their bread.

The atmosphere is so frenzied that I completely forget I'm still wearing a tutu when I'm interviewed on camera by a reporter for NBC. He doesn't bat an eyelid and I wonder if this type of behavior is normal in these parts. If so, I'm emigrating!

The parties are already starting in Boston too. A gang from Missouri who have flown to Boston to run the final stage tomorrow night has been invited out by a group of young locals including none other than Miss Massachusetts herself. Miss Massachusetts! How could I have forgotten about her? Over in Pennsylvania, Scott Allender discovers he is practically neighbors with the guy who shared his brother's New Mexican adventure, and picks Steve Bender up enroute, as he heads for Boston. The pair make up half of a group of misfits who are crashing with a total stranger just outside the city. Among them is Justin O'Connell, a man we are yet to meet, but would soon come to know as a total inspiration. As the five new friends hang out together ahead of the One Run For Boston finale, the excitement is building. "It's like we have become family," Justin tells Scott.

"We've always been family," Scott replies, "We just didn't know it yet."

Chapter 28

Miles is glowing. I am sure of it. The crust of sweat, dirt, vomit and blood can't disguise it. The Duck tape that holds him together cannot mask the strength and vitality that radiates from him. More than a thousand people have touched him, transmitted their energy to him, and imprinted their stories in the layers of grime that now coat his outer shell. Less than 20 miles from the Massachusetts border, the final state in Miles' journey, a group of high school cross-country runners are about to add their fingerprints. As the boys smile and joke with each other, their coach, John Reilly, tells us about his own childhood and his connection to Boston.

"My dad was a runner for 25 years and every year on Patriots' Day he took us to watch the Boston Marathon," John explains. "We would always stand half-way up Heartbreak Hill and witness the anguish and suffering of the runners climbing those hills." John's eyes are slightly glazed and it is clear that in his mind he is back there now. "I think dad took us because he wanted us to see and understand that to obtain something great, you must make even greater sacrifices." John's dad had ensured his kids were well-versed in the legends surrounding the history of the Boston Marathon. He would retell the stories of how Heartbreak Hill got its name and how, in 1967, Kathrine Switzer became the first woman to sign up and run the Boston Marathon, five years before women were officially allowed to compete in it.

When Kathrine told her coach, Arnie Briggs, of her intention to run the Boston Marathon, he told her that no woman could ever run a marathon. But, in a training run three weeks before the race, Kathrine proved him wrong. The pair ran 31 miles together and as Kathrine hugged her coach ecstatically at the end, he passed out cold. The next day, Arnie paid Kathrine a visit and insisted she sign up for the race. She did just that, using the gender-neutral name of K.V. Switzer on the entry. Two weeks later, Kathrine's 235lb hammer-throwing boyfriend, 'Big' Tom Miller, entered the race too. He had done no training but figured, "If a girl can run a marathon, I can run a marathon." On race day, the sight of a girl with a race number pinned to her front triggered more than a few double-takes from the other runners at the start line. But they were pleased for her to be there and made her feel welcome. Crossing the line beside Tom and Arnie, none of the officials picked up on the fact Kathrine was a girl and it wasn't until the photographers on the press truck overtook her and began getting excited about a woman on the course, that the officials took any notice. Standing in the middle of the road, a man in an overcoat and felt hat shook his finger at Kathrine as she passed and made a grab for her hand. She jostled around him, thinking he was a nutty spectator, but then she noticed the blue and gold BAA ribbon on his lapel. Within seconds, another huge beast of a man was grabbing at her shoulder and shouting, "Get the hell out of my race and give me those numbers!" Arnie tried to bat the Race Director away but it was Big Tom Miller who stepped in with a cross-body block, sending him airborne and crashing to the curb. Kathrine pressed on, pursued by a press truck full of journalists whose attitude towards her had now changed. They were willing her not to finish and asking her when she was going to quit. This was all the inspiration Kathryn needed to finish the race and eventually, she did make that right on Hereford and left on Boylston.

"I have run the Boston Marathon twice; in 1996 on the 100th anniversary of the race, and again in 2009," John remembers. "Because of my dad, I know the history of those roads. When you run them, you can't help but feel the ghosts of the legends you are following; Tarzan Brown, Johnny Kelly, Bill Rodgers, Dick and Rick Hoyt. I think if God presented himself to me today and said, 'Kid, I'll give you one more marathon,' for me that 'one' would have to be Boston. There is no other."

In the years when he hasn't run it himself, John has taken a group of kids to volunteer at a water stop at Mile 9. "I think maybe I want them to see the same things my dad wanted us to see. I want them to witness firsthand the graceful manner in which the elite athletes attack these roads. I want them to see and understand the pageantry and the history associated with this day and this race. But mostly, I think I just want them to bring their kids someday, so that they will know that the little things about this day are not so little to me."

John looks across at his son, who is standing with the other boys, and then back at us.

"You know, it's kind of ironic that you Brits have organized this relay," John muses, "given the Boston Marathon link association with Patriots' Day."

We look at him a little blankly.

"You know what Patriots' Day is, right?"

"Uh no, not really."

"It's a public holiday that commemorates the young American patriots who fought the British in the first battles of the American Revolution in Massachusetts." Suddenly we realize that the jovial Facebook posts of the past few days along the lines of, "Watch out! The British are coming!" have been subtle references to the Redcoats of the Revolution! Cheeky yanks.

We steer the conversation back towards the relay itself and get John's boys to sign the banner while they wait. As they admire all the signatures that crowd the six-foot strip of vinyl, John explains to the boys that today they are part of something far greater than themselves. As he does so, we catch sight of that familiar white shape, bobbing towards us in the hands of Kevin Mahon. Whooping and cheering, the boys slap each other's backs and psych each other up for the run ahead, as I suspect they do before every high school race. But as the baton gets closer, rather than escalating, the noise is slowly drowned by a vacuum of silence. At barely a month old, Miles has already accumulated so much history and symbolism and his effect on the boys is quite beautiful to watch. They stare at him with eyes round and jaws hanging slack, as though they have come face to face with the Crown Jewels in the Tower of London.

As Miles changes hands and disappears from view, we make our way to a café, knowing it might be our last chance to eat before the finale in Boston tonight. We also need to get online. The relay is running three hours behind and there are runners and reporters eager for updates, as well as police officers from three or four different departments breathing down our necks. Over the last few weeks, Kate and I have learnt to be relaxed about the delays when they happen. But now, with so many people involved at the finish, the fact we're running so far behind seems to matter a lot more. It's all getting a bit crazy. Kate and Jamie set up a mini office in the corner of the café. Plugged into his digital world, Jamie is in his element. Kate looks less comfortable, juggling the cell phone from ear-to-ear like a hot potato, as she fields call after call on a handset that is literally melting from overuse. She wishes she was back in the desert, away from the hubbub. I just want to get back on the road.

Douglas to North Uxbridge is the first of the eight final stages in Massachusetts and I am super keen to be there. Stalking up and down, impatient to join Miles, I am aware how important it is to me to be present for each and every one of these last legs. I want to rejoin the relay as soon as possible and I feel that Kate and Jamie are wasting time, sweating the details instead of soaking up the bigger picture.

Finally, I drag them from the café and bundle them in to the car. We pass the runners who have yet to arrive in Douglas and I breathe a sigh of relief. I know I shouldn't be, but I am secretly pleased that Miles has been further delayed; it means I haven't missed the hand-off. Slowing his progress are the people who have driven out in their cars to track Miles down. Today's edition of The Boston Globe, New England's largest newspaper, has featured One Run For Boston on its front page. Now it seems that everyone in Massachusetts knows about the relay and wants to have their photo taken holding Miles.

It now looks like our expected finish time of 8pm will be nearer midnight. Gary Allen is suggesting on Facebook that we bring in faster runners to run the last few legs to make sure the baton arrives on time. He is willing to be one of them, he says. But neither Kate nor I have the heart to do this to the runners who have signed up to run these final eight stages and patiently waited their turn, their moment with Miles. And so, despite our concerns that no-one will be awake by the time we get to Boston, we are determined that the relay must continue without our intervention.

The hand-off location at Douglas is a traditional-looking village green. With a large group of runners and their families assembling on the grass, it feels like we've arrived at a church fete in England, except the sun is shining and there is no tea and scones. We work our way through the throng, and as the crowd parts to make way for us, I see her. She tilts her head and looks at me quizzically, as if challenging me to recognize her. Even with the addition of a Boston Strong Duck clipped to her head, it's unmistakably Joan. She's as beautiful as I remember her. I hadn't been expecting to see Joan until we got to Boston and suddenly I feel self-conscious in front of Kate and Jamie. Do they think I've been rushing to

Douglas to see Joan? It wasn't the reason, but it is certainly a nice surprise.

I don't need to worry what Kate thinks; her mind is on other things. With the red hot phone glued to her ear once more, she is patiently explaining to yet another journalist that, "Yes, Miles really has been carried on foot all the way from Los Angeles," and, "No, we didn't realize it was going to be quite so hot when we came up with the idea." We have agreed that Kate will drive ahead to Boston to be at the finish line, dropping Jamie and Sophie at Newton for the start of the final leg. I will run the next stage, then catch a lift with some of the supporters as far as Hopkinton and finish the final 26.2 miles of the relay on foot. But before the Stink Mobile disappears from my sight, there is one last photo to be taken and I have just the picture in mind. The Douglas runners need little encouragement to climb up on top of the car for me to take the perfect group shot. After travelling over 3300 miles through dusty deserts and lightning storms, the windshield is splattered with bugs, the chalk paint on the windows is dripping, stink emanates from each window, every inch is encrusted with dirt and now, after we've done with the photo shoot, there is also a big dent in the roof.

As she leaves, Kate writes our cell phone number on my arm in permanent pen, adding 'Or 911' just in case. "Don't forget to call me when you leave each hand-off," she says.

"But you're taking the phone," I remind her.

"There'll be plenty of people with phones you can borrow. Please don't forget. I've promised I'll keep all the police and journalists updated."

We embrace and wish each other luck. It feels weird for Kate to be leaving my side for the first time in nearly four weeks, almost like a part of me is being taken away. Kate laughs at how stupid I look tattooed with the phone numbers.

"See you at the finish line," I say to her, as Miles leads the runners out onto the road with the Stars and Stripes flag from Missouri bringing up the rear. I stop for one last hug with Kate.

"Off you go, Danny, or they'll leave you behind."

I chase off down the road shouting at the runners to wait for me, "I come all this way and you ditch me at the first opportunity…!"

Without a phone I have no access to Facebook and no knowledge of what is happening beyond the dozen or so people I am running with here and now. I am oblivious to the thousands of people who are glued to their computer screens at home, tracking our progress and willing us ever closer to Boston. I am unaware that there are runners arranging to meet up with other One Run For Boston folk tonight, in towns and cities across America, to mark Miles's arrival in Boston with a celebratory run. I am cut off from the excitement that is building in Boston as, undeterred by the relay running so late, hundreds of runners start making their way to Newton to run the final stage, while John Odom prepares to go to Boylston Street.

The adrenaline pumping round my body is making me even more impish than normal and at the next hand-off I find myself posing for a photo while lying horizontally in the air, held up by a group of runners. I look like a way-out bride in one of those unconventional wedding day photo shoots. It seemed a good idea at the time. I jump in with a supporter to ride the next few stages to Hopkinton, hoping that the confines of the car will calm me down. In search of reassurance, I give Kate a call but it goes straight to voicemail. Immediately I go to redial but am distracted by the flash of blue and yellow on the road in front of us. The painted Boston Marathon start line at Hopkinton is as recognizable as the finish. There is no mistaking where I am. I jump out of the car and into a crowd made up of runners, supporters and television cameras. Instinctively, I throw myself into the arms of the nearest runner, who returns my hug without breaking a beat while attempting to stifle a sniffle.

"Don't you start," I say to her, "Otherwise I'm going to be all over the place."

As I move on to meet the other runners I hear a reporter ask the girl, "So you know him? What's your story?"

"Sorry, it's the first time we've met," she replies, crushing any hopes the reporter may have had of landing a romantic scoop. Signing up to run only a matter of hours ago, Laura Ingalls is brand new to the One Run For Boston scene, but she is taking it in her stride and fitting right in. I look back to see her already deep in conversation with another runner and soon they are hugging too.

I spot Gary Allen in the crowd and make a beeline for him. He sees me coming and shouts out,

"Danny! Come and take a look at this!" As I get closer, he pulls down the collar of his shirt to reveal a small scar on his neck. "I started feeling this pain in my neck when I got home from Texas and it turns out I have this big burn right here," he says, pointing over his shoulder at his neck. "The only thing I can think of is that I must've got struck by lightning while I was running. I remember something around mile 19 that wasn't very pleasant but just thought I was probably tired." It's an unlikely story. I'm pretty certain we would have noticed Gary being struck by lightning if it really had happened.

I can't resist joking with him, "It looks more like a hickey to me, Gary."

"Hey, but I thought you and me only hugged though, right?"

I shake my head, laughing. "It's good to see you again, my man," I say, meaning every word, as I pull him in for another hug. Gary has run the Boston Marathon 21 times and each year he runs the course for fun on New Year's Day. He knows these next 26.2 miles like the back of his hand, or even his neck, and I'm genuinely pleased to have him here as pathfinder. As one of the most experienced runners in the group I ask him if he'll stay at the front and keep everyone to a 10-minute mile pace. He's happy to oblige and I can feel him set his internal speedometer ready.

A reporter calls me over for an interview alongside Dave McGilvray, the Race Director and heart and soul of the Boston Marathon. It is the first time we've met, although Dave has been in the wings throughout our journey, offering us advice and support over email whenever we've needed it. Dave ran across America solo in 1978 and judging by the photos I'd seen of him online, he's a fan of the short nylon running shorts that I have always favored but which were at least fashionable back when he had run cross-country. He had a big black bushy mustache in those days too which had made him look a lot like Magnum P.I. I have to admit, the thrill of meeting Mr. Boston Marathon is ever so slightly marred by the fact that he has turned up today sporting neither a mustache nor a pair of short shorts, but I think I manage to hide my disappointment.

The light is fading as we finally get word that the runners are approaching. We jostle over to the start, like runners on race day, and strain our eyes hoping to be the first to spot Miles. Standing with my toes touching the edge of the blue and yellow line, I am suddenly struck by the fact that I am at the start of the friggin' Boston Marathon. This is where it all starts. The hopes and dreams of thousands upon thousands of runners, the stories, the legends; this is where they all begin. The crowd falls silent and despite the warm evening, my body shudders with goose bumps. I cannot be the only one. Eventually, a single spontaneous whoop breaks the silence as the flashing lights of a police car are sighted, cresting the brow of the hill. It triggers an eruption of whooping, clapping, cheering and whistling as the runners appear in the middle of the road with a trail of traffic behind them. Miles rides into Hopkinton on a sea of emotion, held high above the heads of every runner. Some accelerate for a sprint finish, as if it's the end of a race. Others slow to a jog, savoring every last minute. Finally, Miles reaches the hands of Dave McGilvray. He is almost home.

The crowd turns to me expectantly. They want me to say something, and I have things I want to say but I find myself stuttering as I struggle to get the words out.

"We wanted to do something for Boston," I begin to explain. "We had this tiny idea, but you guys have absolutely made it huge. You have made it what it is." Standing in the middle of a busy road with traffic backing up all around me, I know I need to hurry up, but there is so much going on it's hard to focus on what I have to say. There are TV cameras pointing in my face, flashbulbs going off all around and I can barely hear myself think over the hubbub of reporters shouting at Dave to get in beside me and, "Hold it up! Hold it up!" It is Miles they've come to see.

"Thank you to every single person here," I continue, but am drowned out by cheers and screams. I can feel the blood rushing to my cheeks as I battle to wrap it up and do this moment justice. "This is such an emotional moment; this is the start of the marathon…" My throat is tightening and I'm losing it completely. I step back and throw the ball to Dave who catches it perfectly.

"Danny just told me that unfortunately everyone down the course has decided to drop out, so all of you now have to run all the way to the finish." The crowd whistles and cheers louder than ever. Of course I know he's joking, but with the relay running so late, I can't help thinking it may be closer to the truth than anyone imagines.

As we set off from Hopkinton, I wonder how Kate and Jamie are getting on. Jamie should be at Newton by now and Kate may already be at the finish. They are going to be waiting some time. I probably ought to give Kate a call but decide it can wait until the next hand-off at Framingham.

At seven o'clock, the time when the relay was meant to leave Newton, a photo of two lone runners waiting on the steps of Newton City Hall appears on Facebook with the caption, "Where is everybody?" It will be a few hours before Miles arrives and most of the people running this stage have chosen to sit it out at home rather than arrive early. But the image of the lonesome duo sparks a mass migration of runners to Newton. Suddenly it makes no sense for them to be waiting at home alone when everyone could be hanging out together at Newton instead. So they put on their sneakers and head out the door. Seven hundred runners or more take to the subways, piling onto the trains that would otherwise be empty on a Sunday night. It is standing room only between Boston and Newton. It is easy to make introductions in the crush, especially when you're wearing the same T-shirt. The carriages fill with excited chatter, as runners share their stories of where they're from and how they came to be here. Bit by bit the stony grey steps of Newton City Hall are covered in a sea of bright blue t-shirts. On the flat ground below, the television trucks lie in wait, their floodlights illuminating the car park. Reporters pace up and down taking calls from anxious producers concerned they have airtime to fill and still no baton to fill it.

In amongst the crowd are people who have travelled hundreds, if not thousands, of miles to be here. They have already run with Miles in other states and have pooled air miles, raided piggy banks and cancelled family vacations to be here in Boston to see him reach his final destination. Some of them have become household names among the One Run For Boston community in the past few weeks. Chief among them is Mary Hoatlin, who has flown in from St. Louis with her husband Patrick. The New Mexico collective of Will Allender, Steve Bender and Frank Cherne are reunited again and Scott Allender is there too, excited and proud to be running with his brother for the first time.

As we run from Hopkinton to Framingham and on towards Wellesley I am unaware of what is happening further down the marathon course at Newton. I still haven't rung Kate. I know she is waiting for updates but I can't bring myself to call her for fear she will deliver the news I am dreading; that Boston has given up waiting for Miles and simply sloped off to bed. It is not until we reach Wellesley that I realize I've been fretting unnecessarily. It may be 10:30pm on a sticky Sunday night, but holy schmoly, there are two hundred people waiting for us at the town hall, ready to run to Newton. Despite the late hour there are even a handful of supporters lining the road as we leave Wellesley. It's not quite a scream tunnel and no-one is handing out kisses, but hell yeah – we'll take it.

At Newton a man dressed as Big Bird is pouring water into cups ready for our arrival. At seven feet tall, this bright yellow bird is the first thing I see as we round the corner into Newton City Hall. I wonder if it's another one of Jamie's fancy dress stunts but then I spot the well-trodden face of our digital dynamo grinning at me as he stands in front of a wall of at least seven hundred runners.

"Here they come!" they shriek. "I can see Miles!" The runners surge down the steps and as they envelop our group, I realize that half of them are sporting little red shorts à la Danny. All of a sudden, Big Bird seems quite normal.

Chapter 29

Everyone wants a piece of Miles. The road becomes a heaving mass of bodies as people push their way forward to see him, touch him, hold him, kiss him. I feel uncomfortable and lost. Out on the open road for so long, we've not been used to being among such large crowds of people. People I've never met before are calling out my name and a thousand flash bulbs go off in my face leaving colored spots in front of my eyes. I am smiling but I feel utterly disoriented. I don't recognize these people and yet they know a lot about me. Many of them are dressed like me! It feels strange and claustrophobic. I stare wildly around me, searching for an escape route. But the group is so tightly packed I'm hemmed in with nowhere to go. Then, straight ahead of me I catch site of a familiar face. It can't be, can it? Then again, with that strong nose and grin, it couldn't be anyone else. It's Will! He had made it! Standing next to him, beside a gaggle of girls I don't recognize, are Will's brother, Scott with Steve and Frank. These guys have become like celebrities in One Run circles.

"You're the guy who flew to New Mexico from Pennsylvania?" I hear one girl ask Steve, starstruck. "Didn't you donate your frequent flyer miles to get Gary Allen to Texas?" Another asks, putting two and two together when she sees Will. "That's really cool." Question after question trips off their tongues as they pump the men for more information.

"What was New Mexico like?"

"Just how stinky is the Stink Mobile?"

"Tell us about Danny and the baby rattler!"

I stand a few feet away, not wishing to interrupt. But Will spots me.

"Downhill Danny!" he cries, opening his arms and drawing me in to his chest. I hug each of them in turn and then they drag me through the crowds, back towards the empty steps. "There's someone you need to see." Standing slightly back from the crush, unassuming as ever, is Mary Hoatlin and her husband Patrick.

She gives me a wave and I run towards her away from the crowds. The same Arizonan who had paid for our hotel in New York City, a guy named Andrew Kawakami, had given his frequent flyer miles to Mary to make sure she would be in Boston for the finish. By the sounds of it, she's enjoyed star treatment from the moment she arrived.

"When the hotel found out we were in town for the relay, they upgraded our room! And then they arranged for a limousine to drive us all here," Mary tells me, sounding like she still can't believe it herself.

"All of you?" I ask, confused.

"Yep, there's a gang of us here from Missouri. Skip, Shaun and Richard are around somewhere. Don't you worry, the *Show-Me State* is well represented!"

I want to go and find them but I realize there's no time. It will soon be midnight and we still have eight more miles to run. Thankfully, Jamie has got hold of a portable PA system and we're able to call everyone to attention, just about. I explain that the police have asked us to set off in small waves to stagger the start from Newton, and that we've promised them that every one of us will stick to the sidewalks and run no more than two abreast. But looking round I can feel I'm rapidly losing the crowd's attention. They're eager to get going and I realize how stupid I must sound spouting off a list of rules at the start of this momentous final stage. I attempt to recover with something a little more rousing.

"We came up with a little seed of an idea and we planted it in LA. We had no idea whether it would take root and grow. Watered, nurtured, cherished by the American people it has grown into what you see today. You guys have made it what it is. Without you it would be nothing but a tiny little seed. You're just absolutely friggin' awesome!" It wasn't going to go down in history as the most lyrical speech ever but I hoped people would get the message. The relay really had been just an idea which was developed by the American people and turned into something much more than we could ever have imagined. Over 24 days on the road, One Run For Boston had become a movement that exuded and inspired hope and positivity at a time when both were hard to come by.

"What we started together twenty-four days ago, we're going to finish together. Tonight. Boston Strong."

With that I pass the baton to two women, Denise and Christine, and we set off for Downtown Boston; destination Boylston Street. Much as I'd expected, no one heeded any of the rules about staggering the start or keeping to the sidewalks. Like a coiled snake the 700+ runners packed together, running, bumping and sweating down the middle of the road. The faster runners lead the charge with the slower ones filling in behind, one great big unstoppable mass of humanity. I keep pace with Denise and Christine for the first half mile. The women had been at the marathon finish line on April 15th and had both been thrown through the air by the second blast. Denise tells me that she thought she'd been shot when a piece of shrapnel exploded into her abdomen outside the Forum. Bleeding heavily, Denise ran inside the restaurant with her friend and was guided out the back by the off duty customs official, Richard Coleman, shortly before he realized that he too was bleeding to death. These women are not the only people present tonight who were at the marathon on April 15th. There are many runners in among this crowd who had been on Boylston Street and heard the blasts. They had seen the aftermath and felt the impact.

Others had not made it that far; their hopes of a glorious finish snatched from them shortly after 2.49pm, as officials stepped in to stop the race, diverting any runners still out on the course away from the unfolding tragedy. For many, it is the first time they have been back here since that day. Those who were stopped say they have unfinished business to put right tonight. Others deal with different demons, but are no less defiant.

On this hot humid night, the air is heavy and supercharged with emotion. I find it hard to breathe and my whole body is being squeezed like a plastic bottle twenty meters under water. I long for something to release the pressure and then it rains. It's just a tingling on my face at first. But as we hit Heartbreak Hill the raindrops get fatter and I poke my tongue out to taste them as they trickle down my cheek. The air has cooled, the pressure is dropping and it feels like a miracle. I'm not the only one feeling the relief.

"This rain is so cleansing!" a woman shouts out, to no-one in particular. I run over and hug her. "You know that rain stands for rebirth, right?" She asks me, returning my hug. "One Run For Boston is the rain that has helped us be reborn after April 15th. It's brought people together, and it's helped us to heal. Thank you so much for this experience."

I run on with a spring in my step and catch up with Billy Orman. Together with his dad, Bill, and friend Dennis, Billy had shared four stages of the relay in the Navajo reservation, making up two hours of lost time, and was now back in Boston for college. Enjoying this opportunity to overtake the Arizonan State record holder for the fastest mile, I give Billy a high-five and then leave him for dust. I spot more familiar faces as I run through the group. Skip Mann, the mooner from Missouri, had fallen in with a group of local runners which included Miss Massachusetts herself.

"What did you make of Heartbreak Hill?" I shout to Skip as I pass by.

"You mean we've passed it?!" Skip shouts back, sounding surprised. Running alongside the beautiful Miss Mass., I can understand why Skip might have failed to notice one of the biggest landmarks on the entire Boston Marathon route.

There are police cars at every intersection, holding the traffic to allow us through. Car horns honk out support for the relay, rather than impatience at being held up. As the runners pass by, some drivers get out of their cars to cheer and whistle. Fire trucks have driven out onto the route, hanging flags from their extended ladders for us to run under. Despite the late hour, pockets of people are lining the streets outside their houses to watch the carnival pass by. As residential streets give way to bars and restaurants, their patrons do the same, spilling out on to the sidewalks to high-five and cheer the runners as we pass.

"I can see the Citgo sign!" one runner shouts excitedly as we near Fenway Park. There is little more than a mile to go.

Across the road from Fenway, at Kenmore Square, stands Nicole Reis. This is the exact same place that she was stopped on the Boston Marathon course eleven weeks before, unaware of the tragedy that was unfolding on Boylston Street where her parents, John and Karen Odom, had been waiting for her with her husband. The bombers had robbed Nicole of the opportunity to cross the finish line in front of her proud family. But much more than that, they had severely injured and nearly killed her father. In the early hours of July 1st, Nicole waits patiently in the rain to finish what she started. Meanwhile, a mile down the street, her father is helped out of his car and into his wheelchair by Karen, his wife, and Lori from Boston Strong Ducks. Together they push him to the finish line and wait.

All across America, One Run supporters huddle around their computer screens. They watch the relay's progress, glued to the live tracker map, as Miles makes his way down Beacon Street and into the hands of Nicole. Together they begin the final mile of this epic journey, down Commonwealth Avenue and finally, the famed right on Hereford and left on Boylston. Nicole carries Miles past the boarded-up Forum restaurant, where the second bomb exploded and where her family's lives had changed forever. All over the USA, people are cheering their screens. The finish line is visible from hundreds of meters away. News teams jostle for position either side of it, pointing their cameras down Boylston Street. Groups of supporters crowd the sidewalk. They have stayed up late and waited in the rain so as not to miss this moment. If it wasn't for the fact it is nighttime, it could be Patriots' Day.

Among the crowd, I spot that famous cowboy hat and, underneath it, Carlos Arredondo, high-fiving and hugging every runner who comes by. As Nicole passes Marathon Sports, I see it still bears some of the scars of April 15th. The first bomb had exploded outside the store, shattering its windows along with the hopes and dreams of so many. Tears spill freely down my sweaty face as I watch Nicole head for the finish line. But I see her stop short and look frantically around, as if searching for someone in the crowd. The media scrum that surrounds her blocks the face she longs to see. Eventually they move aside to create a gangway to the finish and we see John Odom, sitting quietly in his chair, waiting to watch his daughter finally cross the Boston Marathon finish line.

"Oh, Daddy!" I hear Nicole say, tears rolling down her cheeks. Bending down to kiss her father, Nicole places Miles in his hands. John looks up at his baby girl, eyes shining, and raises Miles in the air. Cheers and applause reverberate around the packed street as Nicole continues her journey to the finish line, pushing her dad's wheelchair in front of her. They had reclaimed the finish line as their own.

Chapter 30

Reunited with Kate, we stand in the middle of the street cheering every last runner over the finish line. Some stop to kneel and kiss the hallowed tarmac. For others, the emotion is too much. They collapse on the floor with meters to go and are helped over the finish line by strangers from the crowd.

As the final few runners cross the finish, Miles finds his way back to Kate and she presents him to Tom Grilk, the director of the Boston Athletics Association, who had joined us in Newton to run the final stage. Early on in the trip we both agreed that if Miles made it to Boston he ought to stay in Boston and we could think of no better home for him than the BAA's museum. We hook up with Jamie and Sophie and persuade Tom to join us for a drink at the Rattlesnake Bar.

The doorman sees us coming and we are barely within earshot before he says to us, "Can I see some ID please?" We look shattered, bedraggled and on our last legs, surely anything but under twenty-one years old.

"I'm sorry?" I ask, assuming I've misheard him.

"I need to see some ID." Strict door policies are not something we're used to in the UK. I can't even remember the last time I was asked for ID back home. Once or twice when I was a teenager maybe, but in the last fifteen years I'd say never. I look at Kate, she looks at me and we both look at Jamie. We know what's coming. Jamie and Sophie both have ID but we don't. We look dolefully at the doorman. "We don't have any," Kate says, sounding utterly broken.

"Well then I can't let you in," comes the flat reply. We stare through the big glass windows into the bar. It is packed with One Run For Boston peeps, and the party is already in full swing.

"But we're the guys that made the booking, or at least Scotty Gallant made it on our behalf. You've got to let us in, this is ridiculous!" I try to reason with the doorman but he looks at us as if he's heard it all before. By this time, a few of those inside the bar have spotted us standing outside on the sidewalk and cotton on to what's happening. They find it hilarious and start waving their pints of beer at us, as we stand out in the rain looking like a pair of down and outs.

"Maybe we could speak to the Manager?" Kate asks.

"I don't think so."

Things are getting desperate. Tom goes inside to see if he can find someone who can sort this out while Jamie and Sophie make a beeline for the bar. Eventually Scotty Gallant appears with the Manager.

"Come on man, you've got to let these guys in, they're the organizers!" Scotty says incredulous. The doorman looks at the Manager, with a look of contempt, knowing he is about to be undermined.

"Come on in!" says the Manager. We walk through the door and are greeted by deafening cheers and whistles. Jamie thrusts a couple of beers straight into our hands and I think back to Robyn in Arizona. I have an idea.

"Where's Miles?" I ask. Tom has relinquished him so that those who have not had their photo taken with him can put that right. Miles is currently doing the rounds of the bar being kissed and cuddled and otherwise manhandled. "Have a little respect!" I shout above the din, and gesture for Miles to be passed back to me. With Miles in one hand and my beer in the other, I proceed to pour the liquid inside his hollow body. "Cheers!" I say, raising Miles to my lips and downing the contents in one. The gesture receives rapturous applause. It had been a long time coming, but it felt good to finally wet the baby's head.

Postscript / Epilogue

We flew home three days later, on July 4th. As the aircraft took off, we looked out over Boston and could see firework displays lighting up the night sky. It was a shame to be missing out on the festivities, but we figured it was probably best that we leave the Americans to celebrate their independence from Great Britain on their own.

The relay was over but One Run For Boston was not. The spirit of the relay lives on in the friendships that were made and the positive changes that the relay inspired in many people's lives. For me, this legacy is even more important than the money that we raised. One Run For Boston reminded us all of our responsibility to live our lives as fully as we can, with a smile on our faces, dancing to our inner song, doing good when there is good to be done and embracing strangers like we've known them forever. We owe it to those who no longer have the opportunity.

A month later I returned to Boston to present a check for $91,390 made out to the One Fund Boston to the Mayor of Boston, Tom Menino. I had hoped to persuade the Mayor's office to schedule an appointment for me to meet Mayor Menino but his schedule would not allow it. Then someone told me that he would be at the re-opening of the Forum restaurant and so I went along on the off chance that I might get an opportunity to deliver the check to him there. Reunited with thirty or so One Run For Boston friends including Big Bird, I joined the crowds outside the restaurant and watched as Mayor Menino cut the ribbon. We reflected on the moments before the restaurant was last open for business, right before the bombings on Marathon Monday. The restaurant's reopening was, Menino said, a symbol of Boston's resilience and unity. When he finished speaking, I felt someone push me in the ribs and say, "Now's your chance, Danny. Go grab him!"

"I can't!" I hissed, "Look at all the security staff around him. They'll shoot me down before I can get close."

"It's now or never!"

I stood rooted to the ground, paralysed by my English reserve.

As the Mayor turned to leave the lectern, I knew I'd missed my chance. Then I heard the same voice behind me shouting loud enough for everyone to hear.

"No, no, no! We're not finished here yet!" The outburst took everyone by surprise and stopped the Mayor in his tracks. Suddenly all eyes were on the crowd, or more specifically on me and the fiery Hispanic lady behind me who was now propelling me towards the Mayor, clutching the giant check. "Mayor Menino, I'm from One Run For Boston and I have a check to give you for the One Fund," I blurted out, expecting to be bundled to the ground by security guards. But instead the crowd cheered, and much to my relief the Mayor extended his arm for me to shake and thanked me. There is a photo of me laughing, somewhat maniacally, shaking the Mayor's hand as I pass him the check. I can't remember what he said but it must have been funny, even the poker-faced security guards in the background were smirking.

While in Boston I was able to meet up with John Odom again. Seeing John walk into the room made me so happy that I spent the next few hours as we talked, damming my tear ducts. Supported by his family, John's courage and determination had helped him to make such incredible progress in so little time. They were looking forward to returning to their home in California, but were full of love for Boston and the way the city had rallied to help them.

Just as I was leaving, Karen told me in her softly spoken voice that the day One Run For Boston crossed the finish line was the day John could finally start to heal. John nodded his head in agreement and as I took it all in I realized that these few words meant more to me than anything.

Thank you:

My first thank you must go to Kate. She and I shared a vision, a passion for a cause and a very smelly car for three weeks and more. We had some rough times, but mainly we just passed the days as friends on an adventure, like those Enid Blyton books we both loved as kids.

If you found yourself laughing out loud or gasping for breath while you read this book it was most probably one of the many points that Kate added and edited. Thank you, Kate.

Thank you to my buddy, Jamie, for bringing everything to life virtually with your amazing design and knowledge and for keeping me in good humor when things got frantic.

Thank you to our sponsors Poland Spring, Goodwear, Athletes for a Fit Planet, Boston Body Worker and Energy Bits.

The personal thank you list would go on for 3300 miles, but it would start with a big thank you to Mary Hoatlin, who gave up her life for a month to make sure One Run For Boston was a success. Thanks also to Ian Alden Russell, for showing faith in us from the very beginning, for coining the phrase 'Go Team!' and helping us so much with arrangements in New York and Boston.

Thank you to those who dragged themselves from bars and couches to come out and cheer the relay as it went by. Thank you to the servicemen and women who gave up their time to provide escorts. Thanks to the family and friends who supported and cajoled each runner through their designated leg.

Finally I have to thank our runners who left their blood, sweat and tears (not to mention vomit, snot and dirt) on Miles Le Baton over 3300 miles. Thank you for the sweaty hugs and gifts. Thank you for inviting two smelly Brits into your homes, for feeding us and for your friendship. But most importantly, thank you for running, for supporting the cause and for redefining our thoughts and views on humanity. You guys are awesome!!!!

Printed in Great Britain
by Amazon

69623302R00177